SEX AND SENSUALITY IN THE ANCIENT WORLD

GIULIA SISSA

SEX AND SENSUALITY IN THE ANCIENT WORLD

TRANSLATED BY GEORGE STAUNTON

YALE UNIVERSITY PRESS
NEW HAVEN AND LONDON

For information about this and other Yale University Press publications, please
contact:
U.S. Office: sales.press@yale.edu   www.yalebooks.com
Europe Office: sales@yaleup.co.uk   www.yaleup.co.uk

Set in Bembo by J&L Composition Ltd, Filey, North Yorkshire
Printed in Great Britain by TJ International Ltd, Padstow, Cornwall

ISBN 978-0-300-10880-4

Library of Congress Control Number: 2008929983

A catalogue record for this book is available from the British Library.
10 9 8 7 6 5 4 3 2 1

For Anthony, so much more than a reader

CONTENTS

Introduction   1

PART ONE *EROS* **THE TYRANT**   13

1   **Desire**   15
    The way women desire   15
    A theatrical sensuality   20
    An interesting woman   21
    Penelope's time   25
    Sensitive bodies   29
    The philosophy of desire   32
    Love letters   35
    Unpleasant desire   37
    The song of Penia   39
    Insatiable desire   40
    Cause or object?   44
    A river in a vase   45
    Desire as anxiety   48

2   **Pleasure**   50
    Hēdŏnḗ   50
    Democratic life   53
    Shameless living   58
    Érōs kalŏ́s   62
    The Athenian *poīkilía*   65
    Érōs ŏrthŏ́s   69

3   **Bodies**   72
      History of a difference   72
      The erection   79
      Female sensuality   86

4   **Relationships**   89
      Marriage   89
      Having children   91
      Let's get married to avoid litigation   94
      Sex and community   96
      Sex and tragedy   99
      Clytemnestra: Penelope's opposite   103
      Deianeira: Penelope and more so   109
      Electra: Virginity and vendetta   110
      Medea: A mother's passion for her husband   116
      Jocasta: the time of incest   123

PART TWO *MOLLIS AMOR* – UNMANLY LOVE   131
      Dira libido – 'Insane libido'   133
      Arte regendus amor – 'Love must be ruled through art'   136
      Così fan tutte   138
      Saper mentire – 'Knowing how to lie'   141
      Non nisi laesus amo – 'I can only love when I am wronged'   148
      Oh dolci baci e morbide carezze – 'sweet kisses and soft caresses'   149
      Paederasty and puberty   158

PART THREE *PERVERSA VOLUNTAS* – DEVIANT
INCLINATION   165
      Christian watershed   167
      A Greek question and a Christian reply   168
      He that is married careth for the things that are of the world   173
      He that is unmarried careth for the things that belong to the Lord   177
      Marriage is good, virginity is better   179
      It is better to marry than to burn   181
      It is better to burn than to marry   183
      Sensuality and will   185

Conclusion – Indefinite desire   192
Bibliography   207
Index   215

INTRODUCTION

When nature gave all the animals their organs for conception, it equipped those organs with a special facility for creating pleasure, and the soul with a 'marvellous and indescribable desire to make use of them'. By exciting and goading animals, this desire causes them to provide for the continuation of the species, as though they were perfectly wise, while in reality they may be young, foolish and entirely irrational.

This is how Galen, the great philosopher–physician who revived the traditions of Aristotle and Hippocrates in second-century Rome, introduces us to the cunning of sex (*De partium usu*, 14, 2). Sex gives a pleasure whose natural intensity is a paradoxical wisdom. Love exists to provide short-sighted and short-lived animals with immortality. At a time when philosophy, particularly Platonic and Stoic philosophy, had extensively warned against the folly of passion and Christian asceticism was on the rise, Galen reminded people of *eros'* reasons. Irrespective of an individual's mortality and stupidity, sexual intelligence makes the business of procreation attractive and gives meaning to the difference between women and men.

The division of the sexes and their coming together formed the nucleus of ancient reflections on sexuality. These were societies that never forgot this difference, particularly when it came to dividing spheres of activity. Politics, business and war were for men. Rearing children and tending to the household were the task of women. Ritual occasions, such as religious festivals or funerals, could be shared, but, even then, gender roles could not be confused. Moments and places, as well as behaviour and manners, were always either male or female. The social construction of gender through, for example, manly or womanly dress, speech or conduct always took place on this terrain. It was something that no one could be blind to. Mediterranean cultures, particularly those that are central to this book – Greece and the Roman world – extended sexual difference to all aspects of life, and encouraged an extreme sensitivity towards it. The world was sexualised and there was no room for neutral areas.

Were men to act like women or women to intrude into the realm of male prerogatives, this would be always a transgression, a trespassing; never a proof of indifference to gender boundaries. Were a biographical, historical process to entail a transition from feminine traits to masculine traits (as in the case of male puberty), or from manliness to effeminacy (as occurs in the progress of civilization), this would be perceived as a radical change rather than a marginal variation.

The theatre is perhaps the best place to observe the performance of gender roles. In tragedy, Antigone is an exceptionally paradoxical heroine because, in order to perform her womanly duties and to mourn her two brothers, she goes far beyond the attitudes expected from a female. A manly woman, she becomes unbearably threatening for the authority of the ruler of the city. In comedy, the spectacle of an Athens ruled by women is no less hilarious than the idea of a city in the sky, founded and governed by birds. When they step out of their domestic space into the arena of politics, women bring with them their perennial concerns: nurture and sex. Are they going to make democracy really egalitarian? Of course: by enforcing the right to equal opportunity – for the young and the old, the attractive and the ugly, to have sex with the same, handsome, young men. Are they going to fight to impose peace and stop an interminable war? Yes, by denying sex to their husbands – a form of activism which is the most heroic and self-sacrificing they can imagine.

Public rhetoric also offers an interesting standpoint from which to view cultural representations of identities that are well defined, and occasionally exchanged, only to be distinguished even more sharply. In Lysias' *Funeral Oration*, we hear that heroic female warriors may exist – abroad. But the belligerent Amazons were only able to overcome the peoples of the East, not the Athenians, who were the only real men they ever attempted to challenge; and that was to be their undoing. The speech of Aeschines *Against Timarchus* might depict a prominent citizen as a man who uses his body like a woman. But this was the final detail in the biography of an ignominious character: a profligate who deserved the loss of any right to participate in public life.

Athens is a city where female and male appear to be polarised in an exemplary fashion. Protected by a goddess who is virgin and armoured, the Athenians see themselves as the mythical children of a double mother: one fertile, Earth, the other sexually intact and aggressively defensive, Athena. Both mothers make all the citizens siblings and noble. But Athena has to be impenetrable in order to personify and embody the integrity of the city. Her body is sealed, her femininity interrupted.

Genders were neatly constructed because their construction was indeed social and cultural; but they were not disconnected from what we can call 'the real'. The body, in its anatomy and physiology, sets a limit to symbolic arrangements and imaginary creativity. Represented in thousands of statues, mostly in the nude, at least after Praxiteles' Aphrodite in Cnidos, female and male bodies were pervasively visible in ancient cities. Painted on vases and other tableware, they were a constant reminder of sexual difference. Round breasts, slightly curved bellies, soft gestures on the one hand; defined muscles, proud posture and shameless allure on the other.

The polarisation of the two genders, achieved through a diverging stylisation of male versus female details, was part of the aesthetic culture of the ancients. The contrast appeared in visual artefacts, but was also cultivated in the fashioning of the body itself. The gymnasium was the place where the muscular, agile, harmonious features of young men were to be built, chiselled and maintained. To extend that kind of training to girls could only be a striking novelty, as it was stressed in the case of Sparta, where female teenagers used to exercise naked and show their thighs; or in the daring public education designed for Plato's ideal state, Kallipolis, 'City of Beauty'. But then again, physical education was a manner of responding to the challenge offered by anatomy itself, with an emphatic recognition of sexual dimorphism. Males have more muscular mass; their flesh is firmer, Hippocrates and Aristotle claim. Boys will improve their muscles and their joints in the gym. Males are drier and warmer. They will expose themselves to the sun. Females are smaller, softer, more humid and watery. They will stay still, inside the house, and dedicate themselves to pregnancy, nursing and sedentary activities. Proper women had to be pale, and their limbs were painted in white on black-figure vases.

Secondary sexual characteristics, as we now call them, were acknowledged and then enhanced, accented and emphasised. But there is more. The ancients perceived the body, especially the human body, as a model. Social roles, manners, norms and appearances were not defined in opposition to anatomy, as though the symbolic could be separated from nature. Quite the contrary, a few distinctive features turned bodies into a prolific source of metaphors, to be applied in various contexts. From Hippocrates to Galen, for instance, physicians thought of the female body in terms of the male one, as though women had the same genitals turned inwards. The womb was a scrotum, the ovaries were testicles, the cervix was a penis and the vagina was a long foreskin. In spite of this, however, the ancients still looked at a woman's body as something fundamentally apt to accept and accommodate an external object, in order to hold and protect it. Females were containers.

This feature was projected and interpreted in the most unexpected ways. The most obvious association of ideas was the one that perceived women as guardians of the home, responsible for the internal space which conserved the resources the male householder brought in from outside. But the idea did not stop there. Even the soul could become a woman's body when it was considered in terms of its ability to receive into itself, conceive and give birth. Even the male body became womanly when imagined or described in situations of receptive desire, instead of (or as well as) penetrating another body.

Sexual dimorphism had creeping ramifications, which amplified and refined the physical gap between the sexes. This is particularly significant because the feminine body was indeed conceived by analogy with the masculine one, as if its shape and functions could not be thought of independently from the only perfect exemplar of a given species, the male. But that analogy did not result in the idea that genders are interchangeable, equivalent, or equally functional. It was lopsided from the outset, because it posited the male as the reference and the female as an approximate version of it. And, furthermore, it had to be reduced to a quantitative asymmetry, or, in Aristotle's words, a 'difference in terms of the more or the less' – the female being always less strong, less large, less firm, less hot, less mature, less equipped and so on than the corresponding male. That analogy resulted neither in a denial nor even in an attempted attenuation of the division between the sexes. Those accidental female bodies, approximately human, slightly monstrous, and forever infantile were still very different from their better version.

The inability to conceptualise the feminine, except through its position in regard to the male – a position of systematic inferiority, inadequacy and malfunction – can be understood as a deep-seated epistemological obstacle, or a powerful paradigm, or a basic structure, or a transcultural prejudice. We can use different scholarly idioms. But, to put it simply, we can say that the inability to produce anything other than unflattering comparisons between the sexes had a tremendous impact on the cultural common sense of the ancient world. It could justify, on behalf of nature – and with the authority of the physician, or from the podium of a school of philosophy – the most profound distance between the sexes: that of an insuperable failure. Nobody puts it better than Aristotle: sexual reproduction, he claims, as opposed to spontaneous generation, characterises the most complex and differentiated living beings, those capable of motion. The more perfect animals are, the more sexually defined they appear. This is why human beings, because they occupy the highest position in the hierarchy of nature, display the most extreme sexual dissimilarity.

Only if we do not forget the body and do not underestimate its symbolic morphology can we hope to understand how the ancients understood sex and how they came to their stubborn essentialism, the constant reference to *being*, or *having become*, woman or man. Just as contemporary neuroscientists reduce erotic experience to the realities of hormones, cerebral chemistry and evolution, so the ancients founded what we now consider their 'beliefs', 'representations' or 'social constructions' on observations they held to be objective to anatomy and physiology.

We shall examine, for instance, how medical theories of puberty can explain a whole array of concepts and terms relating to the determination of sex and sexual orientation. We shall see how tragedy can connect a woman's erotic passion to gynaecology. Any denial of the naturalistic foundation that the ancients attributed to sex, in the name of a sophisticated and historicist awareness of eros's complexities, would be a betrayal of *their* way of thinking. Moreover, it would mean falling back once again onto that tiresome dualism which separates that which is somatic from something else – be it the soul, the unconscious, the imaginary or the symbolic. Let our approach be a sceptical one, but only in order to understand their dogmatism. Let us not miss their materialism.

Gendered bodies are different and distant. How do they move towards each other, why do they come together? Thanks to that irresistible desire for pleasure which Galen sees as the cunning of nature. Our understanding that bodies were essential for the ancients helps us to recognise how bodies were at the same time, so to speak, 'existential'. On this point, philosophers and physicians of the classical world were more perceptive than contemporary positivists, because they realised that bodies are basic models not just because of their configuration, but also, and above all, because of their openness to the world and their incarnate intentionality. The fact that the female recipient is capable of containing something is not simply a property of her form. Her receptivity is filled with desire; it is a vacuum that aspires to fullness. In Galen's terminology, the willingness to take in and protect what is contained within becomes a strength – the 'power of attraction' and the 'power of retention', which are characteristics of the stomach and the womb. This is why the desire to submit oneself, *epithūmía páscheīn*, becomes the strongest and most insatiable both in women's bodies, where it occurs naturally, and in those men's bodies where it sometimes establishes itself and comes to be a second nature. The protruding rigidity of the erect penis is not simply the condition of its use in penetration. The erection is targeted desire. The ancients had the extraordinary intuition that, for human beings, the body is not simply a thing. Desire is made up of nourishment and representation; material substances for use in specific parts, and perceptions or phantasms. Both categories stimulate, excite and incite in synergy with each other.

Bodies live and are animated in a localised and highly organised manner: the parts where I feel desire have their desires, because a living principle imbues and animates them in a particular fashion. The vitality of sexual organs and the involuntary nature of their movements provided ancient thought with its most interesting challenge. What kind of act is the sex act? Who is responsible for it? What kind of intention is that 'marvellous and indescribable desire' to use parts of the body, whose independent initiative engenders surprise, embarrassment or disappointment? If pleasure is possible and an act takes place, then the latter is the product of a paradoxical event, which is also an act of volition. Sex, it was thought, depends on a particular type of imperious appetite, unthinking impulse and irresistible craving, which poets, physicians and philosophers had attempted to define and classify by examining the evidence of its force, insistence and tyranny. Sexual activity depends on that subjective willingness to desire which we call sensuality.

The sensual, and therefore infinitely desirous, nature of *eros* was a typically Greek theme, and became a crucial Roman one too. Ultimately it was caught up in Christian anguish over the weakness, or rather the power – as Tertullian would put it – of the flesh. The flesh is the body, but a body saturated with desire. It is an enticing voice, a complicit glance or a provocative walk. Sensuality is the body in a desirous mode, and, above all, it is the body when it desires another's desire.

This brings us to the core relationship which provides the title of this book: sex and sensuality. I want to insist on the importance of accepting the (almost imperceptible) lexical shift between these two words. Contemporary historians have distrusted the word 'sexuality' since Michel Foucault emphasised the fact of its nineteenth-century coinage. More nominalist historians assert that, in the pre-Christian world, we can only speak of erotic experience, the use of pleasures and lifestyles, thus freeing ourselves from anachronistic ideas associated with a term which has been excessively contaminated by modern positivism. 'Sexuality', it is true, conjures up the description and classification of behaviours and fixed identities that are common to human beings and other life forms. It smacks of the chemist's shop, the natural history museum and forensic medicine. Those who challenge its relevance support a radically historicist alternative: incommensurable social constructs of gender and erotic experience can be observed in different contexts.

However, something is lost here, and this is the importance the Greeks and Romans attached to both the material nature and the subjectivity of that erotic experience. We need to abandon the clichéd language of sexuality and start talking about, on the one hand, sex – in order to capture ancient materialism – and, on the other, sensuality – if we are to grasp the full range of attitudes the ancients adopted in relation to *eros*. From anguish to its cultivation, from fear to irony and from fascination to disgust, they understood *eros* not as a repertoire of possible acts, not as the 'use of pleasures', but as the body's insistent desire. 'Sensuality' helps us to perceive the intentional intensity of eroticism and its aesthetic and corporeal emanations. There is no Greek word which could be translated into Latin as *sensualitas* or into modern languages as sensuality, *sensualité*, *sensualidad*, *sensualità*. There is no Greek word which could be translated as *sexus* or sex, *sexe*, *sexo*, *sesso*. But it does not matter: what I am going to highlight are concepts which I will define through argument, concepts which are to be found not in the dictionary, but in language itself – in sentences, metaphors, trains of thought and semantic fields.

What is sex? It is the ever magnified difference between two bodies, a difference that irradiates into social habits and cultural artefacts. What is sensuality? It is the moving of those different bodies towards each other, in the pursuit of pleasure. Sensuality is desire, but desire beyond the crude and instantaneous event of what we might describe as drive, stimulation, reflex, response. Sensuality is indefinite, lingering, persistent desire. It is anguish and delight, want and anticipation, attraction and seduction, rapture and strategy. Sensuality is to feel your erotic emotion and to play with it; to desire and to make yourself desirable. Sensuality is to transform the urges of the body into language – be it poetry, letters, rituals, garments, presents or gestures. Sex morphs into sensuality, with the progressive refinement of that system of distinctions, conventions, performances and signs that we call a civilisation.

What is sensual is a boy with feminine limbs, who shoots arrows (*iaculatur*) and makes people fall in love. What is sensual is the woman who emanates love from her entire body (*toto iactans e corpore amorem*, Lucretius, *On the Nature of Things*, iv, 1053–4). What is sensual is the young girl or the young bride who makes herself desirous and desirable in the way she dresses, adorns herself, does her hair and expresses herself through telling gestures such as singing, strolling, glancing, smiling and swinging her hips. What is sensual is the older woman, like Penelope in the *Odyssey*, who would never appear before her suitors without wearing a charming attire. What is sensual in its extreme form is the famous or infamous *cinaedus*, the male with an effeminate, languorous and loose-limbed body. In other words, the sensual is essentially femininity and a libido that is all the greater because it is hidden. It is pure desire to be desired (*tantum cupit illa rogari*, Ovid, *Art of Love*, i, 709). Through sensuality, we shall see, the feminine heart of ancient desire can be recaptured: the womanly 'yes' to the pleasure of one's own body and another's desire.

By recognising that even sex and sensuality are concepts defined against the subliminal backdrop of masculine versus feminine, we may understand many aspects of ancient sexual cultures. Why, for instance, it takes a woman addressing another woman to invent erotic poetry, or why the expertise of courtship and the art of love require from men the acquisition of a certain dose of effeminacy. Sex morphs into sensuality, to be more precise, with the progressive attenuation of a primaeval manliness – that of the blissful men who lived like gods before the fabrication of Pandora, or that of the first humans shaped by the divine demiurge in Plato, before they degenerated into women, or that of Romulus' comrades before the Rape of the Sabine Women – pure virility which, in time, must blend with the feminine if human beings are to form households, found cities and become civilised.

Sensuality, I said, is desire to be desired, longing for reciprocity rather than unilateral possession. It is at the antipodes of rape, harassment or brutality. Aphrodite equips the first woman with *oarístús*, cajoling, coaxing murmurs. Platonic seduction is all about contagious love. Ovid's art is nothing but persuasion. The lasciviousness of the *cinaedus* lies in his avidity to be taken. It is the other's passion for us that matters. If we admit to this, we free ourselves from many dilemmas that unsettle historians of sexuality. Firstly, this jettisons the opposition between passivity and activity: the distinction between the person who aspires to possess an object and the object itself is undermined. According to the dialectics of sensuality, we yearn to be an object of attraction to another, and, if we are desired, we will reciprocate. This is the game of *chărízeīn* or gratification, on which the Platonic debate on love has focused: the moment of delight in seduction comes when a person wins another person's erotic interest. This also diminishes the dichotomy between homosexuality and heterosexuality: sensuality is feminine, whatever the gender of the person who experiences it. It is a boy or an adult *cinaedus* who shoots the darts because they have feminine bodies. It is the woman who dominates the love scene because she is the archetype and because, as Ovid says, adult femininity can provide superior erotic response. A woman – particularly one who has passed the age of thirty-five – offers a *voluptas* which is relentless desire when she asks her lover to resist as long as possible, and supreme pleasure when, completely exhausted, she refuses to continue to make love (*Art of Love*, ii, 681–93).

A history of sensuality is therefore essentially a history of desire. While desire is limited by nature in Homer, it becomes insatiable in Plato, and with the philosopher's vivid language it acquires an explicitly feminine character: the boundlessly seductive voraciousness of a welcoming body. This is the alluring woman; this is also the *cinaedus* – whose womanly limbs personify sex appeal. Tragedy enlarges and exhibits the excess of *eros* by staging women in love. Whereas tragic men develop a consuming passion for sovereignty, revenge or knowledge, women stand out as those for whom 'the bed is everything'. Medea is ready to kill her own children because they are children of a husband who has spurned her love, and Jocasta is willing to keep her incest with Oedipus a secret in order save her marriage. Countless other examples show how women struggle for *eros* or for the family, the institutional consequence of *eros*. Orators turned feminine sensuality into an aggressive political strategy: a man who prostitutes himself with other men enjoys an unlimited and unnatural lascivi-ousness, as though he possesses a woman's body – and for this reason he must be eliminated. Aristotle played down the significance of this, while Epicurus was reassuring: appetites are natural and have their limits; they can be controlled by reason. The Stoics turned them into mistakes in the soul that can and should be avoided.

In Rome, in the first half of the first century AD, Titus Lucretius Carus revived Platonic apprehensiveness over the unfathomable pathology of passion, but only in relation to love as distinct from physiological sexual drive. As a poet, philosopher and early proponent of the Greek Epicurean tradition in Roman culture, Lucretius became an essential reference point for any discussion on pleasure. His eroticism of cruelty – that unbounded craving to seize, penetrate and lacerate the other person in vain – was picked up with clinical precision, by erotic poets from the elegists to Catullus. *Voluptas* (sensuousness) was elusive and ended in disappointment, jealousy and bitterness, because desire is always excessively demanding and unrelenting. The poet warns: 'From the very heart of delight there rises a jet of bitterness that poisons the fragrance of flowers' (*surgit amari aliquid*, Lucretius, *On the Nature of Things*, iv, 1134). This treacherous emotion mars the pleasure and produces apprehension, suspicion and regret over lost time. Even the most exquisite voluptuousness never satisfies.

Lucretius' thoughts were echoed by another poet, a contemporary and also an unhappy lover. 'Lesbia, you ask how many kisses of your lips are enough for me and more than enough. As many as the grains of Libyan sands . . . and as many as the sky has stars . . .!' Only a quantity that cannot be counted could satisfy Catullus' desire (*Poems*, 7). 'Kiss me now a thousand times, and now a hundred more, and another hundred, and a thousand more again' (*Poems*, 5). As with all other things concerning amorous desire, kisses are never enough. Erotic happiness remains unattainable. The object is elusive because it is a subject: its desire always uncertain, and often spasmodic and equivocal. Jealousy is awareness of the loved one's essential freedom.

In Rome, poets were the theoreticians of love, given that they were sophisticated lovers and indulged in sensuality to the point of brushing against detestable *mollitia*, that flaccidity, enfeeblement and effeminacy that the Romans considered to be the secret both to the process of civilisation and to its decadent excesses. Whereas in Greek historiography after Herodotus, sentimental considerations and episodes were treated with contempt and scepticism, in Roman history sex and sensuality acquired a legitimate role in the explanation of social change or political action. The Romans' foundation myths, as elsewhere, were stories of seductions and miraculous births. But there was something more. Even the more thoughtful Roman historians believed that the social and cultural transformations that brought about the collapse of the Republic were principally the result of decline in the thrift and asceticism that Numa, their second king, wisely instilled into their lifestyle.

This wise and peace-loving king had inherited from Romulus a city barely thrown together and inhabited by soldiers, fugitives and coarse, uncouth and bellicose men, whose sexual sensibilities were expressed by the mass rape of the Sabine virgins. Plutarch tells us that Numa attempted to soften the unpolished Romans of the early days by introducing them to pleasures. According to Sallust, sophistication became excessive after the destruction of Carthage and the end of the austerity imposed by the Carthaginian threat, and was the cause of the moral decay that would eventually lead to the Principate. Julius Caesar personified this paradoxical masculinity – both hyper-virile and effeminate, both fierce and flabby. Catullus called him a *cinaedus Romulus* – a 'dancing Romulus'. The history of the Romans is also the history of their sensuality.

In the very early years of the Christian era, Ovid took up the challenge laid down by Lucretius – the mentor he called sublime and whose poetry would die, he said, 'only on the day in which the earth itself shall perish' (*Amores*, i, 15, 23) – and became a teacher of the art of love, as though he had actually learnt some lesson from the pointless tragedies of the poets. The *Art of Love* frees us from the chronic failure of despotic, casual and destructive relationships. We learn to educate love, who is a child and not a tyrant; we learn to seek out the object that can be made unique, the girl to whom one can say, 'you alone attract me'; we learn to use the language of admiration, devotion and idealisation to create a fictitious relationship, whose fiction ends up producing its own truth. And we do all this without foregoing a libertinism that is both entertaining and discrete. '*Ludite!* – Enjoy yourselves as well!', the poet elegantly tells us.

Ovid brought to an end the drama of jealousy, the agonies over the impossibility of possessing the other until one's last breath, the interminable recrimination and the myth of naturalness. When it is deliberately orchestrated, urban love reconciles the poet – the ideal suitor – with virility. In him, male impetuousness is tempered with the correct dose of *mollitia* (softness), which is part of the charm of the poetic art. As he is neither too coarse nor too gentle, the poet knows how to wait for the other person's desire to evolve, because in the meantime he can find the words that overcome modesty and coax love. He is aware of an essential and hidden truth, taught by the classical tradition from Homer to the tragedians, and of which the master poet Lucretius constantly reminds him: all women, without exception, wish to be seduced. It is more likely that the birds would stop singing than that women would cease to succumb to men who sweetly flatter them. The cultured lover is capable of responding to the challenge posed by the concealed and intense female libido with persistence and patience – in other words, with his own form of sensuality. He knows he can count upon the eventual capitulation of the *domina* (the mistress) who deep down is just a *puella* (a maiden). His artful ability to bide his time surpasses that of Penelope's suitors – those aphasic lads of Ithaca – or that of Romulus' pack of bravos who attacked the defenceless Sabine women. The Ovidian model of urban love, civilised love, love in the city, was to become a precursor to courtly love, and a textual influence on it in the context of medieval Christianity.

About thirty years after Christ's death, Paul of Tarsus wrote his First Letter to the Corinthians – the founding text on Christian sexual morality – and in it he replied to the Greeks, who presumably had been educated in Greek philosophy. They were fascinated by Jesus' virginity and, influenced as they were by Platonic and Stoic ethics, they anxiously asked Paul what they should do about their own sexuality and that of their daughters. Paul's reply was concerned not so much with strengthening their asceticism as with calming its fervour: marriage was good, but virginity was even better. Those who marry deal with earthly matters and those who do not marry deal with the Lord's business. 'But if they cannot contain, let them marry; for it is better to marry than to burn' (1 Corinthians 7: 9).

This message was measured, moderate and strategic. From the very beginning, Christian morality embraced 'that indescribable desire' to use one's sexual organs, of which Galen had spoken. It did not attempt to evade the female libido; indeed, the Christian was required to submit himself to his wife's desires, just as she was required to respond to his. The erotic constancy expressed by 'You alone attract me', which the Greeks and, later, the Romans associated with extramarital love, now entered the conjugal space. The Greeks and Romans would never have dared to make that kind of love entirely monogamous, from Ulysses down to the devoted (but discretely unfaithful) Ovidian lover. For Paul, marriage became the exclusive place for a shared sensuality, which the Mediterranean male – indolent at home and unfaithful outside it – could no longer evade. Thus conjugal passion came into existence.

During the centuries that followed, the Church Fathers, heirs to classical and Hellenistic morality, turned this way of thinking into something more inflexible. They did not follow the Platonic line, which argued for the contemptible nature of the body, the insatiability of desire and the impossibility of pleasure, as this would have been dangerous for a religion which attributed to God the creation of a world that had to be considered beautiful and good. Instead, they adapted a fundamental tenet of Stoic philosophy: the idea that desire is an act of acquiescence and therefore of will. The hurried (or overly slow) ups and downs of the penis had represented the most involuntary thing that could happen to a human body. These movements were associated both with the seminal fluid and with the imagination; like the beating of the heart, they were independent of any intention and therefore innocent. They were now considered a 'yes', pronounced in the presence of body and mind, and what were corporeal events became decisions: whether or not to take possession of that object here and now. In Christian literature, the question of inexhaustible appetite became secondary to the question of impatient assent to a future pleasure, and therefore to an immediate imaginary pleasure of anticipation. The Platonic-tragic viewpoint was thus reversed: the Christian was not to subdue sensuality because desire is insatiable and pleasure unattainable, but to distrust it because the libido brings too much pleasure too quickly. The sensual is sensation, the feminine part of the soul which responds impulsively to physical beauty, just as Eve gave her consent to the snake.

This also overturned Galen and Aristotle's rationalisation of sex. They had associated sensual pleasure, sexual intercourse, procreation and immortality of the species. The Christians shifted immortality into the next world, and attributed it to each individual's soul. Eros was no longer required to re-create life. Indeed, lustful flesh creates transient bodies, which live and enjoy pleasure only briefly. On the other hand, Christianity produced an extraordinary eroticisation of its own asceticism: carnal and sensual union became the model for the relationship with God. Virginity, which was abstinence from mortal eroticism, made it possible to savour a celestial *eros*. The soul will enjoy the presence of God through an ecstatic pleasure of eternal life, and anticipates that awaited pleasure through an angelic existence of chastity on earth. In this sublimated version, we encounter the metaphor of *psūché* as a female body, model for infinite desire, and a mystical and patient sensuality.

Greece, Rome and early Christianity are separate cultural worlds. However, for obvious reasons, we have to place them in a historical perspective. A series of texts and ideas flows through them all and, as these are handed down and mixed together, they pose challenges and inspire imitations, comments and objections. In other words, they form what we call a tradition. In the fifth century, St Augustine was still talking to Plato, almost a thousand years after his death. And this was just the beginning.

PART ONE

EROS THE TYRANT

1

DESIRE

THE WAY WOMEN DESIRE

Contemporary woman is something new, but an irreverent French psycho-analyst, Jacques-Alain Miller, reminds us that, if a feminine woman exists, then she is Medea, the woman who demonstrates what a woman is capable of doing – a woman who knows how to be a woman: a player who can, uncondition-ally and extravagantly, lose everything she has. Feminine identity lies in the woman's ability to separate herself from everything that appears to define her social, emotional and personal status: property, acquisition and possession in general. Medea has a great deal: wealth, children and prestige. These things make her the person she is. But she does not cling to them or attempt to salvage all she can when she loses the love of the man she loves, Jason. Instead, Medea divests herself of everything. She kills her own children, ruins her husband, makes herself irredeemably hateful to the people of Corinth, and casts herself out of the city.

On a first reading, Euripides' tragedy supports this counterintuitive interpre-tation. Already at the beginning of her story, Medea has left everything behind her: she has left her family, she has betrayed her close relations and she has torn her brother apart, limb from limb. Her marriage to Jason was not a contract between a man who gives his daughter away and a man in receipt of a wife, but the insolent and freely given gift of herself from a woman in the grip of *eros* (*Medea*, 8). This rebellious marriage did not create an alliance, but separated two cities under the shadow of a bloody feud. Medea had already demonstrated what she was capable of doing and how she was willing to abandon everything she had. Now, after marrying this man and following him to Corinth, the fusion of their two beings has become everything (13). The nurse announces this and she repeats it: this man and husband is everything. Everything she has is in him. Thus, when Jason moves away to marry another woman, Medea reacts with merciless destructiveness, even though he reminds her of how much still remains in her hands (522) and tells her that it is just a womanly illusion to believe in love's ability to represent everything (570). Given that she has lost everything, no one else will be allowed to keep anything either.

Medea poisons Jason's future bride and her father. Most significantly, she slaughters the children she and Jason had together. These children are Jason's, and by killing them she obviously means to inflict a blow on their father (817), but Medea is also destroying what belongs to her (793) – what she herself has brought into this world, her seed (*spérma*, 816). She annihilates what is her own dearest possession – the flesh of her flesh.

Medea is an eloquent symbol, if psychoanalysis is right in defining the feminine in terms of its extreme capacity for detachment. Of course, for psychoanalysis, this lack of instinct of possession, this ability not to identify oneself with what one owns and what one cannot go without, depends on the sexual difference. A man must have in order to be. He has to have a part of the body which symbolises the rest of the world in its willingness to be possessed. And he has to own many things, if he is to feel like a man. When examined in this light, the luxury of being a woman consists in being able to assert complete freedom in passing from everything to nothing, and in being able to allow herself those definitive acts of breaking away, severing relations and shifting from one life to another, which for a psychoanalyst typify feminine fervour. This is because women have a body that does not force them to symbolise their subjectivity in terms of equipment.

If we accept this argument, Medea introduces us to a theory of the feminine and of feminine desire: women are subject to a non-possessive relationship with the world. With their non-phallic bodies, or at least their capacity for pleasure other than phallic, women demonstrate the possibility of another kind of desire.

However, this disturbing infanticide presents us with the very complex question of how women acquire, possess and conserve. It is Medea who bluntly remarks that women are forced into 'buying themselves' a man in order to make him the owner of their bodies. This is a provocative way of redescribing the dowry, which was typical of marriage in the classical era, as though it were not the father who gave it to the future husband, but rather the bride herself who used her money in order to acquire an object. It is also a paradoxical allusion to the relationship between slave and slave-owner, given that, in Medea's words, women allegedly 'buy' the person who will dominate them rather than the one who will serve them. This metaphorical distortion is consistent with the thinking of a woman who has chosen her man by herself and on her own initiative. It is worthy of such women as Helen or the Danaids. In other words, Medea is not only a woman who knows how to relinquish; she is, above all, a woman who knows how to take, choose and impose her active desire.

Jason imprudently attempts to minimise this immense love, and attributes it to the influence of Aphrodite. Born from a double 'foam' (*aphrós*) made up of the seed of Uranus, the sky, and waters of the sea, the 'foaming' goddess, Aphrodite, dominates the stage on which ancient love is played out. She provokes the Trojan War through the adultery between Helen and Paris, and remains involved throughout all the events narrated in the *Iliad* and the *Odyssey*. As the tutelary deity of the heroic world which was created from sexual encounters between men and goddesses and between gods and mortal women, Aphrodite is the source of eroticism for everyone. Her power reaches its apogee in a famous episode of the *Iliad*, in which even Hera had to turn to her to borrow a love charm (in this case, a kind of magic sash worn across the breast), in order to seduce her own husband and distract him from the war. Even the lord of Olympus, a god of triumphant virility, could be captivated by Aphrodite's erotic spell.

Euripides' hero Jason speaks this archaic language of Homeric poems and Homeric hymns, in which *eros* is the effect of a divinity who takes possession of people and carries them along in spite of themselves. It is with this language, which reduces passion to passivity, that Jason vainly hopes to pacify Medea. But she replies furiously with a declaration that she is in complete possession of her feelings. *I* was the one who loved you, assisted you and saved you, she says. Aphrodite has nothing to do with it. Love, Medea claims, is her own experience in all its pragmatic manifestations: to help, to kill, to flee, to live with him, to bear his children. Speaking the same archaic language used by Jason, the nurse also perceives love as an *eros* that has struck the heart of the abandoned wife (8). Yet Euripides' Medea fulminates against the very idea of divine determinism. Her ego appropriates passion and claims it as an act of personal will.

The dizzying magnitude of her loss is for Medea simply the other side of her assertive violence and her claim to be the protagonist of her own emotions. This is not a small detail. It overturns and challenges the traditional image of desire caused by a divine agent. Are we then witnessing an internalisation of the art of love? We may ask ourselves whether this tragedy from the fifth century BC was a decisive turning-point in the history of sexuality. Was this the moment in which love became secularised and ceased to be represented as a form of bewitchment? Was this the moment in which love freed itself from the divine and became a human and psychological affair?

One of the explanations of erotic attraction was the belief that passion was unleashed from an external source upon the individual, and therefore could not be considered the cause of a voluntary and responsible act. This was, more to the point, a central problem in Greek ethics. In his *Rhetoric* and *Nicomachean Ethics*, Aristotle expatiates on the type of action that takes place when a person is motivated by anger or jealousy. Such an act is judged to be voluntary – that is, one for which the agent must take full responsibility. The very notion of intention, Aristotle argues, would be reduced to nothing if everything that one does in an intense emotional state were to be considered unintentional. Whereas we can consider involuntary those errors we commit simply because we lack information – because some essential aspects of their circumstances have eluded us – we have to take responsibility for those acts we carry out when we are angry or jealous. These are our own acts.

Plato perceived *eros* as a tyrant, as the presence of another power – one that is, metaphorically, animal: a volatile and ungovernable horse or a hybrid monster inside the soul, whose only truly human component is reason (*Phaedrus*, 253c–e; *Republic*, ix, 588c–90d). He considered acts motivated by passion to be almost involuntary. Aristotle, on the other hand, asserted the cognitive nature of emotional acts, which according to him consisted of thoughts that we can and must control. The Stoics were even more uncompromising in their theory of the cognitive and intentional nature of passion, and insisted that every sentiment – from anger to desperation and from fear to erotic frenzy – was nothing more than a mistaken and hurried judgement accompanied by a bodily disorder such as warmth, cold, dilatation or contraction. We feel an emotion not because of some instinctive drive, but because of the way we interpret what happens to us: this insult is intolerable, this catastrophe is shattering, that animal is frightening or that person is devastatingly attractive. This kind of hasty and overstated assessment is then followed by an assent, by a 'yes': we accept that perception and make it our own. On this account, love becomes the extravagant overvaluation of an object, one that we decide to agree to. If, however, we were wise, we would see that same object for what it is. Love is a ridiculous exaggeration.

Tragedies written in the fifth century BC played a decisive role in this debate. Theatrical reflection on consciousness and responsibility in human behaviour – a major theme in plays concerned with fatal errors – provided philosophers with a repertoire of cases and ideas. We can see this in Aristotle himself, who systematically drew on Sophocles and Euripides in his moral works, when he wanted to find particular examples of difficult situations. We encounter it in Stoic texts, in which Medea appears as the embodiment of the ruinous damage that passion inevitably causes. Theatre prepared the ground for philosophical debate.

Let us examine for a moment the argument between Jason and Medea: he believed that *eros* came from Aphrodite, while Medea asserts 'my *eros* is myself'. This is not so much a turning-point in the play as a dilemma that Euripides stages by assigning the two theories of desire to the two characters, when the tension between them is most extreme. Their disagreement on the nature of *eros* is the most profound difference that divides them and provokes the horrendous act of infanticide.

The choice between the two theories is not therefore some tedious wrangle: this much is clear from its context in the play as a whole, and also from another play by Euripides, *Hippolytus*. There Aphrodite makes Phaedra fall in love with Hippolytus, a chaste young man whom the goddess wishes to punish for the contempt in which he holds her. This woman is, more than any other, the one he should avoid: she is the wife of his father Theseus, and therefore his stepmother. At the first sight of this handsome adolescent, Phaedra's heart falls prey to a consuming love (27–8). Her terrible passion is not returned by this dependably frigid and insensitive youth. Phaedra is consumed by desire and shame. Dejected, tearful and unable to eat, she tries hard to hide her love but in the end confides in her nurse, who betrays her trust and reveals the secret to Hippolytus himself. Although he reacts with disgust and indignation, he promises to be completely discrete. His lovesick stepmother now risks dishonour for this devastating and unrequited love. She decides to kill herself, but, to have her revenge, she attaches a note to her body before hanging herself. In the note she tells her husband that she committed suicide out of shame, following an attempt by his son to seduce her. Hippolytus keeps his promise of silence and his father, convinced therefore of the boy's guilt, plots his death. At this point the goddess Artemis reveals the nature of Aphrodite's perverse plan and makes possible a cathartic reconciliation between father and son.

Hippolytus is a disturbing tragedy because it displays a woman's erotic and symbolically incestuous disease. The crime of loving a member of her own close kin group – in this case, her own husband's son – is added to that of wanting to commit adultery within the home, while the husband is away at war. Such an affair would have been the most outrageous offence against Theseus. The version of the play that has survived is less scandalous than the first one Euripides wrote, which was subsequently censored. In that initial version, it seems, Phaedra spontaneously fell in love with Hippolytus without Aphrodite's intervention, and took the initiative of declaring her love to her indignant stepson. She was acting just as Medea claimed that she is acting.

In classical Athens, the wider public might find a secular theory of desire to be shocking. Evidently Euripides delighted in testing the limits of toleration. In Euripides' plays, which the ancients already considered dangerously modern, we encounter an unexpected phenomenon: it is a woman who stands out against the 'Aphroditean' version of love, in a dramatic conflict which, if it did not change for ever the theory of *eros*, nevertheless called it into question for an audience which was probably accustomed to Jason's way of thinking.

A THEATRICAL SENSUALITY

What is desire? What is its cause? How different is it for men and women? Men and male gods are overcome by passion, while women consider themselves responsible for their affections. If love is perceived as a form of alienation, then the image of Zeus, bewitched by Aphrodite's spell, and that of Medea, who disdainfully takes responsibility for her feelings and the acts committed in their name, can be seen as opposite extremes.

In archaic discourse on erotic emotions, the male body is more obviously exposed to a swift, unexpected and involuntary surge of sexual arousal. Men fall in love in a more sudden and passionate manner, and are clearly surprised by a visible movement which involves an external part of their own bodies and does not arise from their own intentions. The difficulty in controlling the reflex action of erection remains in the background of stories and scenes of seduction. Because he cannot restrain himself, for instance, Hephaestus spills his semen on the thigh of Athena (and from that fluid, wiped with a tuft of wool and thrown to the ground, Erichthonius, the ancestor of all Athenians, will be born). This difficulty or anxiety is also relevant to philosophical discussions on the nature of desire and eroticism. The manner in which the penis acts independently launches a constant challenge to the precepts of psychology and ethics. We shall come to these debates in a moment.

In contrast, the female anatomy, although phallic by analogy, hides itself in an inner space. The womb/penis is inside and cannot be viewed. In the tragic representation of female passion and sensuality, therefore, the corporeal dimension of erotic desire is less obvious. It needs to be interpreted and always involves the soul as well as the body. The erotic drive is intertwined with all the other aspects of female subjectivity, while *eros* expresses itself symbolically, through acts, words or other signs.

And here lies the subtlety of a playwright like Euripides, who manages to bring to light sensations and feelings that are generated within the body – a space where not only the genital apparatus but also the self can be found – by putting them on stage. Female characters are the more complex ones; for them, sex is not simply a matter of genital arousal and intercourse. It is sensuality. Their excitement manifests itself through a whole range of emotions which, although they arise from *eros*, do not convey it simply and univocally. Women are tortured by jealousy, tremble with humiliation and rage, wait with trepidation for a man who will perhaps return, and either aspire to marriage or regret it. All this is erotic, but also something else. *Eros* becomes many things: resentment, hope, diligence and devotion. The bed, which could be considered the external space into which female desire flows, is a place of pleasure and dignity, sensuality and justice. Ulysses can think nostalgically about his distant wife and, in the meantime, make love to a goddess who cares for him and adores him. His sexual acts occur as natural events, free from all states of mind and scruples. He is unwilling, and yet he does it. He spends the day in tears, looking at his home; but at night he goes to bed with Calypso. Penelope, by contrast, experiences the absence of her husband as sexual abstinence and is unable to separate eroticism from attachment and loyalty. Sex is so unproblematic for Ulysses that he can have some here, some there, with different partners, and never see in this any competition with the legitimate wife. Sex, on the contrary, has so many implications and ramifications for Penelope that she hesitates for three years about accepting a second husband. Her suitors wait patiently for her decision, but in the meantime they have sex with the servants. Jason considered the female obsession with the bed to be a fixed and limited idea. How can she be so narrow-minded? He does not understand that Medea's amorous experience extends far beyond the bed, and that her entire life and identity are made up of love for him.

Precisely because of this complexity, women translate their ardour into acts and words: they externalise something that always occurs inside and cannot be seen. Women hide their feelings and can lie; they are obliged to confess what they feel and can be misunderstood. Hence Phaedra and Medea act and suffer in a state of conflictual and tormented love in which the body and the soul are indistinguishable, and the drive is always partially corporeal but can never be reduced to an unmistakably physical stimulus. The drive has to be questioned, articulated through language and brought to light. And its signs have to be interpreted and played out. In other words, female sexuality is irredeemably theatrical. The theatre is the genre of discourse that represents it, and, by doing so, produces an alternative theory to philosophy.

AN INTERESTING WOMAN

A woman, we can now claim, is capable of losing everything because she is also capable of wanting everything. She is phallic too, but her invisible phallicness makes her the most suitable subject for deep psychological understanding of sexual desire, not so much in philosophical reflections as in the theatre. While Medea represents the female position on desiring and choosing a man, we can certainly associate her with other tragic figures: Phaedra in Euripides' *Hippolytus*, or Aeschylus' Danaids – women who refuse marriage by arguing their right to acquire the husbands that please them. Then there is Helen, who in a beautiful fragment by Sappho is celebrated as the most splendid example of the relativism of aesthetic and amorous judgement. 'What is the most beautiful thing?', asks the poetess, and then she replies: 'That which we love.' Consider that Helen objectively had everything: glory, wealth and the most excellent man in the whole of Greece. Yet Helen followed another man, and her desire took her elsewhere. We will see how the Greek imagination produced several variations on the theme of the wife awaiting the return of her husband from war. For this is the recurrent position of the woman who desires and must decide whether or not to follow her desire.

The reader might object that Helen, Phaedra and Medea are characters created out of excess. They only represent the conventions of the tragic genre and its hyperbolic transgressions. Moreover, tragedy developed in a culturally sophisticated city, fifth-century Athens. The representation of sex and sensuality was therefore transformed in such a place. Medea's modern theory competes on the stage with Jason's ancient one. Let us concede this, for a moment, and see if we can find a meek female figure, discreet and indifferent to sensuality. We shall look for her in the Homeric world, where the Zeus intoxicated by Aphrodite comes from. Let us go and visit Penelope. We shall see whether at least she was imagined as passive and imperturbable.

Penelope is a wife; she is the Wife. She represents legitimacy, loyalty and patience. She seems to be defined by a marital virtue that appears intuitively comprehensible to any reader of the *Odyssey*. Her use of time – her endless weaving and unpicking – is supposed to be a sign of inexhaustible devotion and chastity without malice. We are all meant to be in agreement that she never enjoys the spectacle of that equally interminable banquet at which so many handsome and wealthy young men pass their days in the hope of obtaining her consent. Ulysses' wife is believed to be the exact opposite of Agamemnon's wife, and to be the quintessential anti-Clytemnestra – the steadfast guardian of the home.

Yet all the other characters in the *Odyssey*, including Ulysses, know that Penelope is undecided from the very beginning and until the very end. She is tempted. She is torn between two possible futures, and she hesitates, plays for time, makes her suitors wait. She herself unashamedly confesses, 'so my mind is divided and starts one way, then another. Shall I stay here by my son and keep all in order, my property, my serving maids, and my great high-roofed house, keep faith with my husband's bed and regard the voice of the people, or go away at last with the best of all those Achaeans who court me here in the palace, with endless gifts to win me?' (xix, 524–9, translated by Richmond Lattimore).

Although she was actually faithful at the moment her husband returns, she must have been uncertain and perplexed for a long time. Moreover, the only initiative she has taken is to have launched a challenge so that her suitors can exhibit their power in competition with each other. The best is to become her second husband. An innocent reading, from someone who did not know how it would all end, would not find anything to indicate that Penelope is certain of their collective failure or that she knows that only Ulysses is capable of pulling the string of that enormous and heavy bow she provides as a test for the suitors. This test makes it possible for Ulysses, who has returned disguised as a vagabond, to demonstrate his terrible energy to everyone; but it was not organised as a trap for unsuitable candidates for her hand. Indeed Penelope sincerely and earnestly intends to make her final choice from the men who court her. She says she will follow the one who proves worthy of being compared with her first husband. As she is too intelligent and too expert to be happy with judging the value of the presents offered by each of the suitors, she wants more; she wants a man no less handsome than Ulysses, and a man who can effortlessly achieve the same exceptional deeds (xix, 570–81). Penelope is willing to follow that man, whoever he is.

When dusk sets in, the normally reserved Penelope suddenly becomes talkative and confides in the interesting foreigner whom her son wishes to have as a house-guest, and whom we, readers, know to be none other than Ulysses. She can no longer stand the waiting. She has had a dream that alludes to the imminent return of her husband, but she does not believe in dreams. In fact, it was after that dream that she decided to make her decision: she will marry one of the men who desire her, and she will choose the strongest. Her only regret is that she will have to leave such a splendid, well-equipped and unforgettable house.

Blind to the fact that she alone has failed to recognise the man she is talking to, the archetypal wife tells him that she has finally decided to split from her husband. He encourages her and helps her to interpret her dream. And what a dream! The chaste, sexless Penelope has dreamt that she saw and observed her geese – her twenty geese – leave the water and scratch about intently in the courtyard, pecking corn as they went. She was filled with joy at the spectacle of these beautiful and hungry birds devouring their meal, and she was enjoying running her eyes over them, when suddenly an eagle appeared in the sky, out from the mountains. The bird of prey fell on the harmless and gluttonous birds, and broke their necks with blows of its beak. In her dream, Penelope was frightened and horrified, and she burst into tears to see how the pleasant creatures were treated. Then the murderous eagle settled on the edge of the roof and spoke to her in a human voice. It said that it was Ulysses in person, that the dream was a prophecy and he was about to return to massacre all the men who banqueted and courted his wife.

Penelope wakes up and is too upset to go back to sleep. She jumps out of bed and runs into the courtyard to see if her geese are still alive. She finds them in perfect health in their normal place, where they are still scratching the ground and pecking corn. What a relief! The dream was only a dream. She reflects on the foolishness of dreams, and decides to marry the best of those characters who, in the form of geese with robust appetites, have given her so much nocturnal delight.

The pleasure she experiences in the dream becomes the intention to organise her future wedding (xix, 560–81). The narrative link is immediate. Ulysses listens and continues to chat politely, while she fails even momentarily to associate the arrival of this mysterious stranger with the announcement by the talking eagle. The archetypal wife has decided not to believe in the allegorical meaning of the dream; she has decided to interpret the dream in her own fashion. The human voice of the bird of prey does not refer to anything real. The geese are alive and the eagle is bogus. Ulysses will not return.

Penelope deciphers a nightmare, which explains itself as a preview of the future, in order to infer the opposite of what she is being told. This is not absurd in the Homeric world. Dreams which present themselves as explicit prefigurations of forthcoming events can turn out to be false and misleading, as in the case of the one Zeus sent to Agamemnon at the beginning of the *Iliad*. The naive king of the Achaeans allows himself to be deceived, but not Penelope. With empirical curiosity, she goes to verify whether her geese are still alive and concludes that, if the image in her dream was mistaken about them, then it must have been an illusion about the eagle as well, even though the eagle identifies itself with Ulysses. Her excessive perspicacity leads her to renounce her hopes, which are exclusively centred on that man, once and for all.

At this point in the narration, she is faced with a new prospect: the view of another life, in another house, with another man. It is, however, too late, as we, readers, as usual, are already aware. Ulysses will not return, because he has already returned and is standing before her. He will use the challenge of the bow to enter the game and achieve his aim. But, in spite of our privileged position, we should not be insensitive to the beauty of this moment in Penelope's story in which, for the first time, she imagines putting an end to a period that has been entirely paralysed by the memory of, and the wait for, an absent person. Finally, it seems possible to mourn properly and therefore to attain something else.

If we read the *Odyssey* rather than rereading it, it preserves the pleasure of those moments of uncertainty, in which anything could happen except the outcome that awaits us at the end of the narration. It also allows us to discover the nuances in the Wife's character, which turns out to be much less unambiguous than we are led to believe by following the narrative pattern of the 'return'. The fabric of the *Odyssey* leaves room for a Penelope whose existence is somewhat independent of Ulysses, and who is able to conduct her own game and strategy and respond to her own desire.

What time does Penelope inhabit? Time that has been put on hold. She has stayed at home to wait for a man who may return, but it is not known when. She awaits, being at his disposal. It is the use that the other is making of his time that defines her existence. Penelope is entirely dependent on Ulysses, his decisions and his luck. Will he return? Can he return? Will this occur immediately, soon, in the distant future or never? We cannot be sure, however, that Penelope is allowing herself to be completely absorbed into this dependency. The archetypal wife could be doing something else. In the meantime, while she waits, she has perhaps found a way of making others wait and of making herself desired. To read the *Odyssey* is to follow Penelope in her ability to determine the time of others and to put their days on hold as they await her decisions. This is not her husband's time, but that of the young aristocrats of Ithaca, whom we must stop calling, contemptuously and lazily, the 'suitors' and whom we must sooner or later learn to perceive through Penelope's eyes.

PENELOPE'S TIME

The very first words of the narration invite us to see the *Odyssey* as the adventures of Odysseus, adventures driven by his desire to return to his wife. In Book i, line 13, this woman makes her first appearance, and is the destination of his journey home. We see her from this position; we see her on the horizon shrouded in Ulysses' nostalgia; we see her as unattainable on the island the hero despairs of ever seeing again. At this moment, Ulysses is on another island, Ogygia, and in a highly unusual situation: he is under siege from a sea that is unremittingly hostile because of the anger of a god, Poseidon, and he is detained by a goddess, Calypso, who loves him and wants to make him her husband (i, 15). The first image of Ulysses is that of a man who is being courted and who rejects the desires of a female divinity. This goddess, who is in the position of a 'suitor', does all she can with sweet, tender and persuasive words to enchant him and make him forget the other island. But it is all in vain, because his thoughts go out to the smoke rising from the chimney of his home (i, 55–7).

Ithaca is not only the place that draws Ulysses' attention and the narrative tension of the *Odyssey*; Ithaca is also the scene from which the story unfolds. We readers are not obliged to see it only through the eyes of the troubled traveller. We can observe it during his absence, during the period in which Penelope experiences her patient wait. So we have parallel situations which appear to have been constructed in order to contrast with one another.

In Ogygia, Ulysses is pursued by the lovesick goddess, by her generosity and her promises, but he resists and gives her no grounds for hope. The tears with which he looks on the sea mean that the loving Calypso cannot delude herself about what he desires. They sleep together, but she desires him and he does not desire her. In his own fashion, Ulysses is faithful to both women who love him. In Ithaca, Penelope is pursued by lovesick men, by their generosity and their promises, and she resists. Paradoxically, the repetition cannot continue because the long courtship of the archetypal wife by the young men of Ithaca cannot be described as simple resistance. While Ulysses travels the eventful distance between Ogygia and Ithaca, and between Calypso and Penelope, the rhythm of time is marked out by Penelope's indecision – by her doing and undoing, and her vacillation throughout the intermittent process of seduction.

The action starts in the *Odyssey* when two gods, with the agreement of Zeus and all the other gods convened on Olympus in the absence of Poseidon, take on the task of unlocking the two parallel situations on the two islands. Hermes is to fly down to Calypso and persuade her to let her ungrateful guest go; Athena is to fly down to Ithaca to suggest a set of initiatives to Telemachus, Ulysses' son, who is now a man: to start with, he can launch an appeal to his people and convene an assembly. An assembly, the goddess thinks, will give the timid young man a chance to cope with an unsustainable situation and announce his intentions to change it. He is to proclaim his plan to travel in search of information on his father's fate. There will finally be more clarity about the probability of his return. But the assembly will also provide an opportunity for all the main players to say what they think about the strange paralysis that has taken hold of everyone up until that day. And here the first characterisation of Penelope comes into view.

Standing courageously before the group, Telemachus accuses his mother's suitors of a cruel injustice and cowardice. Those men, he argues, would be afraid to confront Penelope's father and ask him for her hand in marriage. Rather than deal with Icarus, a powerful lord, who would have given his daughter to one of the suitors of his own choice (ii, 52–4), they prefer to plunder a house that has been abandoned to a vulnerable youth in the absence of his father. Their obstinacy has no consideration for the woman's consent (ii, 50) or her son's youth. Telemachus publicly confesses his impotence. He admits that he cannot cope with driving them away (ii, 60–1), while they shamelessly exploit his weakness.

The initial portrait of Penelope is therefore formed by her son's words. From this adolescent's point of view, the mother's position is cut and dried, and free from all nuances: she simply does not want even to hear about this marriage. The wooing upsets her, and there is nothing more to be said. For their part, however, the men involved in this siege see things very differently. They believe that the woman is implementing a strategy of consummate equivocation. She does not openly reject marriage. Instead, she makes them wait. She keeps them in a state of uncertainty. The time they pass in that house and the abnormal duration of their courtship are therefore entirely the result of the cunning of this woman, to whom Athena has given unparalleled talent. She disappoints them and at the same time gives them hope by making promises and sending messages to each of them separately (ii, 90–1).

There are, suddenly, at least two Penelopes: one who does not want them (the impeccable mother), and another who does not want them either but busies herself with not unsettling the situation and engages in several virtual relationships (ii, 110). Antinous reveals that Penelope was secretly cultivating her suitors, disloyally encouraging them and creating clandestine complicities and rivalries. We might naturally suspect that an orator who expresses himself in this manner wishes to disseminate doubt about the conduct of the archetypal wife. These insinuations, however, cannot be lies because another character later says exactly the same things: the goddess Athena in a conversation with Ulysses (xiii, 375–81). Penelope really is acting in this manner. Of course her heart is turned towards her husband, the goddess claims, but her behaviour is another thing. Ulysses immediately understands the atmosphere that awaits him at home. He would have met with the same death as Agamemnon in his palace, had it not been for the goddess' warning (xiii, 383–5).

As an alternative to the exemplary mother, free from desires, who is only moved by her yearning for Ulysses, one of the young lords who wishes to marry her, Antinous, conjures up the contrasting figure of an undecided woman who is reluctant to break off the courtship and is able to play with the constant passion of such excellent men. For her, they have renounced all other possible marriages for three years (ii, 203–7). Why doesn't Penelope release them by unequivocally declaring her faithfulness to Ulysses and his memory? There are no narrative reasons that oblige Penelope to keep all possibilities open. There is the complexity of her character. She does not imitate Clytemnestra, because she does not want Ulysses to meet Agamemnon's tragic end, but she does not act as though she found a second marriage repugnant. The promises, the messages, the delightful dream about the geese and the archery competition, like all the other adventures of this woman who is more than just a wife, demonstrate a wonderfully coherent character.

Besides, no one would demand a loyalty so absolute as to preclude all other amorous plans. Ulysses himself told her at the time of his departure that, if he did not return by the time Telemachus had become a man, she should consider herself free to take a husband of her choosing and to leave the home (xviii, 269–70). Her father, Icarus, is not, perhaps, the tyrannical patriarch of whom the suitors are frightened, as Telemachus claims. Indeed, he is very favourable to a new marriage and, according to Athena, he has already chosen his preferred son-in-law, Eurymachus, who offered the richest presents (xv, 17–18). Even in the case of the young and inexpert Telemachus, the naivety of his judgement of his mother's plans changes into a mature assessment of the possibility that his mother is also a woman.

When Antinous challenges Telemachus to send his mother definitively back to her childhood home, so that her father can negotiate a new marriage, the tender adolescent rebuffs him on two counts. He respects too much the woman who gave birth to him and nurtured him; and he fears that his maternal grand-father would demand compensation. And then there would be the Furies of Penelope herself (ii, 130). Telemachus is to receive such ruthless demands to put his mother out of doors on several occasions (ii, 195; xx, 334–7). And each time he rejects them. However, the reader can note a development in the boy's perception of what his mother might really want. He needs time before he can speak of the possible amorous desires of the woman who brought him into the world. 'I will not send my mother away against her will', he says on the first occasion (ii, 130), unquestioningly certain of her intentions. Later he would say, 'I will not drive her out of the house against her will, but I do not disapprove of her marriage and I invite her to chose the man she prefers' (xx, 341–4). The boy who has become an adult has perhaps finally understood what Athena, disguised as a friend, had told him when she visited him the first time and suggested he allow his mother to remarry, if she so desired (i, 275–8).

There is a father who has already made a decision for her. There is a son who has now grown up and gradually comes to understand the likelihood of marriage, while deep down he also starts to think of his own possessions, which are being plundered because of it (xix, 158–9). There is the memory of a husband who had encouraged her to go away and start a new life. But what does Penelope want personally? To what extent can this daughter, mother and wife impose her own will and desires, surrounded as she is by men who are legally qualified to protect her and highly interested in her fate? So far she has been cleverly playing for time. She has shown her gifts through her delaying tactics. She has defended herself against the pressures of the men who courted her and managed to make them wait patiently. This can only mean that, even though she is a daughter, a mother and a wife awaiting her husband's return, she continues to act as a sexually alive woman and to have herself treated as such. Her mind is made up that she will not deny herself another man forever. However, she now finds herself at a turning-point: her devoted suitors have discovered the trick of the cloth that is woven, unwoven and rewoven, and they have forced her into finishing it. 'I can think of no other ruses', she confides to the stranger whom she fails to recognise as Ulysses (xix, 158). The only way out it is finally to choose a man, because otherwise she would have to renounce a second marriage forever.

Once again, this intelligent woman who thought up the idea of the inter-minable weaving has acted in accordance with her own impulses, in spite of the pressures and her guardians' wishes. If she has to choose one of her admirers, then she is not going to follow her father's wishes; she will not marry Eurymachus simply because he is the most generous. She imposes another game on the suitors. She imposes her own criterion: they have to measure up to the vigour of Ulysses. The challenge of the bow is the sudden inspiration of Penelope the woman.

SENSITIVE BODIES

Telemachus was outraged at the very idea of her remarriage, but he yields to the evidence that this would be more advantageous for both of them (xix, 530–4). Her husband once encouraged her, and her father is anxious to accept Eurymachus' magnificent gifts. She never said that she wanted to be chaste and alone for the rest of her life. All this leads to the final act: bringing the long wait to an end. But Penelope intends to carry out this act on her own, without the assistance of either men or gods. It will be entirely her own choice.

By emphasising the personal and unexpected nature of this act we can reveal exactly how unconventional was the Homeric narration in relation to the world it constructs as its own backdrop. In a universe in which acting, thinking and feeling like a human being were so dependent on divine influences, and in an oppressive situation with competing male powers – father, adult son, husband and suitors – here is a character, what is more, a female character, capable of surprises. Unlike many heroes who can only make a decision when a god puts such thoughts into their minds, the heroine of the *Odyssey* spontaneously uses her own acumen to steer a course through life. She does not ask for permission or advice from her husband, her son, or a confidant. She has a dream, she interprets it in her own way – without allowing herself to be intimidated by the eagle-husband – and then she decides. She is the one who sets up the competition, and she is its only judge. All this must be assessed in the context of what was generally and 'juridically' accepted: 'usually', in the societies described by the poems themselves, it was the father who gave away his daughter in marriage, and 'normally', in myths that narrate a marriage by competition, it is the father who launches the challenges for his daughter. The announcement of a sporting competition independent of the father has no precedent and no parallel; it does not reflect any norm in the archaic world and still less in the classical one.

Penelope innovates. And she does so because she responds in the same register to the desires of the men who have been awaiting her verdict for three years. This is an erotic desire to which she reacts, first, with seductive wiles of messages and promises, and then by inviting them to demonstrate their excellence, not in terms of wealth and social prestige, but in terms of something extremely personal and physical. In order to please Penelope, they have to be on a par with Ulysses in showing the might of their bodies. This final act obviously prolongs the relationship that was established from the very beginning between the woman who is desired and the men who desire her – a relationship the sensuality of which it is difficult not to perceive. The beautiful woman refuses to have sex, but, on the rare occasions in which she appears in the dining hall, the men go weak at the knees. They all think about just one thing: going to be bed with Penelope (i, 366; xviii, 212–13). These are the reactions of lovesick bodies, sensitive to a sexually arousing presence. Not surprisingly, Penelope is to appeal to those bodies. She is to respond to physical desire in the same tone. We will examine in detail the sequence of thoughts, dreams and regrets that will lead her, so to speak, from the memory of Ulysses' body to the body of her possible husband.

But I need to pause in order to deal with a highly predictable objection to this reading of the *Odyssey*. Are we not ignoring the real reason for the suitors' interest in the wife-in-waiting? Are we not perhaps forgetting what has so often been claimed that Penelope, the wife of Ulysses, represents the vacant sovereignty in Ithaca, and marrying her means that one of the suitors will install himself in the absent husband's home and take over his powers, which will be transferred by that marriage? We could be distorting the text by detecting a sexual obsession where there is actually talk of power.

On the contrary. The theme of the sensitive and sensual body is as explicit as the motif of the transfer of sovereignty is out of place. The narration never ceases to repeat that Penelope is not part of Ulysses' line of descent and that she cannot transfer anything, particularly in the presence of an adult son.

First of all, Penelope as the wife was almost an outsider in the house in which she had come to live and follow her husband, and from which she will one day depart if he does not return and she decides to remarry (xviii, 269–70). She has followed Ulysses to that home, but, if she marries again, she will follow another man (xix, 572; 579). According to Antinous, she should in fact have left her marital home and returned to her father, whence she could leave with a new husband once more, for yet another home. By challenging her suitors to compete in the place where they have gathered – Ulysses' home – the independent Penelope is saving herself the extra trip; she would leave directly with the winner. Whatever the case, the suitors are not expecting the chosen man to settle down in Ulysses' house. Virilocality is never challenged.

Besides, her outsider status in relation to the property she has been looking after becomes even clearer when Athena urges Telemachus to be on his guard: the naive young man has to be careful that his mother does not take away precious items when she leaves for her new home and her new life. It is well known how covetous women are in these circumstances (xv 19–26)! Ulysses' son and heir must consider his mother a stranger who would be behaving like a thief and taking possession of goods that are not hers, if she were to take something from the house.

Then there is Telemachus: his father's place is now to be his. His mother's second marriage would smooth his way to the succession, freeing the house of a troublesome presence. The suitors would have immediately got him out of the way if they were only wishing to attain royal title and property. Instead, they wanted to be on friendly terms with him and encouraged him to favour the marriage that would take his mother to another house (xx, 328–37). They do not appear to think that the conquest of this woman will provide one of them with the opportunity to succeed Ulysses and to lay claim to his throne. Only when they are irritated by Telemachus' desire to find his father do they organise an ambush as a collective enterprise: they will kill the young man and share out his assets (xv 383–92; iii, 316), as if the elimination of Ulysses' son and the distribution of his wealth amongst them all was a separate project from that of just one of them marrying Penelope. This is consistent with her having to follow her new husband.

Penelope herself is their objective. The men who court her undoubtedly act with arrogance and baseness, and they dishonour Ulysses. But they insult him precisely because they desire her sexually, in her husband's house, while that husband is still alive. They gorge themselves on Ulysses' food, but they do so because the woman does not accept their persuasive gifts. As previously argued, she responds to their physical desire in the same tone, but in the feminine – with thoughts, regrets, dreams, letters and seductive postures, which give her first marriage, and her possible second one, an intense and sensitive eroticism. The boys from Ithaca are entranced in her presence, feel their knees giving way, and yet, while waiting, they have sex with the maids. They idealise her as the best woman of all, and this is why they compete so unwearyingly, but no one bothers to write her a poem. It is Penelope who, on the receiving side, invents a rudimentary art of love.

Let us examine these moments of Penelope's sensuality in sequence. After the dream about the geese which cheer her and have their necks broken by the eagle, Penelope reflects on the possibility of organising the archery challenge, a test that might make it possible for her to find a man capable of pulling the bowstring of this unwieldy weapon with the same nonchalance as Ulysses (xix, 571–81). She confides her plan to the unknown stranger (Ulysses) and makes it very clear to him that she is looking for a man 'very easily' capable of this act (xix, 577). The following night, she has another dream: Ulysses comes to her bed exactly as he was at the time of his departure, young and vigorous, arousing her pleasure, and she feels that this is an omen and not a dream (xx, 88–90). On awakening from this deceptive dream, she bursts into tears and invokes

Artemis and the death that the goddess could gift her. She declares herself
ready to search for Ulysses even in the next world, rather than settle for a man
'who is his inferior' (xx, 81). The same day, she goes down to the dining hall
and announces the rules of the competition.

Penelope follows her desire and imposes her judgement. Her father's intentions, the gifts and good manners: these all exist in the background, but they
are not taken into account. She has escaped the father who gives away his
daughters in marriage. Motivated by her own dreams and her own thoughts,
she has invented the scenario that will allow her to decide. She wishes to
continue her own life: her second husband must incorporate something of her
first; he must not disappoint her in the area in which the memory of her lost
man becomes most vivid and forceful: the matrimonial bed. She is not acting
against Ulysses by forgetting him or insulting his memory. Penelope is not
Clytemnestra. Although her still ardent love for Ulysses persists, she has now
set out upon a route that leads to another bed.

Thus Penelope quite unexpectedly reveals herself to be close in spirit to
Medea. She is forthright in displaying the restlessness behind her choice, and
she gives voice to the individual perception that marriage does not follow only
the general rules. She introduces a sense of uncertainty into the awareness of
social norms. In a kind of reflective resonance on Penelope's actions, Medea
will ask herself about the criterion that should permit women to decide upon
a husband 'to be bought'.

A woman needs definite signs and evidence on which to make her decisions, given that a conjugal union requires a great deal more of a woman than
of a man, that the obligation of faithfulness weighs more heavily on one than
on the other, and that it is very difficult for a wife to initiate a divorce. In other
words, a woman has to reflect more deeply, because of all those factors that
make marriage a decisive relationship in her life.

But, for Euripides' Medea, there are no signs that can reveal the truth or
value of a man. The ability to pull Ulysses' bowstring effortlessly is to serve this
purpose for Homer's Penelope.

THE PHILOSOPHY OF DESIRE

What is desire? Like the young participants in a Socratic dialogue, we have
reviewed a series of specific situations, but have not yet come up with a definition. We have behaved like bad philosophers, but we have done so intention-
ally in order to conjure up a few scenarios, from a remote cultural landscape.
We have seen how, in the Homeric universe and on the Athenian stage, sexual
desire differentiates between the female and the male. On the one hand, there
is the intricacy of an inner emotional experience that the theatre can best play

out, in the most appropriate language. On the other hand, there is a drive within a part of the body – the penis or the knees – which is manifested in a direct and visible form. In both cases, sexual desire appears as something powerful, but this force takes hold of, and paralyses, men – one might say, petrifies them – precisely in those parts of the body, whereas it affects women internally and externalises those effects in their behaviour. On the feminine side of the history of desire, the connection between *eros* and activity and between *eros* and passions in the form of actions appears to be a constant, from the Homeric world to the world of tragedy. Male eroticism, conversely, is represented as a sudden irresistible stimulus and a loss of control over one's body. This is the ancient theory of love, which philosophy took on the job of rethinking at the time of Plato.

Let us not reduce desire to the simple polarity between active virility and passive womanliness. We have already realised that ancient thought was concerned with *eros* as it came into being, and with its cause. Therefore the erection, inasmuch as it is an event, was more important than penetration, which always constitutes a voluntary act and often an affirmation of power. The unpredictable nature of desire therefore seems to be the most important and problematic aspect of male eroticism. On the other hand, female eroticism is the one that appears diluted in various forms of affectivity and activity.

We will now return to the question of defining 'desire'. One definition can be found in the reading of archaic poetry. *Hímĕrŏs* is the conscious tendency towards an action, a condition or an object. One can desire death, one can wish to cry or one can desire one's own homeland (i, 41). Desire, however, is also what Aphrodite gives to Hera when she lends her the brassiere that will allow her to seduce Zeus. The talisman acts to cause Zeus' desire. Desire is defined as a genre within which the erotic circumstance creates one specification amongst many. *Hímĕrŏs*, however, is not the only term Homer uses to denote amorous intentionality. We are dealing with words, and not with a concept that has been given a single name. *Ĕthélein* expresses volition, a project in general and, in amorous contexts, a consenting desire resonating with another's will. Calypso gives her consent in this manner in relation to Ulysses, who is not interested in her love (v, 155), as does Clytemnestra, whom Aegisthus persuades to follow him (iii, 272). Penelope, however, does not say yes to anyone (ii, 50 and 128). *Āndáneîn*, her refusal to consent to courtship, and the manner in which she takes time to choose the man that pleases her (ii, 114) determine the long wait of her suitors and therefore the passing of time in Ulysses' 'occupied' house. The entire plot of the *Odyssey* depends on the denial of this consent, which clearly contrasts with the consent given by the other two heroines and thus demonstrates the importance of feminine agreement. The only thing the suitors impose on Penelope against her will is the suspension of her interminable work on the loom (ii, 110; xix, 156; xxiv 146).

The same definition can be given to the verb *ĕĕldŏmaĭ*, 'to want', and in some cases 'to want a woman' (v, 209–10); and even to *eros*. Identified as a god, Love does not exist in the Homeric world. Once again, the term means desire in general and, in particular cases, amorous attraction (*The Iliad,* iii, 442; xiv, 294). It is Aphrodite who provokes erotic sensations and situations.

Desire is undoubtedly a sensation which the desiring person experiences and acknowledges. The weakness at the knees accompanies the suitors' intention to go to bed with Penelope. The person who desires claims to be 'enveloped' or taken over by *eros* or *hĭmĕrŏs*. The person who desires is aware of what he or she is feeling. We should remember the corporeal sensitivity of Penelope's suitors in her presence. Although her body cannot compete with that of a goddess in demeanour, charm and loveliness (*The Odyssey,* v, 211–20), she does however emanate beauty of a divine quality. One day, Athena magnifies Penelope's allure with the artifices dear to Aphrodite and applies cleansing lotions with ambrosia to brighten her skin. She makes her taller and stronger, so that she will enchant the men who attend on her (xviii, 187–91). Her attraction then becomes more intense for everyone. Men are immediately unsettled on seeing her standing on the staircase to the hall, and a veil makes her face all the more seductive. Their knees become weak, and their minds are bewitched (*thĕ́lgheīn*) by *eros* (xviii, 208–13).

Above all, sexual interest manifests itself through speech. Desire seeks out the other's desire – that famous *ĕthĕ́leīn* that the young men of Ithaca will never attain, in spite of the rich presents – by attracting, admiring and seducing. Persuasive conversation, in which love declares itself and transforms itself into proposal, expectancy and compliment, is part of the phenomenology of desire more than any other symptom. Poetic words speak of love as it unfolds, like a rhetorical bloom. There is Calypso, who unstintingly struggles with sweet, engaging and ingratiating arguments (*mălăkoĩsi kaì aĭmulíoīsi lŏgoīsi,* i, 56) to enchant (*thĕ́lgheīn*) Ulysses and make him forget Penelope (i, 56–7). There is Hera, who equips herself with the belt that contains, amongst other spells (*thĕlktrĕ́ia*), 'amorous chatter' (*oaristús*) and 'flattery' (*párphasis*), and manages to bamboozle the wisest men (*Iliad,* xiv, 215–17). There is the evil suitor, Aegisthus, who uses alluring words to attract (*thĕ́lgheīn*) Clytemnestra (*The Odyssey,* iii, 263) – not to mention Circe, the enchantress with knowledge of many drugs, who casts her spells through potions rather than words (x, 291), but warns Ulysses against the sirens' call, which is so crystal-clear that it makes the hearer forget his wife and children forever – such is the power of its *thĕ́lgheīn* (xii, 40). Deceit (xvi, 195) and enticement into oblivion make up a semantic field in which desire appears fatally mendacious. Neither truth nor memory of the rest of the world remains intact in the transliteration of love – in its transformation into language.

It is clear, however, that the power of the word to arouse an erotic resonance is not always effective. Ulysses is unresponsive to Calypso's words. His memory of Ithaca and his desire (*hímĕrŏs*) to return home remain unaltered. The epic tale celebrates the resourcefulness of language, but at the same time it demonstrates how language can fail. What is even stranger is that the seduction is narrated rather than depicted. Dialogues with direct speech are rare. The one between Zeus and Hera has an almost comic effect, given that he finds himself in the position of a husband who is being seduced and aroused by means of a non-verbal artifice (the famous belt), but he explains to his wife that he desires her more ardently than he does the other goddesses and mortal women he has known. In other words, it is the declaration of a man who is undergoing the effects of Aphrodite's spells. Zeus has been bewitched, but he attempts to seduce Hera with a rhetoric more suited to maddening her than to making her faint with love.

What does Calypso say to Ulysses? What does Aegysthus say to Clytemnestra? We do not know. We are not witnesses to duets such as the one between Don Giovanni and Zerlina; we do not see gallant persuasion in action. We do not know what is said to the beautiful Penelope by Eurymachus, Antinous and each of the other young gentlemen of Ithaca. Have they ever met her in private? Have they ever written to her? Their collective courtship takes place amongst noisy banquets and moments of silence in which their bodies and their thoughts express love, but a soundless love. Of all the characters in amorous situations, they are the ones who are the most physical and the least skilful in the art of *lógoi* (speeches) used to deceive, ensnare and allure. In the midst of the uproar of that vast and crowded dining hall lacking any room for intimacy, they can never find the good manners to gain her coveted consent. They are uncouth, in spite of all their presents. As we have seen, their clumsy and inexpert sensuality encounters Penelope's surprising response.

LOVE LETTERS

The distance between lovers and the objects of their love will be dramatically bridged by lyrical poetry. An amorous word addressed directly to a loved being, who is often absent, elusive and unapproachable, transforms the description of desire into its representation. In place of a narrated causality – 'Aeneas was filled with Aphrodite's desire', '*Eros* enveloped me' or 'he went weak at the knees' – we suddenly encounter phrases addressed by the person who is experiencing these emotions to the 'you' who is triggering them. Instead of diagnosing his or her own state, the lover speaks directly about it to the other person, in order to transform symptoms into arguments. The poet identifies with the lover and gives voice to that amorous chatter, that enchanting murmur and that ingratiating manner of speaking that the Greeks always associated with eroticism, but which the most ancient poetry has articulated through a kind of theory of love without mimesis.

Then poetry becomes confession for an 'I' that bares its own sentiments, not because it wants to make the public aware but because it wants to move just that person who, as the origin of this passion, is supposed to receive the message. The poet/suitor turns the cause of his or her love into an object, an objective towards which he or she must reach out. The public – the modern reader – has to learn to keep their distance and become a superfluous spectator to a dialogue that does not concern them and is not addressed to them. Poetry shifts the vocative to the person who unsettles the speaker's emotions.

The word embodies a tension. The poem has become a protest and a lament, a prayer and a compliment. The distance of the desired object is the condition for this. Precisely because the beloved is not there, or proves to be unavailable, it is necessary to 'send' her or him a word that arrives at a later time and in another moment. Greek lyrical poetry introduces the celebration of the person who is far away and to whom it is only possible *to write*. We know that the Greeks considered the time factor to be an essential element in discussions of the merits and demerits of writing. Writing makes it possible to enter into a dialogue with someone who is not present and who receives your message much later. Writing means pretending to find yourself face to face with the recipient. Reading means the illusion of listening to a live voice. Amorous poetry, the expression of a desire not yet satisfied, is structurally written: it is, as it were, an epistolary genre.

'He who stands before you, has for me the appearance of a god, while you smile with such sweetness. I know that I am pale, greener than the grass. I feel a burning warmth wriggling through my body. If I wanted to talk, I would be unable, so heavy is my tongue. I feel that I am melting.' These are, more or less, the words of Sappho's 'letter' to a girl she loves, in which we find the essentials of amorous poetry. The poem's voice speaks to a 'you' who is both present and inaccessible, visible and absent. The girl is smiling at another and is entirely absorbed in that other 'face to face' – that other intimacy of looks and smiles. Being engrossed in that complicitous spell and therefore more cruelly distant than if she were elsewhere, the beloved cannot receive the confession the poem expresses in real time. Sappho is speaking to someone who is not listening. And the poem is saying precisely this: 'You cannot hear me and do not want to hear me. You are not here for me. And this is why I have to write to you.' The lacerating torture of the sensations of love – hence the paleness of the skin contrasts with the burning in the veins, and the paralysis of the tongue contrasts with the urgent need to speak – is revealed in order that the beautiful and indifferent woman can have a glimpse at what happens when she is not there, when she is immersed in conversation with another. Sappho wants the girl to know what it means to miss her, and to learn the effects of her absence. The poem conveys the inability to speak – the recipient is unavailable and the lover is not even able to articulate words – and proves, through its very existence, a written remedy to aphasia.

UNPLEASANT DESIRE

As has already been argued, Homeric desire is a conscious tendency towards an action, a condition or an object. It is a movement towards that which has provoked the longing. It is therefore a movement towards its own cause. If the person who desires finally attains that which arouses the yearning – by carrying out the action, achieving the condition or possessing the thing – then the desire is satisfied, appeased and quenched. By coming into contact with its cause, desire disappears. The extinguishing of the sensation of craving coincides with the blossoming of another sentiment, that of enjoying the thing, condition or activity, which shortly before was inaccessible and is now current and present. Pleasure marks the end of desire. This is true for all forms of appetite. The 'heart' is no different from hunger and thirst, which give way to the delightfulness of palatable food and drink; the erotic ache, however strong, disappears at the moment when the loved body allows itself to be taken in the lover's embrace. The duration of desire is demarcated by the advent of pleasure.

It is of paramount importance to understand how desire and pleasure connect. The changes to this connection over time, in different genres of discourse, constitute one of the significant aspects of pre-Christian sensuality. To enjoy and to crave were very clearly distinguished in the Homeric world. The two feelings were opposites: where there was one, there could not be the other. I desire because I am not in the presence of that which could give me pleasure; I start to take pleasure from the moment in which the presence of that which I lacked allows nothing to be desired. Desire is the past of pleasure. Desire is unpleasant. Hunger, thirst, tiredness, sexual arousal, nostalgia, the furore of battle . . . every form of *hímĕrŏs* manifests itself as an urgent, impelling need to put an end to the sensation itself. In its negativity, this sensation – to be *missing something* (an action, a condition, a thing or a place) – impels impatience and rash haste towards its own annihilation. Desire is suicidal. Whatever its cause, I always desire that my sensation of lacking comes to an end. I want to want no longer. That is why I want the thing that has provoked my desire.

Pleasure, on the other hand, is the enjoyment of the present object, as the Stoics would define it. It is relief, but also, the privation that is the essential nature of desire: at last I can enjoy the object of my desire. There is, however, a paradox in this opposition between desire and pleasure. To paraphrase Socrates, we could say that, even though they oppose each other, they are attached to each other like two Siamese twins. Can I enjoy something without having desired it? What am I enjoying, if not that which I felt to be lacking? Do I not need to desire an action, a condition, a thing or a place so that their presence can bring me pleasure? The lack, with the conscious sensation that accompanies it, appears to have the power to indicate that which is capable of making me happy. It is absence and unavailability that identify that which will fill me with joy once it is present.

No Homeric character ever enjoys anything to whose absence he or she would be indifferent. Quite the contrary, the things, persons and situations that are coveted for the longest period of time are also the most sensuous. This explains Ulysses' lack of appetite in relation to Calypso, whom he has no desire to possess, in spite of all the superhuman qualities he acknowledges to be hers. It also explains his passion for Penelope, his distant wife, who is now perhaps beyond his reach. The distance that divides them makes him cry. Penelope is not only a *femme fatale* for the young men of Ithaca; she is also that for her unfaithful husband, with whom she will stay in bed for three days, once they are finally reunited.

You need to suffer in order to experience pleasure. You need to suffer in order to know what brings pleasure. The very absence of what you want plays a fundamental role in the selection of that which, later, will delight you. Something, if lacking, creates a desire; once present, the same thing causes a powerful satisfaction. It is therefore the same thing that causes both desire and pleasure. To say this is to say that joy, sensuousness and happiness are possible, in spite of the importance of a sense of lacking which is required in order to select the sources of joy. Appetites are not insatiable.

This is what philosophy would deny. Apart from Epicurus and the Stoics, classical philosophers believed that desire is insatiable by its very nature. This philosophical theory is profoundly anti-Homeric. However, lyrical poetry and tragedy had already prepared the ground, before Platonic and Aristotelian arguments denied the ancient relationship between negative desire and positive pleasure. Sappho's poetry demonstrates and typifies this: the poetic word, addressed as a letter to the beloved, creates a situation of absence, where the addressee is inaccessible and unavailable. It is a writing full of nostalgia, imploration or admiration, which dwells on the negative moment and stages that period when, separated from you, I can only speak to you in a poem. This time of desire is the one that Homer fills with tears and tireless efforts to reach the destination. In spite of being a skilled bard (and because he is an oral poet), Ulysses does not compose erotic poetry for Penelope, nor does he send her love letters. The same is true of Ithaca's boys. It is lyrical poetry that starts to dwell on this dead time and creates the genre of romantic poetry, if by 'romantic love' we mean a love made up of courtship, expectancy and rhetoric, which is perhaps an impossible love. As for tragedy, it witnesses the almost too obvious triumph of loves without happy endings.

As literary genres multiplied between Homer and Plato, desire gradually lost its capacity to unite with its own cause, which is also the cause of pleasure. The loved person becomes an unattainable objective, the object of a desire which is transformed into language. She becomes the recipient in whom one confides the very difficulty of attainment, in the hope of capturing her attention. Moreover, another story also unfolds in parallel with the literary transformation of the thinking on amorous desire: the one that, broadly speaking, involves political and ethical reflection on human ambitions and on the means to achieve them.

THE SONG OF PENIA

Once upon a time, men lived happily – not human beings, but men in the masculine plural. One day, Zeus decides to ruin their existence because of a series of incidents which recurred through no fault of their own. He orders the divine artisans, Hephaestus and Athena, to produce a beautiful evil, a creature resembling the goddesses who already existed, but specifically designed for mortals. Hephaestus models the body of what will become the first woman, Athena equips that body and Aphrodite makes it desirable. An exception in the genealogical pattern of a theogony (in which everything is generated), the ancestor of all women is a technical artifice and she brings a new way of life to men – men in the dative case, men for whom she was purposefully made. From then on, humanity has to deal with covetousness for riches, hunger for possessions and thirst for abundance. Woman is not satisfied with Penia, and does not make compromises with scarcity and penury. She craves luxury.

For the poet Hesiod in the eighth century BC, the feminine becomes synonymous with insatiability, demanding behaviour and infinite ardour. The first female human being introduced the condition of feeling oneself continuously incomplete, unsatisfied and poor. Woman made men feel for the first time that they lacked something, could be lacking at all, and made them experience their limitation. In her ambitious laziness, woman made men work for her so that they could fill that vacuum. The advent of sexual difference amongst mortals humanises men and makes them irreversibly different from the gods. The 'distressing tribulations' (kḗdĕa lugrắ) – sorrows, unrest, anguish, work and worries – spread into the world in the wake of this female doll. The ability to realise one's wishes and plans, which was so typical of the lives the gods led, became forever lost in a husband's life. Everything has now become difficult and laborious, often impossible.

In the immediate post-Homeric universe of Hesiod, desire comes into existence by accident and as an unmerited punishment. Desire immediately leads to greed, excess and lasciviousness. Very significantly, it does not have a precise cause. It does not arise from the lack of some particular thing. A specific cause would provide a limit. The desire imported by the female presence is indiscriminate, generic and absolute. It is generated by the woman *per se* and affects everything. Hesiod dedicated an entire poem, *Works and Days*, to the ethics of being happy with one's lot, of 'the little more of everything', of prudence and of restraint. It is a morality which attempts to mitigate the fatality of economic want. The destiny of ephemeral human possession is illustrated by the use of earthenware jars in which cereals, oil and wine were preserved. Once the jar is opened and one starts to draw off the contents, one is soon half-way down the jar, and even more quickly at the bottom. If one wants to feed oneself, as one must, then one enters into a vicious circle of constantly filling and emptying one's own jars. Resources are never stable, and therefore one must be vigilant. Poverty always lurks in the shadows, ready to attack.

Starting with Hesiod, an aphoristic literature develops, in which the unlimited nature of human desire played a central role. Insatiability is a fault, but it is principally a curse which is inherent in the human condition. How can we avoid being insatiable, if we have to feed ourselves every day and if things do not have the power to satiate us permanently? Ethical thought appears to lose that Homeric trust in the possibility of experiencing the sensation of plenitude and of not lacking something, which may not be permanent but is real enough, and is something humans share with the gods. Human beings are made in such a way that, when they manage to possess a great deal and to 'fill themselves' with wealth or glory, they find that they have the energy to want much, much more. Solon's political elegies display an obsessive interest in the evil consequences of satiety, *kŏrŏs*. Herodotus' *Histories* follow the pattern of the rise and fall of empires, cities and political leaders, all threatened by self-blindness and greed. As with Homer, satiety is possible, and the emptiness created by desire can be filled. However, Solon and Herodotus perceive, above all, the instability of plenitude. Desires have precise causes that determine and restrict them, but nothing can stop them from proliferating. For every satisfied desire, there is immediately another desire for something else.

INSATIABLE DESIRE

Between Homer and the classical era, an increasing consensus was created around a common assertion, which philosophy attempted to develop and refine. Desire – *ĕpithŭmía* or *ŏrĕxis* – is by its very nature insatiable. One word becomes essential to all arguments on sex and ethics in general: *aplēstía*, the nature of that which cannot be filled.

For Greek philosophers, matters concerning love (the *aphrodísia*) do not constitute an independent field of experience requiring specific treatment in ethics. Quite the opposite. Desiring man is concerned with a plurality of appetites, characterised by the same structure and manner of operating. His first problem is to classify the passions and identify their shared peculiarity in contrast with the other functions of the soul. Sexual drives are part of the *ĕpithŭmíai*, whose cause is a physical object and whose aim is the possession of the said object. This possession involves the body. Hunger, thirst, sexual arousal and greed for wealth come under this definition. In contrast, there are corporeal emotions like anger and courage, which do not tend towards the acquisition of an object, and cravings which, although they involve a yearning to grasp and contain, are directed towards intangible objects, imagined things and ideas that the intelligence takes possession of, without the assistance of the body.

In his *Timaeus*, Plato expounded a theory of the desiring body (70d–73a). Acquisitive desires correspond to the operations of a particular part of the soul, situated in the midriff (whereas the part of the soul that makes us feel anger and courage is located in the heart, and intelligence in the head). The stomach, intestines and sexual organs are its seat, and the place from which the sensation of desire first appears. These areas of the body are also the ones that tend to come into contact with the desired object. This part of the soul, which is similar to a gluttonous beast chained to the body's feeding trough, is supposed to perceive desire as a feeling of emptiness and therefore a wish for plenitude. Hunger, thirst and arousal signify the sense of missing something, and at the same time the reflex action of needing that thing. A certain object is identified as suitable for filling that empty space.

Emptiness is a very important concept for the Platonic understanding of the body and the soul. Our somatic substance is made up of elements mixed together in various proportions. Physically we are an aggregate of air, water, fire and earth, whose particles are interlinked. The aggregate is, however, unstable: each of the ingredients tends to return towards its source by separating itself from the various mixtures. In other words, we are continuously dissolving over time. While we live, our body decomposes. This means that miniscule empty pockets are created. Little cracks are formed simply by the imperceptible evaporation of elements towards their original sites. In order to avoid this unravelling of our corporeal fabric down to the very last atom, we need to eat and drink. To prolong our identity, we have to reproduce ourselves. The need for food and drink requires a digestive system that transforms the ingested material into blood, which, like everything else, is made up of air, water, earth and fire, but with a clear predominance of red fire. Blood irrigates the body and fills the empty pockets left by the dissolution of elements (*Timaeus*, 80d–81e).

The god who designed the body has therefore equipped us with a means of remedying the mutability of matter. And, in so doing, this deity showed great far-sightedness, and even predicted that the human compound would become a greedy, gluttonous and hedonistic being, and would therefore attempt to swallow a quantity of food and drink in excess of the need to compensate for the somatic decay. Hence the god added a kind of safety valve: the intestine. The surplus ingested substances are therefore eliminated in the form of excreta. In order to make the system of discharge even more suited to the predictable intemperance of human beings, the demiurge cunningly obliged the superfluous material to go through a slow, laborious and prolonged passage. This is why the intestine is so long and sinuous. During the food's long transit through its endless meanders, we do not feel the sensation of emptiness that drives us to eat and drink. Thus we are available to think of, and deal with, other things (72e–73a).

Physically, we are constructed in order to be able to use time in a particular manner. Our body helps us to counter its own failings and, what is more, to correct the soul's inclinations. The intestines save us from insatiability and provide us with scraps of time between one meal and another. Thanks to the demiurge, we do not have to live like plovers (*chăradriôi*) – birds which were famous for feeding and defecating at the same time, and unceasingly. This is dependent, however, on the desiring part of our soul not dragging us into an intemperate use of our bodies. If we follow our desires, which are by nature insatiable, we will end up living in a state of perennial movement. Animals whose anatomy creates a shortcut between the mouth and the anus are tubular animals which have no time for anything, like the repellent plover. Paradoxically, the plover represents the way the desiring soul operates (*Gorgias*). If that part of the *psuchế* is nourished, then the person enters into a vicious circle of filling and emptying.

The alimentary and sexual soul (the *ĕpithūmētikŏn*) is systematically depicted through the use of metaphors of unending oral ingestion. In the *Republic*, the kind of life that involves giving in to one's passions, following one's inclinations and seeking out sensual pleasures transforms human beings into beasts. Those who live such an existence resemble violent and voracious cattle who, as they waste all their time on grazing, gorge themselves, mate with each other and gore each other. This brings them no pleasure at all, argues Plato; they think they are enjoying themselves, but in reality they do nothing more than fill a receptacle, which loses substances that are in turn unsubstantial (ix, 586 a–b). They pour non-being into a container that cannot hold its contents. This is unsubstantiality on top of incontinence. Interest in concrete things is futile, because material things *are* of little moment compared with ideas, the only stable reality. This nothingness, which is characteristic of the tangible and the corporeal, is entirely expressed in terms of inexhaustible desire and impossible pleasure. The nothingness of desire is represented by this incessant movement of discharging, for which the equally continuous filling up fails to compensate, even fleetingly. Everything is always in flux.

The same idea appears in the *Gorgias*, but is developed through a different metaphor. Plato compares a frugal and austere man with a pleasure-seeking one. Who will be the happier – the one who goes without, or the one who satisfies all his appetites and his desire for life? Callicles feels that happiness is necessarily linked to one's desires. The more you desire, the more you enjoy. Socrates feels that such an existence would be deadly. That is how the dead live in the nether world, when they are condemned to pour water into a leaking jar and carry it in a colander. Once again, this is how plovers live. How can people think it pleasurable to be frenetically busying around a vase that has to be filled but cannot hold its contents for more than a single instant? Life is pleasant for someone who can sleep peacefully in the knowledge that his jars are full and have been sealed (*Gorgias*, 492).

In his variation on the pitfalls of desire, Plato shows a clear preference for food analogies to express the essential point of his thought: the idea that the various specific objects that come to 'satisfy' specific desires not only fail to calm the craving but actually excite it further. There is an unrelenting mechanism in appetite, which means that it cannot be perceived as something discontinuous and controllable. It does not appear possible to experience one desire after another, halting whenever the person wishes and measuring out a proper intensity of the experience. Desire is tyrannical and imposes its own rhythm on the person, who is now incapable of self-control. At the bottom of the jar, as at the bottom of the desiring soul, there is a gaping hole into which everything thrown inside immediately disappears.

Whereas the body designed by the gods has intestines that remain full for a certain period and therefore placate the appetite for a little while, the desiring soul is analogous to a body without intestines, in which matter flows through incessantly. This anatomy of digestion allows Plato to depict human desire in general in a visual manner in cases where its cause is a material object which can be possessed. Sexual desire comes under this category. While you would expect a visual depiction of erotic and phallic desire to be an image of aggression and protuberance, as we do in fact encounter in the *Phaedrus*, in which lust is an untamed horse, Plato extends the metaphor of the incontinent cavity to male sexuality. Men's desiring soul does not reflect their desiring body. The desiring soul resembles a female body.

CAUSE OR OBJECT?

The most ancient poetic philosophy of love insists on the power that a certain person, body or thing exercises over the person who is in love. Desire appears to be triggered by a specific cause and targeted towards that cause. I have called that movement paradoxical and 'suicidal'. The desire's final encounter with its cause is its end, in the twin meaning of its aim and its termination.

Platonic philosophy of love, however, shifts the origin of the urge to the person who feels it. The reasons for a passion come to depend much more on the way the lover's soul operates than on the properties of what is loved. The cause of the arousal resides in the soul that, according to how it is constructed, behaves mechanically in a certain way. Desire is indiscriminate. The black horse throws itself on the first beautiful body that passes and on all those which are equally beautiful. The uninterrupted filling of the leaking jar never stops in a moment of particular pleasure. In the life of a seducer, that is, the one who follows his or her desiring soul, it is not the quality of the desired things or persons that counts; it is their quantity. Callicles asserts that happiness means continuing to pour in as much as possible, and so much the better if, the more you pour in, the more leaks out. The important thing is to keep the river of desire in full flood.

The logic of this indeterminacy entails an interesting argument: desire does not have an external cause, but rather an object or an objective towards which it suddenly veers. Given that the object is not responsible for the urge, which is generated by human passion itself, it is unable ever to prove satisfactory. The relationship between the desire and the desired object becomes an asymptotic one, given that everything the intemperate person buys, eats, drinks or sexually possesses can only lose itself immediately and flow away in the current that rushes through the jar-soul or the plover-soul. However, if fluidity is absolute and movement can never come to a halt, then pleasure is not possible even for an instant, and cannot therefore exist. Desire runs after an object but never reaches it – sees it being carried away in the flood the instant it comes into view. Desire aspires to a purpose – the possession of its object, satisfaction, and its own disappearance and transformation into delight; but it never achieves this metamorphosis. Hence desire is always there and alive: infinite, eternal and continuous.

Those who live by complying with their acquisitive passions naturally believe they are enjoying life and are happy. They consider their experience of lasciviousness to be wellbeing. But the philosopher steps in to reveal that this is just a laughable delusion. The libertine connoisseur who collects experiences 'does not know', according to the philosopher, that he is calling 'pleasure' an experience which is not pleasurable, and is indeed incompatible with pleasure.

He defines as sensual those moments in which people eat their fill, quench their thirst or satisfy their sexual desires, without realising that the process of satisfying hunger, thirst or sexual arousal coincides with the duration of their hunger, thirst or sexual urge. Their so-called pleasure is made possible by the contemporaneous persistence of desire. One scratches for as long as one feels an itch. While we are filling ourselves up, we are simultaneously emptying ourselves, because the jar is leaking, and that unrelenting emptiness which never ceases to renew itself creates a sense of not having enough, and therefore pain and a never-ending, inescapable desire. Whoever 'enjoys' is always desiring again, desiring more and desiring something else. They are therefore always lacking and suffering.

When the body is involved, Socrates argues, human beings expose themselves to gratifications that are inherently mixed and impure: hybrid sensations that bring with them a vague blend of pleasure and displeasure, or, to put it another way, pleasure and desire. Desire functions as an ever-present killjoy that moderates, alters and impairs that which should be pure and unsullied delight. Without philosophical reflection on what we imagine we are experiencing, we are ignorant of what is really happening. Precisely because, with our material interests, we only and always look downwards, we believe that we have achieved a positive state – that of a real, true pleasure – just as soon as we placate the hunger, thirst or arousal (that is, when we pass from a state of emptiness to a state of relative non-emptiness). But in reality we have only touched a degree zero of non-suffering, from which the incessant action of insatiability immediately removes us. And we re-embark upon our desires.

The so-called pleasure of the senses and possession is therefore spurious, 'algebraically' negative and non-existent. It has no substance. It does nothing more than come into being and become in the movement and change to which it is condemned by desire. Only the possession of intangible objects such as ideas and thoughts procures a true, pure and stable pleasure. For Plato, sensuality is always a vain, cyclical chase after objects incapable of permanence and of being enjoyed. This is the reason why you need to abstain from them.

A RIVER IN A VASE

Sensuality is fluid. Pleasure is not defined as a state but as a process, a shift from empty to full, in a movement which *never* ends because plenitude can never be achieved. This specific temporal dimension to desirous 'enjoyment', as opposed to true, complete and satisfying enjoyment, is the fundamental theoretical argument of Platonic ethics. Sex becomes a philosophical problem for this reason, because it imposes a use of time that is subject to the inability of erotic desire to take possession of its object and retain its hold upon it. Sex is worrying,

because it becomes sensuality and, therefore, wastes your time: compliance
with desires means failing to take notice of anything else. Sensuality wastes
time because it is fluid: there is never any reason to stop, as the pleasure never
terminates the desire; indeed, it is desire that maintains the pleasure in an
unremitting flow.

Platonic ethics is therefore based on an ontological judgement. Acquisitive
passions fail in the realisation of their end, because their objects have little value
and involve little which is of substance. This diagnosis of the weakness of being
implies a connection between being and time: there is something 'insubstantial' about objects whose presence lasts only a short period of time, or objects
which instantaneously flow away rather than remain with us. Food never
completely removes hunger, wine never completely removes thirst and sex
never completely satisfies arousal. We eat but hunger remains, we drink but
thirst remains and we scratch but the itch remains. Pleasurable things are always
transitory. They flow.

The metaphor of fluidity might appear banal, given that we are so accustomed
to its use in connection with time which runs by and has its 'course'. Time is
represented by the continuous movement of the hands of a clock, or the flow
of liquids or sand through an hourglass. It is less banal, however, to realise the
meaning that fluidity takes on in Plato's language. The consistent recourse to
the image of a current demonstrates the coherent manner in which Plato
places the question of sensuality within the context of his theory of sensation.

Plato considered sensations to be forms of knowledge, but inadequate,
imperfect and illusory ones. The perception of sensitive objects through our
sense organs provides us with a confused, contradictory and unstable understanding. The reason for this is that things which can be detected by touch,
sight, hearing, smell or taste – in other words, everything material – never stay
still, never remain the same in time and space, and incessantly change. They
flow. A metaphysics of liquidity explains the experience we all have of our
sensory world. Sensations relate to different points of view, to different times,
and to different states affecting the observer. The same thing can appear hard
or soft, or harder or softer than something else. Until the thing is thought out
and measured, sensory evaluation remains variable and dependent on context
and circumstances.

There were also those who argued that everything – absolutely all the
possible and conceivable entities – is part of this manner of existence: the
sophists, and particularly Protagoras, through their epistemological and percep-
tual relativism, and Heraclitus, through his theory that everything is in flux
(*pánta rheî*). The *Theaetetus* admits the Heraclitean concept of the real as the
metaphysical premise for the Protagorean theory of knowledge. If man is the

measure of all things, it is because everything is in flux. Protagoras leads to Heraclitus (*Theaetetus*, 151e–160e).

Plato took up the challenge of this theory of matter and a theory of knowledge, in which nothing and no object remains true to itself long enough for someone to grasp its nature objectively. If this is true, then knowledge is impossible and there is nothing that can be known. The theory of Forms – real and immutable ideas that remain true to themselves forever and are therefore knowable in themselves and as themselves – was his response to that challenge. Plato therefore rejected the Heraclitean proposition that everything is in flux: ideas are not, and they are protected from the currents (*Theaetetus*, 184b–186e). While it is true that not everything is in flux, however, some things certainly are immersed and carried by the stream. These are sense perceptions. According to Plato, all sensations have a degree of inadequacy and confusion. All things that can be seen, heard, touched, smelled or tasted are characterised by simultaneously contradictory attributes. These attributes vary continuously from one observer to another, and from one moment to another with the same observer. *Apart from* the Forms, everything else is in flux.

This theory is essential to an understanding of Plato's thoughts on the experience of sex as relentless sensuality. Pleasure, pain and desire belong in fact among the sensations, just as perceptions do. Pleasure, pain and desire are also forms of knowledge, and are assessed as such. This is why a pleasure can be 'false' (*Philebus*, 41a–b). This is why pleasure and displeasure are Siamese twins – a couple of opposites tied to each other, with the result that the same person can only feel one in relation to the other (*Phaedo*, 60b–c). This is why desire is for the soul an impression of emptiness which is translated into a movement towards plenitude (*Philebus*, 54d–55a). Above all, this is why everything is in flux in the sensual experience of sex, just as it is in the experience of luxury and gourmandise. The metaphors of the leaking jar, plovers and bestial gluttony provide nothing but a visual content to the logic of flux, which originated with Heraclitus. Let us take a final glimpse at this consistent depiction: the principle of corporeality is represented by a torrential river (*Timaeus*, 43a–b); our body operates in a torrential manner because of the flow of food, the stream of perceptions and the outflow of seed (77c; 81a; 91a–d). We are constructed in a manner which allows us not to be plovers (*chăradriôi*), but we survive as a result of the slow and constant transit of fluids (72e–73a). Heraclitus' river runs through our bodies, just as it crosses the infernal jar.

DESIRE AS ANXIETY

The importance of Heraclitus in the Platonic theory of sensation has been known for a long time. However, I would like to emphasise here the significance of flux (*pánta rheî*) for his ethics. A systematic reading of the texts that deal with sex demonstrates incontrovertibly that erotic desire is modelled on the digestion of food and reduced to an uninterrupted flow, like the other acquisitive appetites. Sex is therefore located within the category of sensory experiences, in contrast with the knowledge of ideas. This explains why Plato emphasised so obsessively the distinction between sex and knowledge, and between dissoluteness and philosophy. Sexual practice competes with the use of reason and thought precisely because it depends on a sensation and therefore, like everything else that depends on sensations, aspires to an impossible knowing or possessing. To cultivate sensation means to embark upon an unending experience: sensuality.

Sexual desire proves ineffective in achieving its aim and therefore, he argues, it absorbs all the time. Its impotence makes it despotic. This is the reason why we have to escape its paradoxical power, otherwise our entire existence is wasted and swept away in the current. For Plato, it is not possible to create a lifestyle in which one can alternate between the pursuits of intelligence and those of licentiousness. The intemperate descends into an abyss of discontent. Sex therefore becomes a way of life and a 'full-time' occupation. Desire is a form of anxiety.

At this point, we come across Michel Foucault's line of thought. We should recall that the volumes of his *History of Sexuality* devoted to the ancient world were entitled *The Use of Pleasure* and *The Care of the Self*. They are based on two theories: for the ancients of the classical period, the ethical substance (that is, the 'material' of questions, worries and concepts from which we compose a morality) is made up of pleasure and the acts that bring pleasure, not of desire and its interpretation. In their codification of the acts, the ancients of the first two centuries of the Christian era speak of care of the self, thereby presenting sexual morality as a style of existence. In *The Use of Pleasure*, Foucault makes abundant use of Plato, but everything we have said about Plato so far leads towards very different conclusions.

Firstly, is it true that sexual acts constitute the essential object of Plato's ethics? The answer is that he never discussed them. Such acts can only appear irrelevant within a theorisation of pleasure which considers pleasure to have been made non-existent and impossible through the persistence of desire. That famous 'scratching oneself', which, with its obvious sexual innuendo, is evoked in the *Gorgias* and the *Philebus* as an example of sensuousness, is reduced simply to an attempt to alleviate an itch while the itch lasts. The act is defined as something secondary, dependent and derisory compared with desire. The act is an illusion. 'For classical Greek thought, this force [of pleasure] was potentially excessive by nature, and the moral question was how to confront this force, how to control it and regulate its economy in a suitable way' (Foucault, 1984a: 60). But pleasure is not excessive. Ethically, the problem is not with the vitality or intensity of pleasure; it is with desire, as I hope I have demonstrated. The ontological judgement of insatiable desire is the reason for constructing an ethics of sexuality. The ethical substance coincides with desire. The use of pleasure is not an essential notion in Platonic philosophy.

As for *The Care of the Self*, it has the considerable merit of drawing attention to the fact that sexuality constitutes a lifestyle. But it was Plato himself who insisted on the link between sexual practice and all the other aspects of existence. The search for pleasure certainly determines a particular use of time. However, sex has this power to become a care, an interest, a dominating and exclusive preoccupation because, once again, desire is insatiable. It is the lack of satisfaction that makes us intemperate and turns licentiousness into a way of life. We continue because we are never content. Michel Foucault profoundly underestimated the ontological factor in Greek ethics: 'The ontology to which this ethics of sexual behaviour referred was not, at least not in its general form, an ontology of deficiency and desire' (1984a: 43). This is why historians of sexuality mistook something Plato based on a nihilistic theory of desire for a pragmatic vision of behaviour.

2

PLEASURE

HĒDŎNÉ

Greek pleasure is sweetness. It is sweetness to the palate: wine and delicious foods. It is the melodious voice of the Muses and the charming song of the poet. Greek pleasure is oblivion. A pleasurable mood is defined by the ability to forget the torment, the worries and the anxieties we have already encountered as some of the meanings of *kêdos* and *kédéa lugrá*. The dulcet voice, *glukéré*, of the Muses makes us forget the *kédéa* (*Theogony,* 97–104). As the daughters of memory, the Muses came into the world with an 'uncaring spirit' (61) and the mission to make people forget their ills and to alleviate anxiety (55). Art is calming and narcotic. It acts like wine or the drug nepenthe, the analgesic and tranquilliser that Helen poured into her guests' cups on a memorable evening. We are at her home in Sparta, the war with Troy is over, and the beautiful woman is reconciled with her husband. Suddenly a shy young man arrives wanting to hear news of the heroes of that war, particularly Ulysses. During the meal, the remembrance of the battles, carnage and death creates a grim atmosphere. Everyone is intent on remembering and renewing the pain of mourning. Helen wishes to distract them from those distressing reflections. She therefore mixes this Egyptian drug into the watered-down wine in a large bowl, and the drug has the power to anesthetise the memory, extinguish grief and placate anger (*The Odyssey*, iv, 220–30). The same is true of all causes of pleasure.

Pleasure is respite, the extinction of pain and an end to unease. Eros is associated with *húpnos* (sleep), as we have seen in Hera's seduction of Zeus. Desire, which we normally see as arousal, was primarily perceived in these texts as paralysis and petrification. Knees that go weak are knees that cannot run or leap forward. The act itself and the sensuousness it produces are a kind of powerlessness and withdrawal from life, similar to exhaustion.

The symposium was the most fulfilling hedonistic ritual for the ancients; it was the setting in which all the ingredients of pleasure came together. When

Plato wants to show what citizens would do in a city governed not by concern for the common good but by the principle of pleasure, he produces the following scene: those who should be dealing with the management of the city would indulge in a life of continuous feasting, those who should be working to produce goods would put on extravagant clothes, cover themselves with jewels and relax in an unending symposium, making the occasional useful gesture if they find it amusing (*Republic*, iv, 420e-421c). The coming together of food, wine, music and eroticism in an event that inevitably costs a great deal of money was a celebration of the triumph of the feral soul and of the disintegrative power of pleasure (*hēdŏnḗ*). And pleasure had to be excluded from the ideal city precisely because it resulted in anxieties being forgotten.

Unsurprisingly, therefore, the ancients associated relaxation, eroticism and conviviality with one posture of the body and one piece of furniture. In Greece and Rome, they slept, made love and dined while reclining on comfortable couches. The frescoes in the House of the chaste Lovers in Pompeii show how a triclinium would have been set out. It is a room containing three beds placed in a horseshoe shape around low tables, on which there are plates and goblets — a dining room. A man and a woman lie in sensuous proximity and amorous languor on each of the beds. Greek vases — the very things which were used at table and were often decorated with scenes pertinent to the table and its universe — depicted relaxation and abandon on couches (*klînaĭ*) in dining rooms between men and boys, or between men and *hĕtaĭraĭ*, sensuous female companions.

Mollitia and *malakía*, which designated yielding, laziness and laxity, were traits of character that were associated with physical characteristics and positions. Resting and lying down — the acts of making oneself soft and releasing the tension in one's body — require something comfortable as support. The convivial *klínē*, with its wide mattress, provided this for men and youths who met in a house for a banquet or a symposium: a place prepared for pleasure in all its forms. Wine, conversation, music, food and erotic titillation: all this was enjoyed with elegant abandon. 'Come and lie on the couch,' the youthful Anticleon invites his father Procleon who, because of his coarseness, is in need of re-education, 'and I'll teach you how to behave at a symposium' (Aristophanes, *Wasps*, 1208–15). Participants at these events had to lie down with grace, by stretching out their knees and languidly slipping down like a gymnast. The Aristotelian author of the *Problems* wrote that you can lie on the left side with pleasure (*hēdĕos*), whereas on your right side you fall asleep. You stay awake while resting on your left elbow because, with the active right hand free, you can make all the gestures you want (vi, 5 and 7). You digest better with your body bent, as a result of the warmth the position allows you to conserve (vi, 3). We can see this in the symposium scenes painted on the pottery used at the symposia themselves: reclining men, with one leg stretched out and the other slightly bent, and with one arm holding up the body and the other free, so that the hand can raise a goblet or caress a drinking partner.

Respectable women did not get involved in such worldly pleasures: to recline beside a table meant also going to bed in euphoric and animated company, which was created in order to abolish distances and expose scantily dressed bodies (the clothing was not stitched) to contact with all the others. For this reason it was generally believed that a woman who frequented banquets was a *hĕtaíra*, a prostitute or mistress (Pseudo-Demosthenes, *Against Neaira*). No husband who cared about his honour would have exposed his wife to such promiscuity. Banquet scenes on vases do indeed show women at symposia, but only in the most unrestrained erotic situations.

Pleasure was hypnotic, and pleasure was lethargy. Plato revived this ancient perception of pleasure, but added an idea of his own: it is impossible to partake of *hēdŏné* in small doses that are compatible with an industrious and balanced life, because desire is insatiable. Once you give in to desire, you sink into a different kind of existence. The power of sensuousness does not therefore depend on its intensity, but rather on that continuous movement of want, refilling and want again, which ends up absorbing all the time of those who live like plovers, grazing cattle or jars with a leaky bottom. The symposium of those who abandoned themselves to the game was full-time indolence.

The problem of pleasure, let me insist, is not its excessiveness – its excessive intensity, duration or beauty. Indeed, pleasure paradoxically becomes illusory and unreachable in its purity because of the desire that pursues it asymptotically. With its despotic and inordinate demands, appetite prevails and renders satisfaction impossible. The excess, therefore, is to be found in desire and not in pleasure (*Laws*, 783a–b). This is why Platonic ethics cannot be reduced to a simple call for moderation, as though it were a matter of curbing an overindulgence; it actually proposes ascetic abstinence. The guardians in the ideal city have to renounce property and a private life in which they would be able to express their taste for luxury. They have to eat communal meals precisely in order to avoid the exquisite ambivalences of symposia. They have to form sexual partnerships that are unrelated to their erotic inclinations. The city has to be happy, but its happiness is not the one its citizens aspire to, which is individual pleasure. In other words, they have to prefer something else. The black horse has to be tamed.

Thus, regarding erotic pleasure, sexual acts themselves are not the substance of ethics, because what matters is, rather, the risks inherent in *la dolce vita*. Sexual acts were perceived as the effects and expression of a certain kind of persistent inclination – what I call sensuality. Although each one can be isolated and described, they all depend on a yearning for a state of completeness that can never be achieved.

DEMOCRATIC LIFE

Platonic thought was a corrective, polemical and paedagogic response to a particular vision of human existence. Callicles, a character in the *Gorgias*, speaks for those who believe that happiness is made up of powerful passions, which come together in a continuous enjoyment of life. Unless you want to live like a corpse or a stone, the movement of appetite must never be halted. Life is desire and the satisfaction of desire. As we have already seen, Socrates responds to this Heraclitean manifesto with one of his usual dramatic reversals of ideas. Who is really living like a dead person? Aren't the dead – the souls of the Danaids in the underworld – those who pass their time vainly filling leaking jars? Is not this continuous filling the opposite of what we really want to obtain, which is plenitude? The soul of a pleasure-seeker is like a holed jar – it is like a plover. Callicles obstinately refuses to agree. But then happiness would be like being hungry and eating, being thirsty and drinking and feeling the itch and scratching oneself all the time. This argument has no effect, and Callicles continues in his beliefs. At this stage, Socrates uses a less paradoxical example: the *cinaedus*, a type who was well known to everyone. He asks whether such a person could be considered the model for a happy life. Callicles finally surrenders. The public image of such a contemptible and ignominious person removes all doubts. No one would dare to support such an idea, even in jest.

The *cinaedus* represented an extreme, and typified covetousness in all its forms, but particularly shameless sexual frenzies. He was the human equivalent of the plover – an inexhaustible body, always hungry for pleasure. He had a male body that resembled a woman's. We encounter this in a speech Aeschines delivered in 346 BC: *Against Timarchus*.

Those who had committed one or several of the following crimes were banned from speaking in the assembly by Athenian law: abandonment of one's shield on the battlefield, that is, desertion; mistreatment of, or failure to maintain, one's parents; dissipation or waste of inherited wealth; and prostitution. A citizen who dared to stand up and give a speech to the people after having committed one of these acts was liable to face legal action. If the accusation was confirmed by the courts, the guilty party could lose his civil rights, including the right to be elected or chosen by lots for political and religious offices, and even the simple right to take part in the assembly of the people. He could be punished by *atīmía* (19–32).

The law on *atīmía* followed a logic which provides us with a crucial element for understanding what the Greeks, or at least the Athenians, thought of individual and private life. It affords us a glimpse into a question which is increasingly relevant for contemporary societies: the importance of sex for the integrity and credibility of political actors. When ancient and modern democracies are compared, it can be argued that the law and Aeschines' comments demonstrate the existence, already in the ancient world, of a distinction between the private sphere and the public and political one. The absence of legal norms affecting private life demonstrates the Athenians' great concern with negative freedom or freedom from oppressive rules. Prostitution is not prohibited: the only violation of the law occurs when someone who has committed this act appears in the assembly. The law did not interfere with those who minded their own business in the privacy of their own home (Wallace, 1996: 127–215).

Following this argument, the city's restraint in not interfering in such activities as management of the home or the use to which one puts one's own body confirms Pericles' proud boast in his famous *Funeral Oration* (Thucydides, ii, 37). Under Athenian democracy, citizens did not look on each other with mutual suspicion when it came to everyday behaviour, lifestyles and forms of pleasure. People did not get emotionally involved or become irritated with their neighbours simply because the latter were living in a particular manner, just as they pleased. The Athenians did not ill-treat others even with attitudes which, stopping short of actual injury, could hurt or make life unpleasant. In other words, the Athenian was discrete and had an open mind, free from envy. This meant that all those habits and manners that we associate with the personal and domestic sphere – how we dress, how we eat, how, when and where we make love, and how we bring up our children – were left to individual choice and preferences: everyone was free to behave as they thought best. This assertion can be found in a whole series of texts on the nature of democracy. Democracy was by definition a regime, the only regime, in which everyone lived as he pleased (Lysias, xxvi, 5; Isocrates, vii, 20; Plato, *Republic*, viii, 557a–b; Aristotle, *Politics*, 1317[a] 40–[b]14).

When comparing the freedoms of the ancients and the freedoms of the moderns, however, we need to be aware of a much more radical distinction. In democratic Athens, nobody claimed that the city should allow complete sexual freedom to all consenting adults. One could not find in the Athenian constitution a fundamental right to privacy. (Rahe, 1992: 196). One of the proofs of this theory is precisely the speech *Against Timarchus*. Hence the comments of such philosophers as Plato, Aristotle and Isocrates concerning the licence that democracy allowed to proliferate in the private sphere, must be considered polemical exaggerations by critics of the *dêmos* and its *laissez-faire* (ibid.,

189–90). Athens was an 'illiberal democracy', a pre-modern state that knew nothing of the principle that a state must allow its subjects to behave freely, pursue their own happiness and live in safety.

Without any doubt, the ancients were aware of a symbolic and real separation between *tà ídia* and *tà dēmósia*: distinct spaces, specific activities, and different levels of intrusion by the law. This distinction is, however, compatible with a constant and fundamental relevance of the private in relation to the public and political. As Paul Rahe asserts, the right to privacy – that is, the right to respect, principally consisting of non-interference in people's preferences and habits, which are considered irrelevant outside the home – could not become a value in a society which linked so closely together what a man did in his bedroom and what he said before the people. This connection goes to the heart of the law on *atīmía*: a way of life – one involving waste of one's own money, selling off family property cheap, failing in gratitude to one's relations and, above all, using oneself and one's body for mercenary reasons in an erotic lifestyle – engenders a discrimination in public life. To be more precise, it creates an absolute and drastic exclusion: the law deprived those citizens who dared to do these things not only of their right to election to particular positions, but also of their right to the most fundamental activity in a system of direct democracy: the freedom to speak in the assembly.

The private therefore had a very heavy impact on political activity. In his rhetorical use of the law, Aeschines reminded his fellow citizens of their familiarity with what it was that linked those two worlds: prejudice and reputation, the instruments of shame. Let us see how the use of one's body relates to political ability.

The management of one's own house is relevant to the holding of high office and to the expression of one's opinion on communal decisions. Aeschines asserted that this was because the private and the public are similar or *paraplēsioi* (*Against Timarchus*, 153). It is possible to infer or predict (*manteúŏmaĭ*) how a person will act in political life from the way they have acted in their own home (127). How has this man treated his relations, his inheritance and, most importantly, himself – his *sôma*? That is the way in which he will treat the city. The past gives a foretaste of the future, and the manner in which he looked after himself will be reflected in the way he looks after the common good (153). An elementary semiotics makes it possible for anyone to assess the qualities of a politician in advance.

There is an ethical aspect to this view of sexuality as something politically significant. To judge a man in his capacity as a citizen meant examining his life in its most intimate moments, as though political competence were a component of the person taken as a whole. At stake is a man's integrity in the literal sense of his wholeness, and this presupposes that the individual has a coherent, homogeneous and unchanging identity. The actions a person carries out at different times and in places are supposed to follow a repetitive pattern: they are always the same because the person is the same. Desire for pleasure is the thing that unifies all of Timarchus' actions. And reputation is the thing that gives the impression of continuity. Aeschines warded off possible difficulties: no one was supposed to ask him to refer to particular deeds as everyone knew what Timarchus' behaviour was like (*Against Timarchus*, 89–122). His listeners had acknowledged the kind of things he got up to, by laughing at him in a recent assembly (*Against Timarchus*, 79 and 85).

This focus on the entire person, from head to toe and from the beginning to the present, was unsurprising, because democracy – whose spirit the orator attributed to his public – rejects in principle any criterion based on social status (27). Pericles proclaimed in his defence of the aristocratic Athenian democracy that obscurity or origins lacking in prestige or renown do not interfere with the opportunity to acquire reputation and glory through personal merit (Thucydides, ii, 37). Aeschines took up the same theme to introduce his political attack on Timarchus and his defence of the democratic values shared by his listeners. He asserted that the Athenians did not ask that those who took part in politics be descendants of generals or noble ancestors; they simply asked that they should live a decent life. Instead of aristocratic virtues, which were the product of education in childhood and of a particular social environment, democracy demanded personal guarantees from individuals. Their deeds, habits, manners and life histories became the exclusive source on which the people based their evaluations. Public trust therefore depended on private matters.

This is why, for all the claims concerning the fundamental freedom of behaviour inherent in the power of the *dêmos*, it proves to be mercilessly intrusive towards this very behaviour. Morality, habits and customs were the sole material by which the politically active democratic individual could be judged. There had to be complete transparency. Reputation and gossip were its instruments. Through Rumor, who, as Aeschines reminded his listeners, is a goddess (*Against Timarchus*, 127–31), the community came to know how each person lived. There was nowhere to hide. *Tà ídia*, one's private affairs, ended up being exposed to the eyes and ears of everyone. The rumours that circulated about an individual – the people he mingled with, the places of ill repute where he went at night to have his fun, and the things that happened to him when he got drunk – provided the information needed to assess the dignity of that individual in relation to the workings of democracy, once the right person had been able to collect it and present it to the public in the proper place, which was a court of law. What kind of man would live like that? How could he make himself useful to the city, if he behaved in such a destructive and dishonourable manner towards himself, his people and his things?

The Athenian democracy was prying and puritanical in the name of the rejection of class distinction, as Thucydides admitted when he examined the popular resentment against another famous pleasure-lover, Alcibiades. The same exemplary fellow citizens whom Pericles idealised for their lack of envy and for their capacity not to interfere in other people's affairs displayed extremely intense feelings when it came to this young dandy, with his hair after the Spartan fashion, his horses and his life wasted amongst *hĕtaîrai*, young men and banquets. While admitting his great skills as a general, people were offended by his extravagance, intemperance and luxury to the point where they entrusted the state to others and hence, concludes the historian, brought about its ruin (Thucydides, vi, 15, 4). What is evident here is a criticism of the regime's stupidity, as it sacrificed the best interests of the state to vulgar emotions – resentment, indignation and envy – which might have had nothing to do with a policy based on more politically appropriate emotions, or rational choices. Was this a manifestation of human nature in historical events? It was certainly the emergence of a contradiction inherent in ancient democracy.

If what counts for political participation is the individual, irrespective of his origins, then it must be his life that counts, hence his acts and their methods, because this is what the essential person comes down to. But this means that an individual is not free to live exactly as he pleases. He is going to be judged in accordance with a shared sense of proper behaviour, and this traditional and collective perception will prevail over an assessment of his intelligence and competence. It was democracy's boast that it attributed value to a man on the basis of his merits, in contrast with the aristocratic perception of excellence as the product of a certain genealogy and a given *paĭdeîa*, which can only be obtained if one has the good fortune to be born into a noble family. The democratic man was a competent adult, born on Attic soil, who was responsible for his own qualities and was only accidentally someone's son. He was not born well, but he lived well. However, his value depended on the values of those who had the power to acknowledge it, that is, of the *dêmos* in the sense of the 'people'. It was the people who sat in judgement of individual decency in the *dŏkĭmăsĭaĭ* (the examinations of candidates or retiring magistrates) and in trials like the one against Timarchus. The individual thus had to conform to communal standards of morality and passions. Above all, he had to know how to show contrition.

In an ancient Mediterranean city, which was a relatively small community where everyone more or less knew everyone else, shame and fear of other people's opinion – *aischŭnē* or *aidŏs* – act as the most important factors in social cohesion and moral control (Cohen, 1987). Shame means experiencing displeasure over what others might find deplorable in our behaviour. It means that our happiness becomes dependent on other people's opinion, and especially on received beliefs. This is not an entirely passive apprehension, because we are only sensitive to the opinions of people we respect and with whom we share precisely these same opinions. We relate to others in a reciprocal manner through the use of restraint and embarrassment, but only in so far as they represent the values we believe in (Aristotle, *Rhetoric*, 2, 6; Williams, 1992). Someone who knows no shame also fears no one. If we cannot blush, then we do not belong to a community.

Democracy can only accentuate the role of the public dominion. Shame becomes a fundamental passion, because of the importance of the way the *dêmos* judges individual and politically acceptable behaviour. And sex becomes a political matter. Indeed, shame concerns sexual behaviour more than any other aspect of life. The sexual organs were called *aidoîa*, or (in Latin) *pudenda*, *parties honteuses* ('shameful things'). Dishonourable behaviour (*aischrá*) included unions with inappropriate persons at inappropriate times and in inappropriate places, because such transgressions resulted from incontinence (*akŏlăsía*) (Aristotle, *Rhetoric*, 2, 6, 4). Timarchus' entire life was ignominious (*aischrŏs*): as his behaviour was as shameful as he was shameless, he had lost all fear of other people's disapproval and was no longer able to blush (*Against Timarchus*, 28 and 38).

SHAMELESS LIVING

In 346, Timarchus was a prominent politician. He and Demosthenes accused Aeschines of having betrayed the city's interests during the famous embassy to King Philip II of Macedonia. He thus exposed himself to the public gaze, and Aeschines wanted to get his revenge and destroy an undesirable opponent. His personal attack was cynical and purely concerned with the end result. It was, however, an opportunity provided by the law on *atīmía*, which made it possible to eliminate a political adversary with arguments of a personal nature. This was the punishment that Aeschines wanted the judges to inflict on Timarchus: he wanted him to be condemned to disappear from the political arena because he had continued to speak in front of the people after having wasted a considerable paternal inheritance, after having ill-treated an ageing and infirm uncle and, above all, after having shamelessly sold his body and having been unrestrainedly maintained by other men. Timarchus was culpable of every single one of the ignominious acts detailed in the law.

We are interested here in an extreme interpretation of the law, and the relentless ferocity with which an orator managed to provoke his listeners, the *ándrĕs Athēnaîoi*, into feeling repugnance at the simple rehearsal of something they were already well aware of, as everyone was talking about it. Democratic rhetoric, by echoing gossip, manipulated that quintessentially social emotion we call shame, in order to destroy a man completely. There is, however, a special fierceness in the arguments about sex. Aeschines examined Timarchus' sex life in its most intimate details – using prurient insinuation and euphemistic reticence – and exploited those details as his main argument. They were supposed to be infinitely more important than Timarchus' squandered inheritance and his poor neglected uncle when it came to excluding him from public life.

Since his early youth, Timarchus had indulged in ceaseless erotic pursuits with *hĕtaîrai*, youths and mature men, one after another. This craving of his was the cause of his dissipated fortune, of the ease with which he could be corrupted and of his habit of selling off his assets cheap. But, the culmination of this insatiability included behaviour without which Timarchus could not have been arraigned (rather than simply gossiped about): that behaviour was prostitution. The fact that he had sold his body – in other words, himself – to other men was the central point to Aeschines' rhetoric.

Now this is the really interesting problem in our argument: what was so despicable about Timarchus' love life? What persuaded the Athenians to deprive him of his honour (*tīmḗ*)? Was it the fact that he allowed himself to be penetrated sexually and that he subjected himself to a humiliating power that debased him and his identity as a citizen (Dover, 1978; Halperin, 1990; Foucault, 1984a; 1984b)? Was it his general dissipation, which included his passions for fish, gambling, courtesans, female flautists, extravagant dinners, and so on (*Against Timarchus*, 42)? If this was the case, then Timarchus was simply a bottomless pit and a slave to his insatiable desires, which needed to be paid for by someone else (*Against Timarchus*, 75–6; Davidson, 1997).

When we consider the violence and vehemence of Aeschines' speech, which commented on the law using general assertions on sexual morality, we have to ask ourselves whether it was the venality or the actual sexual behaviour that made prostitution incompatible with political activity. Now male prostitution was not only a form of immoderate hedonism, like the mania for flautists and mullet: it was a sexual transaction. This was the point that rhetoric managed to magnify and dramatise. The only important relationships were those between Timarchus and his various male partners, because these were the only ones that involved money, gifts and maintenance in exchange for sexual favours, and these were the ones that were presented as truly scandalous. The other things fleshed out the depiction of his lifestyle, but this was the decisive factor as far as his public disgrace was concerned.

The law referred to selling oneself, not to having sex with another man. It is also true, however, that we do not know of a law inflicting *atīmía* upon men kept by women. And it is also true that Aeschines spoke of other things and extended his attack far beyond the financial aspects of Timarchus' sex life. The speech ends by vilifying the kind of relationship this man created with other men. Timarchus, Aeschines insists, has made his body impure and therefore unacceptable within the confines of the political space (*Against Timarchus*, 188 and 195). He has used his male body in unspeakable positions, as though it were a woman's body (185). He has cultivated an unnatural sexuality, *parà phŭsin* (*ibid.*). All this went beyond the simple act of prostitution and threw a disturbing light on the intolerance that the orator wished to arouse in his public. Precisely because he was so keen to demolish the reputation of Timarchus, we have to assume that he was using plausible arguments and could count on the sympathy of those who were listening and preparing to make their decision. By using words that stigmatised unnatural, effeminate and impure eroticism, Aeschines was touching on what must have been a sensitive matter for the Athenians.

We do not know exactly what these unmentionable acts were, but the allusion to femininity and nature suggests they concerned anal eroticism. In fact it was considered against nature (*parà phŭsin*) for male bodies to behave like female ones and to wish to be passive (*ĕpithūmeîn páscheīn*). In the section on sexuality in the Aristotelian *Problems*, we find a detailed explanation of the changes that desire undergoes in certain people (iv, 26). In naturally effeminate men (*phŭseī thēlūdríai*), the tubes that carry semen to the penis and to the testicles are obstructed either because of a congenital malformation or because these men are eunuchs or impotent. The fluid therefore flows towards the posterior (*hĕdra*), where it accumulates and creates a store of material which is sensitive to erotic stimulation. In contact with a depiction, perception or thought, that is the area that experiences the desire to be rubbed. The pleasure of the sexual act is also experienced there because that is where a secretion of semen occurs, as is demonstrated by the fact that during the sexual act the anus contracts and the surrounding tissues are consumed.

This is analogous to what occurs in active males – those who act (*drân*) in the sexual encounter – because it involves a redirected ejaculation. Effeminate men always remain men, and they can have short erections (otherwise they would become women). Their partial mutilation makes them only similar to women: like women, they are insatiable (*áplēstoí*) because the seminal liquid does not come out with sufficient force to empty the anal area completely. They therefore remain permanently in a state of erotic sensitivity and potential arousal: their erogenous zone always retains a little stagnant material, ready to respond to stimulation. This is why their sensuality is pure lasciviousness (*lagneía*). Anyone who desires to be the passive partner, either all the time or on alternate occasions, has a physiology which can never free itself from desire: it is like having a constant itch, in the manner of the Platonic hedonist. For Aristotle, the itch is the exact model for erotic pleasure: it is an enjoyment that culminates in the expulsion of a fluid full of hot air, which was trapped in the body against nature. The expulsion of semen is the ejection of a humour of this kind in accordance with nature (*Problems*, iv, 15).

Men who desire the passive role are insatiable because their bodies never dry out. Their bodies never manage to expel the humour completely for an anatomical reason: the anus does not have the necessary force to eject it all. It is not designed for this purpose. The natural function of the penis is to fill itself with hot air and liquid in quantities sufficient to eject the semen that has accumulated in the testicles (*Problems*, iv, 21). In a very hot and humid body such as that of hirsute, lame, melancholic or young men, the abundant outflow of semen is accompanied by a great capacity for replenishment and by an intense sexuality, which inevitably involves a series of erections (*Problems*, iv, 30 and 31; v, 31). The anus, on the other hand, is inadequate, just like the female sex organs. Its weakness is effeminacy. Its lasciviousness has a timing which is quite unlike that of the penis: this is the consequence of the residues that constantly impregnate its tissues.

This physiology applied to both Plato's *cinaedus* and Timarchus. The *cinaedus* is the paradigm for insatiable desire (*áplēstos*), because he passes his life 'scratching himself', maddened by a chronic sexual itch. He is like the plover, the leaky jar, the grazing cattle. Timarchus had extravagantly indulged in all manner of pleasures, but the pleasure of pleasures remained the sexual voracity of his youth, which drove him to let himself be maintained by several men, in spite of being rich (*Against Timarchus*, 95). The young Timarchus was not driven to humiliate himself by need; he was not forced into an involuntary slavery. He chose that life (160) because he liked it and desired it (95; 191). He gave it up only when his faded beauty ceased to be profitable. Then he sold his properties and continued to live as he had done. It was the hedonistic gratuitousness of his lascivious nature that strengthened his enemy's hand.

The application of Aristotelian physiology to Timarchus poses a problem. Are we attributing a theory of sex founded on nature to the Greeks, or at least to the people to whom our belligerent orator addressed his arguments?

Like Plato, Aristotle perceived sexual pleasure as the drive for procreation (*Problems*, iv, 15; *History of Animals* 8, 1). And procreation is the work of the *phúsis*. Sexual dimorphism exists in order to allow the transmission of life, while the intestine has a different and specific purpose. The use of the anus for erotic purposes does not fulfil the natural duty to procreate, but if this act is possible as a sexual act – if anal penetration is pleasurable and can be desired – then there must be an explanation. How can sexual pleasure shift to that area? The answer is: through the redirection of the flow of semen, which is a material that acts specifically upon the erotic *diánoiă*. This shift therefore results from processes that occur within the body, and these can be either congenital or the product of habit. We have a dilemma: anal eroticism is in the body, but it is still unnatural. Let us examine this point more closely.

Those who are exposed to sexual relations in adolescence conserve a memory of those acts and of their associated pleasure. By acquiring a habit, they come to desire passivity as though it were natural. In many cases, habit becomes nature. If the person is also lascivious, weak and humid, then this process occurs all the more quickly (*Problems*, iv, 26). This artificial nature, which could be defined as the product of inurement, is indeed a modification of the body: the pleasure of those who acquire the desire to be penetrated occurs because they enjoy and secrete semen in a particular place (*ibid.*, 879b34–5). The acquired nature becomes a memory which is both psychological and corporeal. However, this is not enough to make it natural in the sense of conforming to the ends of *phŭsis*. It is the *body* in which the semen is not directed towards the penis that is defined as 'not in accordance with nature' (*mě katà phŭsin*, 879b6).

Let us cast Aeschines' speech against the background of this Aristotelian theory. His insinuations portrayed Timarchus as the perfect example of a man who had given himself over entirely to effeminate and unnatural pleasure, both because of his lasciviousness (his repugnant nature) and because of his assiduously cultivated habit, which in turn had resulted from his uncontrollable desire (*Against Timarchus*, 95). Like Plato's *cinaedus*, he had a desire for passivity, which explains why he voluntarily engaged in prostitution.

ĚRŌS KALŎS

We have therefore come to the very core of the most widely known question concerning ancient sexuality. What was the attitude of the Greeks towards sex between men and youths? It is an attitude, I will argue, that depends on the social environment, and changes radically between the rarefied world of the enlightened aristocracy and that of the ordinary Athenians, engaged in the performance of democracy.

This question is usually posed by taking Plato as the starting point. But, with Plato, the setting is that of the palaestra and the symposium. In the gymnasium, naked young men ran, threw javelins and wrestled. They sweated, covered themselves in oil and sand, and then dried themselves by running a strigil over their thighs and biceps. They would sit on the ground and leave traces of their genitals in the dust. Older men would look on, admire and comment upon them. They would meet and socialise. And then a youth comes in: he is of such beauty that everyone, older men and peers alike, are unsettled and turn to look at him (Plato, *Charmides*, 154b–d). In the symposium, grown men and youths reclined on beds in pairs, in studied proximity; they chatted, drunk and listened to music. The only women present were flautists and the *hĕtaîrai*. There was warmth and euphoria. It was then they asked themselves about the nature of *eros*. And it was then, in the company of nobles and philosophers, that they eulogised Love as though it had nothing to do with women and the dilemmas of passion and chastity, and as if pleasure and devotion were a matter exclusively for and between men.

Timarchus' trial projects us into an entirely different world. Here we meet the people and find ourselves in the midst of the *dêmŏs*. Pleasure is something else. There are no women, but the men are family men, mostly landowners, who had time to engage in political activities while their slaves worked their fields. Here the ancient and still current argument of 'nature', contamination and disgust could be used with impunity. Aeschines became the mouthpiece for frightening intimidation, secure in the knowledge that he was stroking the beast in the direction of its fur: his public was going to follow him. It was the same public that laughed at Aristophanes' crude obscenities: the playwright, too, liked to direct his sarcasm against love between men. In this context, Timarchus, who ultimately wasn't that different from Alcibiades, had reason to be afraid.

However, the public was mixed, and you never knew who might have wormed their way into the crowd. Aeschines cunningly reckoned that he had to take at least one precaution. He asked the people to imagine what would happen if a general, one of those pompous and pedantic characters who frequented gymnasia and symposia, were to come to the court. Such a man would most probably see the thing in a completely different fashion, and appreciate and cultivate male love in its refined form as in its noble and literary history. There had been mythical couples, like Patroclos and Achilles, and historical ones, like Harmodius and Aristogiton, the tyrannicides. The general might have referred to that authoritative and aristocratic image of heroic excellence associated with erotic friendship between men. He would have demanded his right to teach his fellow Athenians that this type of *eros* is good. In the name of this tradition, he might have wanted to defend Timarchus and his various partners.

Thus there was another sort of listener. The general represented a potential public, whose presence could not be excluded in the anonymity of the audience. In response to this objection, which came not so much from a particular person as from the circles that frequented gymnasia and symposia where love was considered in exclusively male terms, Aeschines admitted that such noble forms of love exist. But, of course, Timarchus' ignominious sexuality had nothing to do with them, as they were ultimately dissociated from sex. That *eros* was good because it was chaste, just and legitimate (*Against Timarchus*,

136–7; 139–40). The wise moderation (*sōphrŏsŭnē*) that typified it was the exact opposite of the overindulgence in pleasure.

During his rhetorical peregrinations, Aeschines addressed two very different audiences. First there was the Athenian multitude, which was ready to snigger at his portrayals of Timarchus wandering outside the city walls at night (80–4), inclined to blush at the spectacle of his all too public exposure in that memorable assembly, and sensitive to the disgust (*bdĕlŭría*) which his actions and the marks it left on his body provoked (189). It was all right to speak of unmentionable acts against nature and of defilement in front of such people, because they were already disposed to receive these kinds of argument favourably. The other possible presence, as I have said, was that of people who thought differently because they lived differently. The general and people like him would have been well disposed towards Timarchus and willing to defend him against Aeschines, by associating him with famous historical and mythical male couples. As they would have been disinclined to accept the orator's premises and conclusions, he challenged them by dwelling at great length on the two types of *eros*, the chaste one and the ignominious one. Aeschines, in sum, attempted to head off the arguments by insisting that love can only be virtuous if it is Platonic.

By distinguishing between the two types of listener to whom he had to address his oratory – the aristocracy and the commoners to whom Aristophanes appealed – Aeschines has provided us with two very distinct sets of beliefs on sexual morality in Greek society. A Greek who stood up in defence of a man with an intensely erotic past, a pleasure-seeking individual who loved grown men as well as youths, and accepted gifts and money would have approved of anything, including venality, and regarded these activities as insignificant detail. This was the viewpoint expressed by the famous general, in whose eyes Achilles, Patroclos, Harmodius, Aristogiton and Timarchus shared the same kind of sex life. Any form of sensuality between males was welcome, whether it was active or passive, mercenary or not. On the other hand, a Greek who fiercely criticised Timarchus for his prostitution, ridiculed his nightly escapades and showed contempt for his unnatural effeminacy was attempting to stir up revulsion against that kind of sex, both in itself and in all its various aspects. Such a Greek would end up feeling nauseated in the presence of Timarchus, not just because he had sold himself but also because he engaged in that kind of eroticism.

According to this logic, those who prized love between males perceived it as an affair between partners both of whom were worthy of respect, and those who scorned it reduced it to nothing more than an inherently imbalanced and ruinous relationship: destructive for the youth, who would lose his good reputation forever (160), and ignominious for the grown man, who would be the cause of such dishonour. The general spoke clearly: the magnificent fame of couples – Patroclos and Achilles, or Aristogiton and Harmodius – had to be defended against Aeschines' vulgar attack on Timarchus. It would indeed have been unjust to harm the handsome young man for the beauty which exposed him to the desires of others (132–6). It was not a crime to be attractive, because comeliness is involuntary and irresistible: it was well known that you could run into that terrifying animal, the beautiful young man, in the world of the palaestra and symposium, and the only solution was to flee abroad for a year (Xenophon, *Memorabilia*, i, 3, 13). Aeschines, who had to answer for his own loves, replied in the affirmative: there can be a wonderful *erâsthaî*, the state of being loved which becomes noble passivity (*Against Timarchus*, 137). But allowing oneself to be loved for one's beauty falls into the same category as loving with elegance: it is a just, lawful and chaste love.

In other words those who speak in favour of *eros*, whether or not they perceive it as sensual, praise the whole relationship. Those like Aristophanes or Aeschines in his speech to the *ándrĕs Athēnaîoi*, who wish to make it hateful, start by distinguishing between the active role (*práttein*) and the passive role (*páschein*), and then go on to discredit both. Both members of the couples which were formed – first Misgolas and Timarchus, then Timarchus and Hegesander – came out pretty poorly, according to the portrayal Aeschines gave of them. By accepting money and gifts and allowing himself to be maintained, Timarchus placed himself in the position of a wife or, in other words, he renounced his virility and revealed his effeminate *phúsis*. By engaging him for money, Misgolas behaved in a shameful manner (41). The enjoyment of a body which has been hired is the act of an arrogant man (*hubristḗs*) who lacks education (*apaídeutos*) (137). In their case, neither avoids criticism.

THE ATHENIAN POĪKILÍA

The fact remains that allowing oneself to be bought and to become *pĕpŏrneuŏ́mĕnŏs* led to the notorious exclusion from political activity. Aeschines' blend of rhetoric demonstrates the mentality of the Athenian middle classes – those non-aristocratic property owners whom democracy included in the political process and mobilised in assemblies and trials. It reveals the degree to which they were willing to hold in contempt the *eros* between males. Aeschines won his action against Timarchus, and therefore his arguments were both pertinent and effective.

We must, however, take note of the general's voice. There was an environment, we said, in which beautiful love, *érōs kalŏ́s*, united older and younger men. The dynamics of their amorous relationship needs to be explored and further examined.

The speech of Pausanias in Plato's *Symposium* has the appearance of an anthropological reflection on Athenian sexual mores. While the barbarians despised paederasty because tyrants feared the heroic loyalties it inspired, whereas the rustic Greeks of Beotia and Elis cultivated it without ceremony, the Athenians, according to Pausanias, had a more complicated, *poīkílŏs* approach to it. Adult men looked out for, and courted, beautiful young men, but, in their capacity as fathers, they protected their sons from the disgrace of a physical relationship. These conflicting intentions and interests might appear to be a double standard: within the same society, adults defended their own sons but did not hesitate to ruin the reputation of other people's sons, while young men found themselves the object of widespread sexual advances but had to reject them in order to defend their honour. The young man who was the object of such desires, *ĕrōmĕnŏs*, had the task of containing within certain limits the active desire of the person who took the initiative, *ĕrastḗs*. According to the generally held standards of decency, the former would be stigmatised for not being able to say no, while the latter would be absolved for an enterprise which was considered normal and even admirable. If this was the 'complication' of Athenian custom, then the moral climate was similar to that of Victorian England, in which men had the right to court while young girls had the duty to resist (Dover, 1978: 84–9).

The complication was, however, even more complicated. According to Pausanias, there were two types of love – two versions of Aphrodite. Aphrodite Pandemia, who was earthly and of the people, engendered the love between men and women, made them desire the body, showered them with gifts, money and social favours. In exchange, the lover expected to receive sexual pleasure (*Symposium*, 181a-b; 183d-e). Aphrodite Urania, on the other hand, inspired love only between men, made them desire the other's soul and offered wisdom (184c). This is disinterested love, which requires no gift in exchange. It is therefore shameful to give in to the desires of a 'vulgar' suitor, because such a person acts in an offensive manner (*húbris*), like a seducer of other men's wives and daughters (182a). Granting him favours means allowing oneself to be enmeshed by self-interest, in an avowedly utilitarian relationship (185a-b). Conversely, it was good to satisfy the 'uranic' or 'celestial' suitor, because the only advantage to be had was in the wisdom this lover dispensed freely (184c). In courtly love it was good to give something back, because reciprocity was not demanded.

The Athenian complication was not simply the sexual overture on the one hand and the resistance to it on the other, but rather the manner in which the suitor made his pass and how the object of his desires responded. To be more precise, what counted was the end – the stake the *ĕrastḗs* placed upon the relationship. It was seemly for a youth to surrender to his suitor if the only thing he stood to gain was intellectual and moral edification. It was unbecoming to do this for material gain, under the influence of the gifts and advantages that the lover provided as part of his strategy to make a conquest. In both cases, however, the *ĕrŏmĕnŏs* gratified the *ĕrastḗs* – he satisfied his desire.

What is the nature of this gratification, this (*chărízĕsthaĭ*)? Pausanias – who was known to have had a long amorous relationship with the poet Agathon, in whose house the symposium was taking place – spoke in euphemistic but nevertheless quite explicit terms. When the purpose of the surrender was purely intellectual, then it was all right to concede anything to the *ĕrastḗs*. It was worth giving up everything in order to become wise and good, *sŏphŏs* and *agăthŏs* (184d-e; 185b). Hence erotic gratitude could be considered acceptable and virtuous (Dover, 1978: 91).

This interpretation of the circumstances in which a young man could agree to make love to a man who courted him after having put his 'uranic' or 'celestial' intentions to the test – love for his soul and not simply for his good looks, paedagogic generosity and selflessness – was shared by Clinias' son Alcibiades, a young general who was notoriously fond of the palaestra and the symposium. At the end of the evening in Agathon's home, just after Socrates' speech in praise of Eros, a drunken and euphoric Alcibiades burst into the room in the company of friends. The symposiasts told him the subject of their discourse and he embarked on the strange story of one of his amorous misadventures. He had been under the impression that Socrates was precisely that kind of *ĕrastḗs*, a miracle of wisdom, to whom one had to show gratitude in an erotic manner. Alcibiades therefore made himself available and indeed took the initiative, almost reversing their roles. He invited him to wrestle in the palaestra and then to supper, having dismissed his slaves. He arranged it so that they would be alone together until late and had to sleep in the same room, even under the same blanket, throughout the night. But it was all in vain. The supremely beautiful Alcibiades was unable to make Socrates seduce him, and he felt that this failure dishonoured him (*Symposium*, 216c-19e).

Alcibiades confessed his embarrassment with the frankness and garrulousness of a drunk. In such company, before his own friends and, for that matter, in Agathon's home, this inability to have had himself seduced was just as shameful as the opposite would have been for the vulgar rabble, *hoi pŏlloĭ*. There was a certain logic to Alcibiades' account and his misunderstanding of Socrates' intentions. The philosopher had placed himself in the position of *ĕrastḗs* in relation to the young man. Yet his *eros* was entirely different from that of the Athenians, even in its more sophisticated form, *poĭkílŏs*; it was a completely unprecedented and paradoxical *eros*. Socrates' love was triggered by corporeal beauty, which is the only visible form, but it shifted towards the beauty of the soul and then towards beauty itself, without dwelling – even for a fraction of a second – on the gratification (*chărízĕsthaĭ*) of the sexual act.

While Alcibiades had the same idea of noble love as Pausanias – and therefore thought that, at a certain stage, once the celestial nature of the other's desire had been ascertained, one went to bed together – Socrates redefined the very notion of *eros*. Paradoxically, he did not scorn the attraction to physical beauty; indeed, it was the body that triggered the very first movement of admiration which was to culminate in devotion to beauty itself. Beauty is indeed attractive. It was therefore to be expected that Alcibiades, who was well known for his striking good looks and was fully aware of this, should detect the attraction he exerted on Socrates. But the attraction to beauty is attraction to a form. The beautiful young man failed to understand that the philosopher would not use his wisdom as a good reason for making love to that body. He could not foresee that this eccentric mentor would reject him and shatter the ethics argued for by Pausanias. As the young man's advances became increasingly intense, Socrates asked him what he, the older man, had to gain by allowing Alcibiades to enjoy his soul in exchange for his enjoyment of Alcibiades' body (218e-219a). With his usual irony, the intellectual and 'disinterested' *ĕrastḗs* actually calculated profit and loss. Pausanias' ill-concealed utilitarianism was now out in the open.

If Socrates were just a refined *ĕrastḗs*, inspired by Aphrodite Urania, his behaviour would make no sense. Socrates was attracted by the beauty of bodies. There was no hypocrisy in his declaration that he was always in love (Xenophon, *Symposium*, 8, 2) or in his being constantly aroused by beautiful people (Plato, *Symposium*, 216d). He confessed that he found all adolescents beautiful and Charmides in particular a magnificent young man, whose physical features he had suddenly glimpsed under his cloak, while the two were conversing in a palaestra. The philosopher was enthralled (Plato, *Charmides*, 154b and 155c–e). The distinction between the two Aphrodites was not really significant for him. His Aphrodite was primarily terrestial, and desire for bodies was a reality. That reality was a challenge which had to be met and overcome.

Socrates lies in bed with Alcibiades' arms around him, but doesn't give in to the desirous part of his soul. He is dominating the black horse, while controlling, we may suppose, his erection. This is the perfect idea of Platonic love, with all its acrobatic tensions. This was the situation Plutarch had in mind when he defended Plato's morality and psychology against the Stoics. If we believe that reason can be constantly on its guard, even in moments of sexual attraction, then we can understand how it is possible to resist in the presence of beautiful young men and women and not respond physically (Plutarch, *On Moral Virtue*, 422e). Aristotle would probably have explained Socrates' composure as the failure to respond, typical of an ageing body with little vital warmth. For Plato, it was the triumph of intelligence over *Ĕrŏs tŭrannŏs*.

Alcibiades knew nothing of this and, while he told his story, he still did not understand the workings of Socrates' mind: he arrived late and missed his encomium of Eros, in which the philosopher quoted the words of Diotima of Mantinea, a priestess who possessed what Dante called the 'intellect of love'. The pleasure-loving young general had mistaken the paradoxical Socratic asceticism, which starts with physical desire and ends with abstinence, for the elitism of Pausanias, which commences with desire for the soul and concludes with a sexual gratification (*chărízĕsthaĭ*).

ĔRŌS ŎRTHŎS

We can now compare the different arguments on the question of pleasure being compatible with a noble *eros*: Aeschines, Pausanias, Socrates and Plato. Pausanias represents the point of view of a man of the world. He had lived for many years with the same lover, in a lasting and tender relationship which had borne fruit. Having been Pausanias' *paīdikă* since his teenage years, Agathon had become a prominent young playwright, sufficiently famous to merit parody by Aristophanes (*The Women's Assembly*). His life as part of a couple was a success story. In the world of the palaestra and the symposium, this was love at its most sublime – a love made up of a beneficial affection for the whole person in the interests of that person (not a predatory passion), as well as sensuality. This was the *eros* that Alcibiades, the archetype of that world, enthusiastically believed he could experience in the company of Socrates. This was the *eros* that was evoked by the other mysterious general (of which Aeschines spoke) in order to defend Timarchus and his lovers in the name of Patroclos and Achilles.

Aeschines did not belong to that world. Indeed, Demosthenes, his constant adversary, often made him the object of offensive, sarcastic and somewhat undemocratic barbs about his humble origins. In court, Aeschines' attack on Timarchus, who was Demosthenes' friend and political ally, contained highly demagogic arguments to incite the crowd to revulsion against unnatural sexual acts. Aeschines could be considered the main exponent of the ideology of the 'democratic body', the corporeal registration of the citizen's identity (Halperin, 1990: 96). He referred specifically to the morality of those who frequented the palaestrae and the symposia, but only in order to rescue an expurgated version of it: for the masses, it should be said that love between males was only acceptable if it was all sensible moderation (*sōphrŏsŭnē*) and no pleasure, as in the *Iliad*. In public, there was no room for the many nuances within Athenian eroticism which were discussed in Agathon's house.

Plato infiltrates Socrates into the world of the palaestra and symposium to subvert its morality. This strange man, forever out of place (*átŏpŏs*), went everywhere in search of young men to educate. And where did he go? He frequented precisely those places, the symposia and the palaestrae, where he could meet the right candidates – young men who were already receiving an Athenian education and who believed in the possibility of receiving a good *paídeía*. They were prone to intellectual attraction, full of admiration for cultured people, and infused with the values of liberality and gratitude. Socrates appeared to be part of the game and to wish to seduce them; he was not sparing in his allusions and pretended to take up the part of the *ĕrastḗs*. He manifested his desire for beauty. However, he suddenly held back when it came to playing his role of 'professor of desire' and to accepting the sexual favours of those young men who felt obliged to return his gifts and thank him for his self-lessness. Once in bed with Alcibiades, it was no longer a game. The lesson started once he was in the arms of the most attractive *ĕrṓmĕnŏs*. This extra-ordinary display of self-control in the most perilous circumstances demon-strated what he meant by *eros*.

Socrates expressed in practice his concept of sexual pleasure, by resisting Alcibiades, and Plato recorded this in a very clear and analytical manner in his political works. One can see in the *Republic* what a just love (*ĕrōs ŏrthŏs*) would be – that is, directed at a beautiful and elegant object, and experienced under the ægis of chastity (*sōphrŏsúnē*) and culture (*mousikḗ*). This love would mani-fest itself by frequenting, touching and kissing the *ĕrṓmĕnŏs* like a son (*hŏspĕr huĕŏs; Republic*, 402e-403d). This idealised *eros*, with its more tender features, categorically ruled out sexual relations, unless one wanted to introduce an element of incest, as 'like a son' meant precisely this. It was entirely admissible to love young men in the perfect city, but within the limits of friendship and restrained gestures. In the *Laws*, the Athenian, the character who takes the place of Socrates, argues for an unambiguous regulation: sexual acts between persons of the same sex are against nature (636a–c; 836c–e). Unions that can lead to procreation are natural. Unions that are justified by the inability to control one's desire for pleasure and induce men to act like women are unnatural. Aeschines' rhetoric is not so different from that of Plato the political philo-sopher, who was concerned with reforming public opinion and the common morality. This Plato would not even jokingly compromise himself with the ethics of the palaestra and symposium. This Plato reasserted the rights of the *phúsis*.

When seen in this light, the dialogues on love, *Phaedrus* and *The Symposium*, appear in all their ironic asceticism. We also have a better understanding of the end of the conversation in Agathon's home. The strangeness of attributing Socratic thought to a woman, the learned Diotima of Mantinea, can be explained as a stratagem: the reintroduction of the difference between the sexes and the language of procreation in an entirely male circle, in which everyone was convinced that the most interesting love is between men who have something to say to each other. Alcibiades had the thankless task of exemplifying through his own experience – and of narrating in his own words – a theory of love that he had never understood and probably never would understand. He even turned up late at the symposium, after Socrates had reawoken Diotima's voice. He shared his friends' illusion in a supposedly selfless *paīdeīa*, which associated voluntary sexual submission with the supposition of another's wisdom. This handsome general represented the values of a world to which the elusive philosopher could never belong. Socrates was merely passing through as a curious guest, able to leave calmly the following morning with his sober head held high after having drunk wine, his mind fresh even after a sleepless night. Alcibiades did not have the last word, because the last utterance and most eloquent gesture is that of the philosopher who leaves Agathon's home, and goes on his way.

3

BODIES

HISTORY OF A DIFFERENCE

We have followed the paradoxically paradigmatic nature of women from female desire to the female model of desire and to effeminate desire. Just as the body of a goddess – Aphrodite, who preceded little Eros – was formed from drops of semen that sprung from the severed penis of the sky and fell into the sea, so the phantom of female sensuality – the image of the insatiable body – emerged from the world of male sexuality. We will now examine how this body started to differentiate itself.

Sexual difference did not go back to the beginning of time. Women were a supplement, a late addition to the world's panorama. Sexual anatomy has a history. In the beginning there were no women. Gods and goddesses were generated by the primary couples of Earth and Sky or Earth and Sea, or by the Earth on its own: the world was already full of divinities. Men were also in the world, although it was not clear how they got there. Men existed and apparently lived in the company of the gods. One day Prometheus, one of the Titans, decided to indulge in a practical joke. He had to divide an ox for a banquet at which both men and gods were to eat. As he cut it up, he hid the red meat under the animal's stomach on one side, and on the other he covered the bare bones with a layer of fat. Thus the good portion looked as though it were offal, and the fatty side suggested the presence of steaks where in fact there were only bones. Zeus, at whom the prank was aimed, was mortally offended. He took it out on the men, who were not to blame, and he suddenly stopped striking trees with lightning, thereby depriving them of the fire that was so necessary to their survival. Prometheus recovered the fire for the harmless mortals, and an even angrier Zeus decided to make those 'bread-eaters' really suffer. He ordered the manufacture of a snare, an evil thing with an attractive and deceptive appearance: woman (Hesiod, *Theogony*, 535).

This is the first version of the invention of woman. In a work called *Theogony*, which narrates the genealogy, or rather the anthropomorphic biological birth, of the gods, woman first made her appearance as an artificial object created by an act of craftsmanship. She was fabricated, and she was covered with artistic, contrived ornamentation. Woman was not natural and was not nature's spontaneous issue. She had been modelled. And she was a plague, a torment that would prove insufferable. She brought with her into this world an excessive covetousness, a craving that despises poverty and seeks out the fulfilment of all one's desires. Woman was demanding; woman epitomised all that is demanding. Like a drone, she remained comfortably at home awaiting her husband, who would bring food and wealth.

The second version of the manufacture of the female human being can be found in another poem by the same author: *Works and Days*. Here the first woman was called Pandora (All-Gifts), because all the inhabitants of Olympus gave her as a gift (60). The work, which was ordered by Zeus, was carried out meticulously. Here was Pandora, decked out in seductive jewellery, equipped with handcrafted abilities and furnished with tremendous skill when it came to deceit and mendacity. As soon as the work on her was finished, she was offered in marriage to the god Epimetheus, Prometheus' stupid and impulsive brother. No sooner was she in his new house than she committed an irredeemable act: she lifted the lid on an earthenware jar and released its contents. All the distressing cares (*kḗdĕa lugrắ*), worries and anxieties which, since that day, have afflicted mankind swarmed out of the jar. Upsets and sorrows spread amongst men in great numbers, and the land was filled with evils, as was the sea. Illnesses visited men night and day in silence and without warning so as better to catch them unawares (99).

This version, which is more detailed and complex than the account given in the *Theogony*, makes it much clearer that the late arrival of sexual difference was responsible for making human beings really human. The invention of woman created the human race. Before that, the poet tells us, the tribes of 'men' on the earth lived safe from evil and free from hard work, stress and fatal illnesses (93–6). Following Pandora's reckless act, men started to experience difficulties, tensions, suffering, fragility and, more generally, those distressing cares which define the existence of mortals. While the manufacture of woman may not appear to be an anthropogony, because the men were already there, it needs to be interpreted as a variant of the creation of the first humanised beings, as we are now: anxious and vulnerable. The idea that *Cura* (*kḗdos*) – concern and restlessness; worry and anguish – is that which distinguishes mankind was in fact an essential component of the Greek concept of the advent of humanity.

A Latin fable from Hyginus' collection offers yet another version. Cura was one day crossing a river, when her attention was caught by the mud at the bottom. Lost in thought, she picked up a handful and started to model a small figure. While Cura was reflecting on what she had done, Zeus appeared and asked him to give life to her statuette. Zeus gave Cura's creation the spirit of life, but their collaborative efforts led to an argument: both Cura and Zeus claimed the right to give this new artifice a name. While they were arguing, Earth rose up and also demanded the same right, as it had provided the material. How were they to name an object shaped by Cura, given life by Zeus, and made of wet Earth? The three contenders consulted Saturn, who pronounced the following verdict: because he had given it life, Zeus would receive its dead body. Because she had manufactured it, Cura would possess it for the duration of its life. The name it was to bear would be *Homo*, because the material of which it was made was *humus* (Hyginus, *Fabulae*, 220). The origin of humans was therefore 'muddy' and 'slimy', and their name bore the memory of their 'humble' (*humilis*), humid and sludgy corporeality. As for their existence, humans were to remain in the hands of Cura for every day of their lives – in those hands that originally modelled them and made their life possible for the first time.

This late and prosaic tale is an anthropogony based on artifice and craftsmanship, just as is the story of Pandora. When faced with a divine power capable of creation, human beings define themselves primarily as something that receives life, breath and movement by a demiurgic act, not by natural genealogical transmission. The divine craftsperson in this case is Cura. For Hesiod, all the inhabitants of Olympus contributed to the creation of Pandora. And just as the story of Pandora, Hyginus' fable makes a connection between living a properly human life and taking care. All-Gifts introduced the 'distressing cares' into the world for the first time: she altered mortal existence forever and created the human condition as we know it today. Cura, namely Care personified, is the inventor of *homo*, and is destined to hold him as long as he lives. This is a philosophical fable in the mould of Heidegger, one might say, given that the author of *Being and Time* considered this striking myth a proof of the pre-philosophical intuition that being in this world means always and in all events relating to care, be it attention or anxiety, occupation or preoccupation.

Hesiod's variant insists on the sexual element, which is what interests us: disquiet, curiosity and suffering enter this world together with femininity. It is Woman who spreads anxieties amongst men. That which Woman brings about in the *Theogony* – the obligation incumbent on men to work for her and to suffer in order to satisfy her demands – has to be included in the category of what *Works and Days* defines as distressing cares (*kḗdĕa lugrá*). Work is quintessentially effort, apprehension and worry. Work is the opposite of that state of indolence, and indifference which typified the time that preceded Pandora's epiphany – a time when everything was easy and free. The logic of the narrative presupposes a primordial humanity, before sex, when life was perfect, almost divine. But that life before sex was actually before the addition of one sex – the feminine one, that beautiful evil – to a humankind which was all-male, not a-sexual. The myth does not recount the transformation of originally neutral human beings into females and males, but that of males into females and males – the latter being now as distant from the gods, and therefore human, as they can get.

There is a powerful connection between human identity, sexual difference and the loss of perfection. For Hesiod, to live careless and carefree and never to experience anxiety meant living like a god or living in an ideal past, a golden age, and before the existence of women, sexual difference and sexual activity. A portrait of this existence is provided in *Works and Days*, immediately after the events surrounding Pandora. 'I shall tell another story', the poet announces, and he narrates the succession of metallic 'races' and generations of men created by the gods. The first was of gold: the race of golden men lived like the gods. They passed their days in banqueting, and their bodies always remained youthful. They died sweetly in their sleep and they were free from all cares. 'They lived like gods with carefree hearts and away from all toil' (100). In this primordial time, Earth produced fruits and food spontaneously. There was no need to work. Everything was given and on offer. Suddenly and for no apparent reason, Zeus had those blissful people buried, and the gods manufactured a second race, this time of silver. These new mortals were very different from the previous ones: a child remained a hundred years next to its mother before it grew, aged and died. The men were violent and did not sacrifice to the gods as they should have done.

Something was lost in the transition from the golden race to the silver one: the loss of carefreeness and happiness, and the discovery of the sacrificial distance between mortals and immortals. The relationship between the time before Pandora and the time after Pandora is the same as the one between the golden age and the silver age. Sexual difference does not appear to have existed in the society created by Cronus; it only appears in the decadent silver race, which reproduces itself through maternity – a particularly showy and cumbersome maternity. Sexual difference and sexuality come into existence at the same time as the suffering and the unavoidable worries of the post-Promethean age. The myth must be read as a variant on the manufacture of Pandora, as though the transition from gold to silver presupposed (or narrated in another fashion) the creation of the first woman and the foundation of sacrifice. But, if this is true, how are we to envisage procreation for the golden men? There is something missing from Hesiod's portrayal of the Age of Cronus.

Plato provides us with a more sophisticated response. Borrowing the language of myth and its temporal perspective, philosophy continues a reflection on sexual difference, which associates its belated appearance with decline and decay. In the *Statesman*, Plato claims to reconstruct the history of humankind by reconnecting scattered elements of the mythological tradition. History started at the time of Cronus, which for Hesiod was the golden age. At that time, the god was personally involved in the movement of the universe and in the existence of living creatures. The portrayal is even more idyllic than that of Hesiod: animals did not attack each other, the land produced food spontaneously, people received all their necessities as a gift, the grass was so soft that it provided natural beds to lie on, and the climate was so stable that clothes and houses were not required. As this god was taking care of humans, they had no need to look after themselves. There were no cities, no marriages and no procreation. All the people grew out of the earth, just like any other wild fruit (272a).

Plato fills the gap left in Hesiod's myth of the age of Cronus. Hesiod has no word about women and procreation, but Plato emphasises a nature that germinates not only plant structures, but also human bodies. Just as plants are born automatically, without agriculture, so the human beings come up into existence without seed. The earth carries the work of generating the living, thus conserving the humans' energies and keeping them free from worry. This hyper-civilised pre-political world had no need of marriages in order to create alliances. Harmony was entirely natural and spontaneous, because ultimately it depended on divine action. The universe benefited from a constant renewal of life by a god who took care of it (270a). If we follow Plato's claim that this is a cosmology which is created out of scattered scraps of myths, and which reveals their inner logic, we can project the image of this enchanted world, as yet free from the city, wives, sexual differences and sexual relations, and as yet unaffected by Pandora, onto the universe, and onto the reign of Cronus. Before women existed, men grew and blossomed like plants. If there is care, it is that of the gods for carefree human beings.

Both Hesiod and the author of the *Statesman* associate the appearance of the female with the establishment of a regime of hard work and anxiety. Inseminating a woman was part of the *érga*, the wearying productive activities that marked the separation of men from the gods. Both Hesiod and Plato articulate the addition of femininity and the loss of divinity in the history of human life; the presence of women and the distance of gods, on earth. Women appeared in the world to introduce a new internal division within humanity, which reinforced the separation between the human and the divine. Procreation became sexual when Zeus stopped striking ash-trees with lightning to light fires (Hesiod), or when Cronus abandoned the movement of the universe to its own devices (Plato). This coincidence is structural, and bears consequences for the conception of sex and sensuality. One of the counterintuitive implications of this narrative pattern is that sexual pleasure was not a paradigm for happiness. Lingering at the banquet table to savour delicious food and exquisite drink provided an exemplary model of a sensuous life, but making love did not. Sex, or at least the heterosexual version, presupposed the difference between men and women, and that difference was perceived not merely as something secondary or derivative, but as a calamitous accident. And sex was to be a chore.

Another Platonic myth presents yet another variant of this same lesson. When the divine demiurges manufactured human beings, the first generation started to practise and experience different ways of living. On the death of these primitive males, those who were guilty of cowardice and injustice were reincarnated in the second generation in the form of 'women'. Those who had proved to be foolish and frivolous were transformed into birds. All those who had looked downwards by concerning themselves with material and corporeal endeavors ended up as quadrupeds, reptiles or fish, and so lived in a physical 'baseness' proportional to their inclination to what lies below. The taxonomy of living things is therefore determined by a system of retribution which creates meaningful and symptomatic anatomic realities. As in Ovid's *Metamorphoses*, which illustrated the original configuration of plants, animals and stars, change creates a body which has never been seen before, but it does not create it out of nothing but from some deviation or accident which has occurred to a human being and needs to be remembered. The form that appears for the first time expresses visually a micro-history, a biographical fragment: the event that triggered the transformation. The new body is a portrait of a life and therefore has to be 'read' as an eloquent yet non-fictional, version of a story. Having no legs and being obliged to cling onto the earth, a snake exposes the baseness of the man it used to be; deep under the sea, a fish reveals the abysmal ignorance of a previous existence within a human skin.

The female body speaks of injustice and cowardice. Being fragile, weak and less combative, a woman's body is still that of a human being, with two feet and no wings, but one that has lost its defences, rather like a soldier who abandons his shield and flees the field of battle. Woman is borderline between the original human being, who was originally manly, and the next living creature, which does not belong to the species: the bird, which flies up in the air, covered in feathers. This has nothing to do with the simple fact of being equipped with primary sexual characteristics. In this version of the late appearance of woman, we find Plato imagining what the men, *andres*, were like before sexual difference and how their anatomy and physiology were later adapted to the task of sowing the female furrows. This happened in the second generation, when the first women appeared and the demiurgic gods made the necessary alterations to the bodies of both 'men' and their newly arrived companions so that they could carry out the work of procreation. Sexual organs were therefore added to 'male' and 'female' bodies as an adjustment and an improvement, in order to use the difference between *anér* and *guné* for reproductive purposes. In the *Timaeus*, we could say that the distinction between the genders – male as courageous and just, female as cowardly and unjust – preceded the differentiation between bodies with sexual functions and dissimilarities.

The sexual organs are, moreover, two supplementary beasts, one inserted in the abdomen and the other attached to the abdomen externally. The womb is a little creature, desperate to fill itself with the minuscule animals which can be found in sperm and which develop into babies within it. If it is kept waiting for too long, the womb loses patience and starts wandering around and provoking disturbances and various other symptoms, particularly suffocation. The other animal, the external one, is undisciplined and disobedient, because the fluid that flows through it is anxious to get out. This humour is animate indeed, and provokes in the penis the desire to procreate – that is, the desire to ejaculate the liquid itself and the invisible animalcules which are carried within it. When the two beasts meet in sexual intercourse, which should be thought of as a snout-to-snout encounter between the womb and the penis, the latter spits out the animate liquid and squirts a microscopic little person into the matrix, like a seed into a field. This little person is nourished by the uterine earth and grows like a vegetable (*Timaeus*, 90e–91b).

Erotic desire appears in this case to be a by-product of man's degeneration towards the female. Given that some new living beings, hereafter called 'women', are formed by metamorphosis, the demiurgic gods decide to put them to work. They will collaborate in procreation, another novelty. Conceptually, it was a kind of recycling: the adaptation to an end of an unexpected and unwanted accident, for which no particular purpose had been envisaged, except punishment. Given that there are now these humans, which had not undergone a change so radical as to constitute another form, the gods adjusted both types of human body to allow reproduction. Heterosexuality was again presented metaphorically as a kind of agricultural labour, while desire was explained by the indiscipline of the two little beasts, the impatient womb and the rebellious penis.

The fabrication of sexual difference culminates with the sartorial fashioning of two more living beings: two pets, so to speak, attached to the body and yet self-moving. The movement of the erection, with its irrational and capricious pace, disconnected from the will, corresponds to the equally uncontrolled movement of the uterus, which Hippocratic medicine described as hysteria, and which had to be understood as an irresistible attraction towards an object.

In both cases the erotic sensitivity betrays the presence of an animal motility which, as a result of the appearance of women, now contaminated men as well. Because they had acquired a penis, the original *ándrĕs* had lost something of their wholeness: at the very least, they had lost control of their own bodies.

As we have seen in the chapter on desire, the Platonic body was programmed for a particular use of time. The intestine was long and sinuous to make the passage of the remnants of food towards the anus interminably slow, because of the psychological craving of human beings, who would try to eat and drink unremittingly. Having foreseen this lack of moderation, the gods had designed a remedy: a length of intestinal tubing that prolonged the interval between meals during which men could devote themselves to the use of their reason. The body therefore was intelligently designed, while taking into account the excesses of the soul and the need to counteract them. But now the degenerative accident that caused the appearance of women modified the rationality of the body. The penis and the womb introduced the mindlessness and the beastly nature of the appetitive part of the soul into human anatomy. Whereas the intestine was intended to curb an excessive appetite, the sexual organs were merely incarnations of sexual immoderation and in no way attempted to restrain it. With sex, in sum, the body itself becomes feral. Or, in other words, sensual.

If we link the narrative of the invention of sex in the *Timaeus* with the vivid depiction in the *Phaedrus*, of the soul as a flying chariot, dragged by two winged horses and driven by an athletic charioteer, we can follow a consistent metaphorical argument. The addition of sexual hunger to the passion for food and drink makes the task of the charioteer most difficult, and he has constantly to rein in the impetuous, impulsive and untamed horse of acquisitive desires. *Eros* is the most tyrannical of all drives. *Eros* – the baleful consequence of sexual difference – torments mortals with the violence of a passion in which want makes its influence felt. As Hesiod said, the first woman would not content herself with poverty and would avidly seek repleteness. In Plato's opinion, this compulsion corresponds exactly to insatiable desire: a desire that did not exist among the homogeneous, original men, before the advent of the first unmanly beings, women.

THE ERECTION

Michel Foucault placed great emphasis on penetration and erection, particularly in his writings that led up to *The History of Sexuality*. The ancients are supposed to have been more interested in the sexual act and its circumstances, which were significant in terms of power, whereas Christians are supposed to have shifted the attention to desire, of which the penis' uncontrolled movement (or immobility) was an expression. In a startling historical montage, Foucault compared Augustine and Artemidorus Daldianus, the second-century author of *Oneirocritica* (*Interpretation of Dreams*), in order to demonstrate the crucial transformation that Christianity brought about in relation to ancient thought.

Artemidorus describes a series of dreams in which the male organ appears to be involved in various situations. He interprets these oneiric images strictly following the principle that they all symbolise something other than the thing that manifests itself to the dreamer. He therefore reveals meanings that have nothing to do with sex, but generally relate to power and possession. Foucault enthusiastically appropriates this system of dream interpretation, which is perfectly non-Freudian. Instead of apparently banal objects being revealed as phallic symbols, here are actual male members standing for the only thing that was truly significant for the ancients: domination. The comparative argument also shows that, when the ancients considered the phallus, they concentrated on its predatory and despotic activity once the erection had occurred, whereas Christians, and St Augustine in particular, anxiously examined the penis' hesitancy.

In the third part of this book, we shall discuss that marvellous text, *The City of God*. For now, suffice it to say that, taking Genesis as his starting point, Augustine concludes that God inflicted the erotic urge on the first human beings as a punishment for original sin. It is a myth concerning the invention of desire and the occurrence of the first spontaneous erection, but it is also a myth that owes a great deal to Greek ideas and to ethical and biological reflections on the tendency of the phallus to initiate action by itself. How does the moment in which penetration becomes possible come about? Why do we get there unexpectedly on some occasions and on others we cannot get there at all? What language must we adopt when speaking of this mystery: that of the will, that of self-control or that of pure chance?

It is highly questionable that you can take a work like Artemidorus' *Interpretation of Dreams*, which belonged to a marginal genre in relation to the mainstream philosophical and medical tradition, and turn it into a manifesto for Greek theory on erotic experience centred upon penetration as a symbol of power. We need to compare St Augustine with Plato, Aristotle, Plutarch and Stoic philosophy; these were texts that really did constitute an *episteme*, to use one of Foucault's own terms – voices of a knowledge with which the Church Fathers entered into a genuine dialogue. This must be emphasised, not so much for philological or genealogical reasons, although those are important enough, but because the focus on Artemidorus creates a false perspective. If you read the texts just mentioned, you realise how absurd it is to assert that the Greeks ignored or neglected the erection and, more generally, the other manifestations of the erotic drive in its initial stages, just as it is not true that they meditated less on desire than on the economy of pleasure. The mechanism of insatiable appetite provided them with the most important reason for being wary of sex. The mobility of the penis posed a challenging problem for a definition of desire, for the soul and for the body.

Let us return to Plato's narrative in *Timaeus*. When men were alone, they had no penis, even though they were *ándrěs*. Their masculinity, from which the femininity of the first 'women' differentiated itself (although they too lacked their sexual organs), was actually their manliness: they had a more combative and better defended body. This was a distinctive feature of gender and not of anatomical sex. Only after the metamorphoses of some men into 'women' did the demiurgic gods decide to fashion the reproductive organs by adjusting the bodies of both men and women. Only then did the penis make its appearance, and it is an anxious, tyrannical and rebellious beast, which always makes up its own mind and refuses to obey reason (91 b2–c1).

This text was to have a fundamental place in ancient ethics and indeed in the ethics of other societies, because Augustine developed his commentary on Genesis precisely in relation to this passage – a commentary in which the erection becomes a sign which original sin left imprinted on the body. The philosophy of the erection, which was so significant for Christian theory of the flesh, had its roots therefore in Greek thought. In the Platonic context, the autonomy of the penis outside the body makes visible the irrational and anti-rational nature of the sexual drive, and therefore the permanent hostility that divides *eros* and intelligence. The penis is a separate animal, and it is not a pretty, benign, tame or docile one; on the contrary, it displays all the characteristics of the savage beasts that Plato used as metaphors for the appetitive part of the soul. The penis is undisciplined, disobedient and stubborn like the wild black horse of *Phaedrus*. The penis is ungovernable like the riotous Chimaera of the *Republic*. Desire is both impetuous and mechanical, and it is radically different from reason, which is represented as a man inside the human soul. When any beautiful body comes into view, the rowdy black horse of the soul launches into an assault. It acts as though it were independent of reason's control, but its movement is always the same – always a predictable reflex. Thus the sexual organ is rebellious but goes in search of the same thing, the discharge of its semen. Freedom of movement betrays necessity. The male member was called *anágkē*, which means 'need'. In the logic of the Platonic interpretation, the imperious nature of its reactions is symbolic of the tyranny of *eros*.

In Aristotle we find two registers of reflection. The erection is both a physiological phenomenon, whose mechanism needs to be understood, and a corporeal manifestation of desire that needs to be explained coherently with a theory of spontaneous movement or, in other words, of the 'self-mobility' of living beings. As a manifestation of desire, the erection is one of the sudden changes that accompany or immediately follow the impulse towards an object. It is not a movement of the whole body but only of a part of it, comparable to the leaps the heart can make in the breast. But how can these two organs, the heart and the penis, move by themselves?

Aristotle acknowledged the existence and vital role of a set of activities that are not consciously willed. Whereas breathing, waking up and falling asleep are simple non-voluntary actions (*ouch hĕkoūsiaî*) and transformations, the movements of the heart and of the penis are *in*voluntary (*akoūsioî*) because their cause is a *phantasía*, a representation, but one without a command from the intelligence (*Movement of Animals*, 703b1–10). Like the heart, the penis moves 'automatically', in response to particular images and representations, without need of deliberate consent – of decision and volition. The heart and the penis are two organs so sensitive and so quick to react that they can be considered two animals, two separate living beings. The reason is that the heart, being the source and origin of life itself, contains blood, the cause of all sensations (Aristotle was a cardiocentrist), while the penis – when filled with that concocted blood which is semen – causes the continuation of life, and therefore that of sensations, in another being. The indication of this is in the fact that a seminal force is derived from it like something alive (703b20–6). Now blood and semen are full of life because they are full of *pneûma*, warm and moist air or vital warmth that acts as a support to life. The heartbeat and the erection result from the variable quantity of material, blood or semen, they hold (703b36–704a1). Ultimately, those involuntary movements depend on the abundance of *pneûma* (703b22–3).

Aristotle insisted on the autonomy of the penis, just as Plato had done, but he accepted its naturalness and, in a sense, its innocence. His tone and language were very different from those of his teacher. For Plato, the untamed exuberance of sexual appetite constantly challenged reason to impose its control and restraint, thus creating a dramatic conflict. The chariot of the soul travels in fits and starts with this unbearable black horse always on the point of bolting, while intelligence pulls hard on the reins and occasionally slackens them only to swerve again, without being able to relax its concentration for a moment. The more reason releases its grips, the more a potential and always vibrant energy ready for action will be emboldened. Untiring desire is a repetitive impulse. Only thought – an external and contrasting force – can hold it back but without ever definitively taming it.

For Aristotle, the conflict between rational thought and passion certainly exists, but it is not unceasing, nor does it almost destroy human beings. Pleasures and desires are natural, and that naturalness is not experienced in the same way as tyranny, savagery or some inescapable evil, but rather as an element of life that has to be accepted and kept to the right dosage. Reason is a matter of experiencing emotions at the right time, in the right place, with the right person. This is why, at the most noble level of ethical behaviour, a person desires what it is appropriate to desire, whereas the repression and control of urges which are experienced but ought to be barred constitute a form of second-rate morality (*Nicomachean Ethics*, 1099a, 7–20).

Sexual desire was reassessed primarily with a view to procreation, as something necessary and precious for more complex animals. The more perfect and distinctive a living being, the more marked the difference between the sexes must be, and that difference is based on the distance between the male, which is the superior sex because it is the origin of life and form, and the female sex, which provides the material (menstrual blood) and the space (the uterus) for procreation. It is therefore indispensable to have some mechanism to bring these two together. Erotic attraction is a means to the most essential purpose of life: its conservation beyond the death of individuals through the reproduction of the paternal form within the female body (*Generation of Animals*, 2, 1).

However, this argument plays down the moral drama of sexual desire. Like all passions, love is part of the human experience and, if it were not part of it, we would no longer be human. Sex should be experienced as long as a proper intermediate space can be found for *eros* between excess and insufficiency – the secret of a well balanced existence. In this context, the erratic movements of the penis are judged with indulgence and curiosity. It is a good thing that the generative organ is sensitive, because its involvement is crucial to the conservation of life. It acts like the heart, the most important and valuable part of the body: it prolongs the heart's work by transferring life from one generation to the next. It is not a problem if, like the heart, it reacts so promptly; this is the inevitable result of its welcome and youthful vitality.

For Aristotle, the movement of sexual organs in response to the perception or the imaginary contemplation of an object becomes a functional advantage: for life to reproduce itself, there has to be a specific instrument similar to the one that ensures survival of the individual. What is required is a live organ which is capable of action without having to receive an order every time there is an intention to make it work. The penis is full of energy, and can take the initiative its owner expects of it. Its 'spontaneity' should be seen as perfect obedience which occasionally results in an excess of zeal, but with a view to a fundamental end: *phůsis* itself. In short, the penis is like an ideal slave: almost separate from the body of the person who owns it, it is capable of sensing its owner's desires and carrying them out automatically – without any specific commands. *Érōs* is no longer *túrannŏs*. *Érōs* works in the service of nature.

The erection also becomes something essentially virile. With the polarisation between the two prime causes of generation in the coupling of the opposites, maternal matter and paternal form, the ejaculation of sperm becomes a specific feature of the male genital apparatus. Female blood is regularly deposited in the womb in order to overflow into menstruation every month. A little is always left in the uterine repository, where it awaits fertilisation. So, just as there is always wood ready for use in a carpenter's workshop, the material required for life is always available. Thus only the penis must become erect in the arousal, in order to ejaculate the fertilising substance at the right moment. Just as the artisan comes and goes from his workshop to carry out his plans and to use the raw material that awaits him, so a father provides the maternal blood with life and form, in accordance with his own time requirements (2,4). Pleasure is the thing that attracts the male to carry out the work of procreation, whereas, for a woman, pleasure becomes what might be called a collateral result, which is not necessary to the ejaculation of semen, as was believed by Hippocratic thinkers. Pushing to its extreme the analogy of male and female genital apparatuses: these attributed an enjoyable emission of seminal fluid to the phallic womb.

The swelling of the penis became a problem in Stoic ethics. This was a morality based on the act and on the moment of consent – the 'yes' that we grant both to representations and to thoughts and decisions. All our actions presuppose that we have accepted them, approved them and therefore wanted them. Desire is, in fact, a form of will, whereby will is understood to mean the conscious and deliberate movement towards something. Every desire contains a thought – a thought about the value of the thing which is desired, and there-fore about its desirability. This thought might be an incorrect assessment – and we might therefore consider it irrational – but it is a judgement and an opinion. The second I say 'yes' to the idea that a certain person is attractive or sexy, I am in a state of desire because my desire is made up of that idealisation I have chosen to adhere to. Is this an overly intellectualised interpretation of passion? Certainly, but it is also a sensual interpretation. As my intellectual activity is linked to my body by permanent interaction, the thought that a person is irresistible results in my inability to resist. The overestimation of the pleasure which the presence of that person can give me does not remain confined to the imagination, but enters the circuit, as it were, and becomes flesh and then *pneûma* as it moves towards the penis. This is an erection which says the same thing that I am saying to myself, but it says it in body language. It says, 'yes, it's true; those shoulders are splendid, that curve is sensual even if it is just between me and myself'.

For a Stoic, this erotic response demonstrates promptness, presence of spirit as it were, of a soul which entirely transforms itself from reason and intelligence into emotion and agitation. The key concept in Stoic psychology is that the soul cannot be divided into different parts, each one responsible for a specific function, as was the case both with Plato, and his tripartite soul of intellect, ardour and appetite, and with Aristotle, with his distinction between an appetitive, a vegetative and an intelligent soul. The Stoics believed that *psuché* is a homogeneous whole, and that it shifts from rational behaviour, in which it takes time to assess objects and situations, to errors of judgement, in which it recklessly succumbs to its own overestimations of things. A passion is nothing more than an incorrect and hurried decision, accompanied by an alteration of the body.

Rapidity is crucial here. Using a language inspired by physics the Stoics perceived emotion as a sudden, irreversible and irresistible movement. This is why the *motus turbidi*, the confused movements, of psychological perturbations have to be prevented – blocked even before they start, because otherwise it is too late. Once it has been triggered, the whole soul is directed towards an excessive and obsessive thought. Like a swimmer caught by the current or a stone thrown into a ravine, it cannot stop half-way and turn back. Our detailed knowledge of this theory is based on the critique of a philosopher who favoured a return to Plato's ideas. In his treatise *On Moral Virtue*, Plutarch very carefully examines the so-called monism of the Stoics – namely the idea that the soul is one and changeable, rather than multiple and conflictual. He concludes that they were wrong and Plato was right. In order to salvage the idea that intelligence can control and curb the impulses of desire, you need to believe that there are distinct parts which are in conflict with each other. It is pernicious and wrong to consider the soul to be a whole which occasionally becomes all passion, because this is to admit that, in certain circumstances, reason completely disappears. On the contrary, our own behaviour demonstrates that the ability to make rational choices is always there and always operative, even when the appetite is at its most pressing. We know that in the presence of beautiful young men and women we can feel desire and yet suppress it, thereby preventing an erection, something which would be impossible if the entire soul has allowed itself to be taken over by this consent (*On Moral Virtue*, 422e).

This critique of automatism in the name of conflict can also be applied to Aristotle. In spite of his distinction between desire and intelligence in the way the soul is structured, Aristotle perceived the erection as a spontaneous and, above all, immediate motor reflex. Desire, *órĕxis*, normally involves both thought and will (*On the Movement of Animals*, 701a26–702b1): I think I need something to cover me; in order to be covered, I need a blanket; I get a blanket. In this kind of practical syllogism, calculations and acts follow one another fairly rapidly. The time factor is obviously crucial: the less time I spend on connecting ends to means, the sooner I start to take action. There is therefore an intrinsic risk in every kind of action: promptness, which is useful, is at the expense of due consideration. The extreme case of promptness of spirit is the vitality of both the heart and the penis. These parts of the body, so full of life and so highly strung, are, unsurprisingly, associated in the imagery of instinctive movement with male sexuality. These literally self-propelled organs, like individual animals, respond without intelligent command, and therefore in record time. Plutarch could have countered Aristotle, just as he did the Stoics, by reintroducing Platonic psychology, where reason is always vigilant whatever the 'acceleration' of sexual appetite and the penis. If the black horse suddenly rears and escapes the control of the charioteer, it is because the latter's distraction or weakness has resulted in his being overwhelmed by the animal's despotism, and not because he no longer has a role to play.

FEMALE SENSUALITY

The advent of the difference between the sexes left humanity divided into two anatomies: one body strikingly equipped with a disobedient organ and one body secretly inhabited by that same instrument. This was the myth, but what was medicine saying, and how did it believe that this hidden device worked?

For centuries, doctors considered the 'fact' that a woman's body is not really different from a man's to be a clear and irrefutable anatomical phenomenon. For them it was simply a thermal and spatial variant (Sissa, 1983). Because of a deficiency (or an excess) of vital warmth, women have inside them what men have outside them. Both kinds of genital apparatus have the same structure and the same function. From Hippocrates (fifth century BC) to Galen (second century AD), with the sole exception of Aristotle, the dominant medical theory interpreted the female body by taking the male one as its model (Laqueur, 1990). Therefore body and desire, even when female, should operate in the same way. Female pleasure must depend on an invisible erection and an internal ejaculation.

We can see, however, that the analogy between the sexes was continually weakened by their difference. Let us start with Aristotle. As has already been mentioned, Aristotle's biology made women less phallic, because his arguments contrasting male and female as the necessary elements of procreation required a relation of opposition between the active paternal principle (the genuinely procreative one) and the purely material, receptive and passive maternal principle. In anatomy and physiology, this meant that women did not ejaculate semen during sexual intercourse – as was believed in the Hippocratic tradition, which Galen would revive – and, in sexual terms, it meant that a woman's enjoyment was not indispensable for procreation. What mattered was the ability of the womb to ingest the semen deposited by the penis in front of its orifice. Aristotle was the philosopher who endorsed the notion of female passivity and passive femininity. Here is a body that can conceive without desire, eroticism or arousal.

However, the Aristotelian woman is aware of sensuousness, and indeed seeks it out. Her erotic desire – now optional and uncoupled from the procreative function – manifests itself in an extremely intense manner. Although her pleasure is incidental, it is frequent and serves a purpose.

Greek woman is therefore never frigid or lacking in passion, even in her most passive version. Could it be that her sexual sensitivity – her sensuality – is simply a residue of phallicness? If there is a seeking of pleasure, we might ask ourselves whether the female morphology remains to some extent phallic for Aristotle. If this were true, we could confirm the dominance of the male body and its mechanisms in sexual imagery.

Aristotle admits that the cervix secretes something similar to male semen during sexual intercourse and this secretion produces pleasure. The sensation is the same for the two bodies: it depends on the expulsion of a fluid (*On the Generation of Animals*, 739a31–5). The uterus expels a humour which is deposited in the place where the male semen is deposited (739a35–b2); that, too, is a secretion (727b33). The pleasurable experience is entirely the same in both cases (727b33; 739a33–4). The resemblance also concerns the phenomenon of wet dreams (739a23–4). It is true that Aristotle insists on this systematic analogy. However, he also insists on the fact that the female secretion occurs not always and in varying quantities, and is more copious in women not when they are more masculine in their features, as you might expect from an extension of the parallel with male semen, but when they are more feminine and have fair hair. 'Some believe that a woman emits sperm during sexual relations because a pleasure similar to that of men is produced in some women and there is a humid emission at the same time. But that humidity is not spermatic; it is a local secretion, which differs in the case of each woman. It mainly occurs in blondes of a feminine aspect; it is not to be found in masculine women with brown hair' (727b33–8a4; *History of Animals*, 583a8).

Feminine passivity, even the most extreme, is therefore desirous. Although it is ancillary, the role of the female body in procreation is still accompanied by great pleasure in the act – a sensation of a womanly type (given that the most feminine and delicate bodies feel it more) – and by great desire, which is kept alive through the memory of past pleasure. Erotic delight is not finalised to the purpose of generation for women: for that, they have the extra blood of menstruations. It is sheer, gratuitous gratification. Aristotle demonstrates that, when it comes to sensuality, Greek thought was unable to conform to the male model of sexuality. Sensuality is spontaneously female. And it is an end in itself.

It is even more interesting to observe how Galen defines the operations of the genuine phallus which is, for him, the neck of the uterus, surrounded as it is by the vagina as though by a foreskin out of all proportion. In his summary of Hippocratic and Aristotelian traditions, he produces his own detailed theories on the workings of this mysterious genital apparatus, which remains atrophied in the womb. The penis and the neck of the uterus, or cervix, become erect in a similar manner, but, by becoming erect, the cervix dilates in order to *receive* the semen the man deposits in the vagina while the maternal semen is secreted within the uterus. In other words, the purpose of the female erection is to collect and not to ejaculate. So that it can carry out this function, nature has decreed that the womb should be elastic and relatively soft, and above all she has provided it with the appropriate features: the power of attraction and the power of retention (*On the Utility of the Parts*, x–xi; *On the Natural Faculties*, iii, 2–3). These notions of Galen confer a physical existence, albeit a qualitative one, on that eagerness which characterises the *ĕpithumía páscheĭn*, the desire to be acted upon, from Pandora to the voluptuous *cinaedus*.

The polarisation of the sexes was an unstoppable process, central to the theories which appeared to assimilate them. We will now examine how those separate bodies could move towards each other and come together.

RELATIONSHIPS

MARRIAGE

Imagine a city in peacetime – a happy city whose happiness manifests itself in a party. Chariots career along the streets, carrying flaming torches to shouts and singing. It is a wedding party. When it is not destroyed in war, society regenerates itself. By making weddings a public and convivial festival to symbolise the prosperity of peace, ancient Greek society celebrated the union of distinctive sexual bodies on which its reproduction and very existence depended. In the beginning there was sex, and in the beginning there was the difference between the sexes. The sexual act between a woman and man is the cause of procreation. This is a biological fact. Marriage and the begetting of children, with their rules and rituals, are legal and social phenomena. Above all, they are the institutions whereby a society acknowledges its debt to *eros*.

What we know about the matrimonial rite, from the ancient period to the classical one, is sufficient to demonstrate that, in the nuptial performance, the Greeks symbolised the dual nature of marriage both as an erotic event and as the foundation of a legitimate family, with the resulting alliance between kinship groups. There were many public aspects of the wedding party that alluded to the sexual encounter: the procession that took the veiled bride from her father's home to that of the husband, the banquet which ended with the bridegroom lifting the veil as though he were seeing his bride's face for the first time, the songs which accompanied first the procession and then the first moments the couple had together in the intimacy of their bedroom – songs supposed to drown out the cries of the deflowering (Sissa, 1987). The visual representations that abound on vases and, in particular, on the vases used during the ritual depict the presence of a small winged god, Eros himself, who flutters around the future bride as she dresses up and makes herself beautiful. Mirrors and caskets decorate the conjugal space in order to emphasise the flirtation, seduction and amorous expectancy. Marriage is a euphoric event.

Female and male sexuality found in marriage an ideal stage on which to act out their exemplary roles. Socially, the bridegroom carries out the active role of taking the woman and receiving her from the father or from another member of her family, who acts as her guardian. When it comes to being an erotic player, however, the young man who is about to marry is subject to the uncertainties of desire: thus the ritual is also a game which gradually draws the two together, while the man slowly besieges the female body through an unveiling which is public and, later, private. From the perspective of law, the woman has to be considered a minor, being under the guardianship of a man who then hands her over to another man, in order to procreate legitimate children. As a sexual body, however, the bride enters the scene in hiding. She shows herself in a veil, as the beautiful Pandora did before men and gods: a mysterious object whose decorated and well adorned surface promises beauty and pleasure. She is inside the chrysalis of the veil, and only gradually comes out of it during the wedding party. Her desire is represented by this ritual flirtation: the bride knows that she is not only an instrument of reproduction, or she knows that she can become one only if something else happens too. To consummate the sexual act, there needs to be an event that produces the embodiment of desire. We should not forget that her desire is also an erection, albeit an internal and invisible one. She has to manifest it. By making herself beautiful and slowly undressing, she offers herself to male desire, but also reveals her own. She too is an erotic player. The ceremony is one of seduction.

The wedding feast culminates in the first sexual act. While the ritualisation of this act in other ancient societies required proof of the bride's virginity up until that moment, the blood of deflowering was not of great importance in Greece. The Greeks had a notion of virginity as the integrity of a body that had never been penetrated, but they did not identify this state (*parthĕnía*) with the presence of a membrane, which obstructed the female organ and was torn on the first penetration (Sissa, 1987).

The violence inherent in the first heterosexual intrusion was a recurring literary theme – alluded to in the tragic events of the Danaids and examined very explicitly in the Hellenistic novel (Goldhill, 1995). The blood, however, is not necessarily explained by the piercing of the hymen. Greek doctors, from Hippocrates to Galen, were ignorant of the existence of this membrane. The silence on this subject extended to Aristotle, in spite of his meticulous attention to genital anatomy. The first time a gynaecological text mentioned it, it was to assert forcefully that this part of the anatomy does not exist. Soranus, a doctor writing in Greek but active in first-century Rome, argued that anyone who believes the female sex organ is naturally closed off by a membrane which is broken on the first penetration is simply wrong. His reference to people convinced of its existence needs to be put in the context of Roman culture. Most probably these were midwives, rather than physicians. After Soranus, even that most fastidious anatomist Galen – who believed firmly that nature makes perfect and complete bodies – could ignore the hypothesis of a virginal seal. All the anatomy and physiology of women concur, let us remember, on the destination of femininity: to admit or take up, and to hold, the semen; to let any blood in excess flow out periodically. This body is open (Sissa, 1987).

There is no exhibit of blood in the Greek wedding, but sex is pervasively present. The first penetration remained the high point of the wedding, irrespective of the hymen, which for us is supposed to act as a seal capable of indicating and guaranteeing a woman's sexual purity. It might surprise us that the famous nuptial song that accompanies the initial phase of the wedding feast is called *humĕnaĭŏs*. Couldn't this be an allusion to the hymen? In actual fact, this is a later interpretation, probably a Roman one, based on a lexical coincidence. Hymenaeus is a mythological character, who has great difficulty in getting to his wedding and dies on his wedding day. The song celebrates his heroism and laments his death. The identification of the unfortunate bridegroom with part of the bride's body (*humĕn*, membrane) does not appear ever to have occurred to the Greeks (Sissa, 1987).

HAVING CHILDREN

Sexual intercourse produces children – sons and daughters. The difference between the sexes means that maternity and paternity were two profoundly different relationships for a son and for a daughter. We should now follow these processes of socialisation and acculturation of a human being, from the mother's womb to paternal and civic acknowledgement of men and women. We will examine legal and medical attitudes in the classical era, as these two forms of thought were influential and normative. Law is made up of rules, and medicine is an authoritative profession, whose beliefs are turned into advice and prescriptions.

Let us start with the law and the most corporeal of all relationships, that of a child with the mother's body. Maternity had to be defined primarily in relation to the legitimacy of the children, and therefore of the marriage. Marriage turns a natural phenomenon into a social reality. Children who were defined as 'natural' could not inherit and were not citizens: they were not acknowledged in terms of kinship or citizenship. Without a father who 'makes' (*poieîn*) his son or daughter, the child in question did not belong to any social group. Nothing, the son of nothing, as Euripides says. *Ápŏlis, ápatris*: deprived of father, fatherland and city, as one of Demosthenes' characters complains. A nameless body, without person.

If there was no marriage, with its ritual sex between man and woman and the ensuing alliance between two families, maternity was socially sterile. It did not create a recognised bond. The discovery of a mother–son relationship between two people who ignore each other or treat each other as strangers is the tragicomic theme of Euripides' *Ion*. This is the most ambiguous aspect of Sophocles' tragedy *Oedipus King*: Jocasta does not realise that, when she marries for a second time, her young bridegroom is in fact her son. It is as though the lack of paternal acknowledgement blinds mothers to their children's faces and bodies. A 'natural' mother appears incapable of recognising the similarity between herself and her son.

As always, we know the Athenian case best. When maternity occurred within marriage, it provided the material for the making both of a son, who was acknowledged by his father, and a citizen, because only a son who had been accepted as such could be registered in a phratry (kinship group) and later in a deme (*dêmŏs* or country district). It also provided the material for the making of a future legitimate mother of legitimate children, because to be born well meant to be born to a woman who had been given away in marriage, in accordance with the rules, by a father, a consanguineous brother or a paternal grandfather (Demosthenes, *Against Stephanus*, ii, 18). Only a woman born to a married woman (and not a concubine) and acknowledged as a legitimate daughter by the father could be given away in marriage in accordance with the rules. Only a woman acknowledged by a father *had* a father capable of giving her away in marriage. A woman could not marry in her own right; she needed someone to give her away. Let us not forget the situation of Penelope in Ithaca, and her daring initiative to challenge her suitors, personally.

Legitimate maternity was therefore essential for the transmission of social identity. This was part of the chain of matrimonial legitimacy, legitimacy of the resulting births and legitimacy of the subsequent marriage, at least as far as the daughters were concerned. And it was literally in the oath sworn by the man who presented a son or daughter to the phratry: he declared himself father and swore that the child was born of a married Athenian woman (Isaeus, vii, 16; viii, 18–20; *Sylloge*, 111, 371, 45, 921, 109–10). It did not matter whether the woman was his wife, but she had to be the legitimate wife of someone and therefore a woman whom a responsible male had given away in marriage, acknowledging her as the daughter of a married woman, and so on. The father had to be a legitimate son, because otherwise he would not have been there as a member of the phratry, to which he must have been introduced by his own father.

This chain of events and the wording of the oath demonstrate in practice what the undifferentiated filiation under a predominantly patrilineal system meant in Athenian society. It was an asymmetric system, because only the father had the prerogative to acknowledge children and bring them into existence socially; but also a bilateral one, because the legal status of the mother as a married woman of acknowledged paternity was indispensable for the transmission of identity. A man could not acknowledge a child as his own simply as the descendant of a single line – a child born in whatever manner and not of a married woman. Moreover, the man had the obligation to declare the existence of a married woman who was mother of the child he intended to accept as his, and therefore could not appropriate his children as though they only belonged to him. The presentation to the phratry acted as a double acknowledgement: one for his children and one for their mother.

It is important to insist on this crucial point, as it has been the source of spectacular misinterpretations: the relationship between a child and its mother was not based on evidence as a natural fact, but has to be acknowledged symbolically by the father. A child was presented to the kinship group as the child of a legitimate mother. This bond was established once and for all, whereas paternity was purely symbolic – a ritual certified it and another ritual, adoption, could cancel it. An acknowledged maternity was indissoluble. This is demonstrated by the case of an adopted person: the person would acquire a new father and lose the previous one, but the mother would remain the same. There was only one mother.

This did not so much express an increasingly rigid moral code as enhance protection for Athenian identity. We are in fact talking about the effects of Pericles' famous decree of 451 BC, which restricted citizenship to children whose parents were citizens on both sides. This decree made it illegal to marry a foreign woman: it prohibited giving away in marriage a foreign woman to an Athenian in accordance with procedure (Pseudo-Demosthenes, *Against Neaira*). Consequently marriage became the mark not only of a legitimate (as opposed to an extra-marital) birth, but also of Athenian parentage. When a woman was given away in marriage, this was also a demonstration of her being an Athenian. Her children could now inherit membership of this same polity.

In the context of asymmetric but bilateral parentage, maternity was valued because it contributed to ensuring the transmission of Athenian identity, as well as the transmission of property within a kinship network. Women inherited in Athens, but in what might be called secondary situations. Firstly there had to be no sons. If there were, then they would inherit equal shares of the father's assets on his death, while the sisters would only receive a dowry at the time of their marriage. In the absence of brothers, married sisters with children would inherit equal shares (Isaeus, vi). As far as inheritance by collateral lines was concerned (in the absence of either sons or daughters, and of a will or an adoption), men and the descendants of male lines had precedence over women and their descendants; all the agnates, that is, relations of the deceased on his father's side) had precedence over the cognates, that is, relations of the testator on his mother's side). In this case, the estate was not divided up but went to the relation who could demonstrate the closest kinship to the dead man in accordance with these rules. If a group of brothers found themselves in that situation, the eldest one would have precedence over the younger ones.

LET'S GET MARRIED TO AVOID LITIGATION

The difference between the sexes was treated with systematic asymmetry, which manifested itself in its simplest form in the inequality of male and female heirs of direct descent in relation to the paternal estate. A sister's inferiority, which resulted in her being her father's child to a lesser extent than her brother, raises a very interesting legal and anthropological problem.

Let us take the particular case of a young woman who finds herself obliged to 'follow' her father's estate when, in the absence of brothers, her father dies intestate: such a daughter was called *ĕpíklērŏs*. In this situation observance of the priority of the direct line entered into conflict with the principle of collateral rights of inheritance. On the one hand, the daughter was not an heir with full entitlement, *klērŏnŏmŏs*, because she was not a man, but she was nevertheless in the direct line. Furthermore, she was potentially the mother of a son who, in the future, would be the direct heir of the maternal grandfather. On the other hand, the closest collateral male kin could claim the right of succession, because there were no male children, and he too could inherit the estate. How was this dilemma to be resolved? By allowing the devolution of the estate to the male who was first of kin to the deceased, on one condition. He had to marry the woman and have a son by her, who would then be given in posthumous adoption to the deceased, in order to become his mother's 'brother' and therefore the primary heir of the disputed estate. In effect, we could redescribe the *ĕpíklērŏs* daughter as an *ĕpíklērŏs* mother – a potential mother, that is, of a direct heir who would be born from a later generation. Should an *ĕpíklērŏs* be married to a man outside the family, and were she to beget a male child, then the closest kin – cousin or uncle – would find himself at a disadvantage and threatened by a law suit. But if the girl's issue were also his son, then everyone's interests would be reconciled.

It is important to place the particular case of the *ĕpíklērŏs* daughter in the context of father/daughter inheritance and in contrast with the rights of married daughters. In absence of living sons married daughters who had already become mothers would normally inherit from their fathers, as if they were *klērŏnŏmoĭ*. Having married men outside the family, they already had sons who were heirs to the maternal grandfather in the direct line. The estate, therefore, could only go in one direction. Where possible, the direct line prevailed over the collateral line. The law sanctioned this principle and consequently accepted both the division of a dead man's estate between his daughters – just as it would for sons – and its dispersion into various homes, as long as these heirs were married and had become mothers. It was therefore normal for the inheritance to follow that line and descend through them to its most legitimate claimants. The grandsons of the deceased (the sons of his daughters) disqualified all other relations. There was no competition and there was no conflict.

In the case of the *ĕpíklērŏs*, on the contrary, we encounter a considerable predicament. Where should the inheritance go? Should it go down the direct line, even if this is represented by a female who is for the moment unmarried? Should it be diverted to the closest relative amongst the collateral males? That is indeed a strong candidate, partly because he (probably an uncle or a cousin) would have legal responsibility for the fatherless daughter. He would become her *kúriōs*, which amongst other things involved being the appointed administrator of her property. The woman's status as a minor, unable to inherit with full rights of ownership, creates a situation in which the estate is at risk of being devolved elsewhere, to the benefit of another line of descent. However, the principle of precedence to the direct line would have been seriously undermined if a collateral could prevail over a child, albeit a female one. A daughter still remained a direct descendant of the first degree. The problem was to reconcile these two concepts – the priority of men over women, and the priority of the direct line over the collateral line – without renouncing either.

Athenian law, as we have seen, resolved the dilemma through a compromise. It allowed the closest male relation to inherit the deceased's estate, but on condition that he did not neglect the potential mother of a future heir, namely the *ĕpíklērŏs* daughter's son. When a cousin or uncle was willing to receive the inheritance, the law obliged him to marry the fatherless girl and consummate the marriage in order to produce an heir. If, for whatever reason, the candidate had no interest in the marriage and managed through a private agreement to obtain the assets without having to carry the burden of an unwanted wife, and the daughter married another man, then the collateral heir would almost certainly face a court action brought by any son born of that marriage (Menander, *The Shield*). The conflict between the two competing lines of descent would then come into the open.

In other words, the law was not primarily concerned with keeping assets within the 'family', by which we might mean a homogeneous group, because in that case women would never have inherited at all. Instead, the intention was to defend a weakened line – a line temporarily represented by an unmarried woman – from the legitimate but provisional demands of the closest collateral males. The issue was one of time: the time the woman would need in order to bear a male child to her own father. According to this principle, a pregnant widow would find herself, like an *épíklērŏs*, under the protection of the eponymous archon, the authority charged with maintaining stability in Athenian society and protecting private property. Her pregnant body acted as an intermediary between the dead husband and his child soon to be born, who would re-establish the continuity of the family line. The law took care of women, and the city watched over the domestic space.

Inheritance law prescribed a kind of exchange. The uncle or cousin took advantage of his status as a male, but had to put it to use by marrying and impregnating the daughter of his deceased relative, in order to re-establish the dead man's family line. The daughter's rights as a potential mother were recognised, and her femininity was used in the service of 're-masculinising', as it were, the father's line of descent, which she had damaged simply by being a woman.

Women did participate in the process of inheritance, as mentioned, but this was obscured by the fact that they were represented in court cases by their *kúriŏs*, and were therefore invisible to their judges and to those of us who read the speeches made in their names. However, the phenomenon existed. Women received wealth and assets, which gave them power and prestige within the home. However, the right to inherit did not put them on a par with men. Moreover, this right depended mainly on their ability to act as an intermediary between two generations, and therefore on their having become a mother or having prospects of becoming one later. They would leave the assets received from their fathers or collateral relations to their sons, as well as their dowries. When a mother died, the dowry was inherited by the sons (Demosthenes, *Against Boeotus*, ii, 50 and 56). If a woman died childless, her dowry was returned to her family of origin. If she divorced with or without children, she took her dowry with her. However, a woman could make a claim on an inheritance of, for example, a dead cousin with or without children (Isaeus, vii, 11–12). All this meant that women made possible a continuous circulation of assets through dowries and inheritances that passed from one line to another.

SEX AND COMMUNITY

The importance of women as agents in the transmission of assets must be understood in the context of economic interests as well as social ones. Women created family ties made of affection and solidarity, not just personally but also through the 'diplomatic' role of marriage. Marriage is an alliance. This idea is crucial to Lévi-Strauss' structural anthropology. There sexual coupling is the basic instrument for creating social bonds, by which we mean new relations, which do not derive from genealogy but imply exchange and reciprocity, a more or less formal contract and therefore a cultural acknowledgement of nature. The circulation of women given away and received in marriage constitutes the primary factor in socialisation.

Greek thought on kinship confirms this theoretical insight in an exemplary manner. In Athens, marriage created a group of allies who shared a preferential friendship and formed a community, *koinonía*. This association brought about a stable and instinctive solidarity between its members. Whereas brothers and consanguineous relations were always potentially in competition over family assets and dynastic powers, brothers-in-law found themselves in an ideal situation: they had nothing to fight over. The gratitude generated by the act of exchange itself appears to have contributed to the emotional atmosphere of the newly formed group, in contrast with the permanent rivalry within a consanguineous group.

A marriage also created a community between the spouses: the couple formed a *koīnōnía*. This is how Xenophon presented the relationship between Ischomachus and his wife in the *Oeconomicus*. In his *Politics*, Aristotle defined the constitutive heterosexual relationship in a home as *koīnōnía*, whereas Plutarch, in his famous *Conjugal Precepts*, idealised this portrait of the married couple as an intimate and indivisible fusion – or, again, *koīnōnía*.

It was procreation that consolidated the marital community. Children, one orator asserted, are common to both parents and promote reconciliations (Demosthenes, *Against Boeotus*, i, 23; ii, 29). Shared children are an instrument for creating cohesion: for this reason Plato wanted them to be held in common by an entire generation of 'mothers' and 'fathers' in the 'Hawaiian' city of the *Republic*, in which kinship terms became purely classificatory. On the whole, children embody the indivisibility of the conjugal space, beyond divorce and separations. As we shall see in *Medea*, they always remain the surviving residue of a broken marriage.

More generally, a recognised sexual union between a woman and a man played a conciliatory role and prevented conflict. According to the orator Isaeus, marriage could be used to resolve disputes between relatives, and not just relatives, because by agreeing to such a transaction – the gift of a woman to a man – the parties to the dispute entrusted what they held most dear to each other. This was the result of the legal construct that regulated the marriage of the *ĕpíklērŏs*: no reason for a fight, once the heiress becomes her paternal kin's wife and they share the same children. This was the role explicitly attributed to marriage as a means for ending political hostilities (Sissa, 1990b). This was also the value implicitly recognised in marriage in such tragic stories as those of the Danaids and Antigone. The daughters of Danaus were expected to marry the sons of Aegyptus. This would put an end to the two brothers' quarrels. However, only one of the fifty women plays by the rules. The others murder their new husbands during the wedding night. Antigone becomes an *ĕpíklērŏs,* when her two brothers kill each other. Already an orphan, she is now under the tutorship of her closest kin, her uncle Creon, the ruler of Thebes. Her irreconcilable clash with him, over the burial of one of her brothers, culminates in the failure of her scheduled marriage with Creon's son, Haimon.

Now, to return to the gendered aspect of the Athenian system of kinship – which is undifferentiated and yet predominantly patrilineal – let us restate that the bilateral nature of inheritance, the married couple as a model for social interaction founded on consent and indivisibility, the conciliatory effects of alliance and marriage, all this took place, however, within the context of inequality between the sexes. The difference between the sexes was a source of collaborative sociality, but it was defined by inequality in law. A daughter was not equal to a son. A sister was not equal to a brother. A wife was not equal to a husband. At any age, a woman was a statutory minor. Approximately like a man, but never quite.

We have seen that this train of thought can be found also in ancient biology and medicine. Let us now look at how these different discourses, that of a positive knowledge of the body and that of the legal apparatus of the city–state, converge in framing the idea of sexual difference. The theories of procreation explain the material underpinnings of the *koīnōnía* between man and woman: the physical substances that brought about the transmission of identity.

According to Hippocratic doctors, genetic transmission is bilateral, as has been mentioned. However, there are two types of semen, one male and one female, which are mixed together during conception. Doctors believed that during sexual intercourse there is an emission of fluids from both the penis and the cervix, as a result of the warmth that creates pleasure. The two doses of liquid are mixed together and the mixture is sucked into the womb, where the development of the embryo commences. The sex of the child is decided by whether the mixture is made up of prevalently male or female semen. This theory associated a clear concept of genetic bilateralism (there are two seminal contributions) with the idea of a symmetry that was almost, but not quite, perfect. The male semen was in fact stronger than the female semen.

Following the *Corpus Hippocraticum,* the next great work on biology was Aristotle's. The philosopher constantly referred back to the theories of the *Corpus,* and he criticised it on one fundamental point: there is no female semen identical to the male one. The role of the maternal body in procreation is to provide the inert matter, which receives warmth, movement, form and life from the male semen. For Aristotle, the female matter is blood, the blood that normally flows from the body every month. This blood contains the body of the potential embryo. This theory resonates with that of Apollo in Aeschylus' *Oresteia*, as we shall see in a moment. Only a father is a parent, understood as a source of identity, the god argues, while a mother plays an ancillary role: she provides the place where the living being in progress needs to be sheltered, the rough material and the food necessary for growth. Here the notion of a predominance of the paternal line overshadows that of bilateral descent.

Greek thought was prepared to admit that the cooperation of two sexes was the natural cause of the construct of kinship, which is legal and social. But biology as well as the law could perceive the difference between the sexes only in its asymmetry. For the Greeks, it was undeniable that women were inferior. Inferior and yet undeniable. Not quite the protagonists, but always playing a second role in the script of procreation. A result of this way of thinking was the admission that mothers are, so to speak, more 'real' than fathers. The symbolic construct of kinship, through the power of men to acknowledge their sons and to adopt, was very different from the bond that united children to their mothers. As has already been said, an adopted son acquired a new father, but kept his own mother. For all the arguments about its being subsidiary or weak, maternity was intangible – it could not be touched or touched up. In the *Oresteia*, the last word on kinship is with the goddesses who keep alive the frightening memory of a mother, murdered by her son at the orders of Apollo.

SEX AND TRAGEDY

Having explored the norms which translated into habits and rights the difference and the connection between sexually different bodies, let us now examine very different texts: literary texts, written to be staged and enjoyed in public. Let us turn to tragedy. It is intuitively clear that tragedy is concerned with sex and sensuality. Whenever we recall tragic plots we conjure up the image of intense erotic passions: boundless love, reckless adultery, forced abductions, unintentional incest and virginity desperately defended. There is, however, a more profound reason for the significance of sex in tragedy than the simple presence of characters with strong emotions. It is there, in Aristotle's *Poetics*.

What is a tragedy and how can we define it? A tragedy is a well constructed tale, capable of provoking strong feelings of pity and fear in the audience. Something violent must occur to produce such emotions, but the violence must not be of a predictable kind, for instance between enemies, because in such cases there is no reason for pity when one of them is killed. This would have been normal. Aristotle claimed that the plot had to concern *phíloi*, friends that is, or dear ones, if the audience was to feel pity – in other words, if the play was to be a tragedy. In their case, the antagonism, the confrontation and the spilling of blood are disturbing, regrettable and pitiable. A murderer is only a tragic figure if her crime affects someone she should love and not an adversary or an unknown person. Death has to occur as a misfortune, an accident, something unexpected within the space of *philía*, the friendship that connects the members of a group. It cannot be a deliberate choice; it has to be a mistake.

For the tragic to be defined by this type of violence, there has to be an aggressive society that is relatively at ease with death and has few qualms over murdering a stranger. Within the city, of course, the circle of *philoí* extended to all citizens and their friends. In the theatrical universe, *philía* was understood almost exclusively within the context of kinship. An example of tragically pathetic violence is that of Oedipus who believes he is attacking passers-by – which would not have disturbed anyone – but is, in fact, killing his own father. Infanticide, parricide, uxoricide, fratricide: these were the recurring themes of theatrical violence.

Now, we can use Aristotle's definition to understand the anthropological thinking which occurs in tragedy. The assertion is Aristotle's own and has to be interpreted first within Aristotelian thought, but it is also the conceptualised expression of what an intelligent spectator could see. Aristotle was right because his normative definition captured what we do in fact find in tragedies, or at least in extant tragedies: stories of families, violence among blood relatives, tensions between man and wife or parents and children, and victims murdered by their spouses, sons, mothers, brothers or fathers. And obviously we encounter the large doses of jealousy, desire, love and hate required to bring these relationships into existence and then to explode them. These relationships are built upon sex and sexual difference. In other words, the *philoí* provide a hotbed of actual and institutionalised sexuality. Moreover, precisely because kinship provides the framework for tragic events, women (wives, lovers, sisters, daughters and, above all, mothers) are necessarily the protagonists of those events.

While we have examined the fundamental principles of socially symbolised sexuality, tragedy allows us to look behind the scenes, where the rules, yet to be imposed and accepted as normal, come into conflict with other possible rules. In the theatre, the very definition of someone 'close', as opposed to a stranger, proved to be uncertain, indeterminate and open to discussion. The nature of closeness was not obvious. It is an appalling thing to kill one's mother, but what is motherhood? It is a terrifying thing not to bury the body of a brother, but who is a brother? It is a terrible thing to set a murderous trap for one's husband, but what is marriage? It is an unspeakable thing to knife one's own children, but whose are the children? Who is the issue of a sexual encounter? Using variations on mythical themes, tragedies produced a wide range of situations, intrigues and catastrophes which demonstrate the options and transgressions that eluded the normalisation of sex.

By showing this spectacle, tragedy invited viewers to look into the social and legal systemisation of sex in the past. In fifth-century Athens, the stories of Clytemnestra, Medea or Electra were remote; their use of retaliation was obsolete. The temporal distance allowed the playwrights to explore what erotic passions might have been – and what they might become – without well established norms. The stage exposed the sphere of subjectivity, which normally remained invisible; this sphere was the source of desire, where emotions were translated into words. The uncertainties and deviations from the norm were in fact linked to irresistible or, to use our key term, insatiable urges. In the theatre, *aplēstía* came out into the open. In the theatre, the feminine inner self was revealed. Given that women's emotions were mostly erotic, rather than political or intellectual, the theatre was the place where female sensuality triumphed. Tragedy was paradoxically pornographic. The Greek theatre, a place of exposure where light was thrown on the unknown and the invisible was put on exhibition, never ceases to be an optical device. Priapus was not tragic, but Phaedra was.

In its representation of subjective sexuality – that is, the sensuality of characters who express sentiments and passions – tragedy demonstrates the immense importance of relations between the sexes and the richness of ancient thought on female love and love for women. A strict reading of Michel Foucault might lead us to believe that the Greek problematisation of sex was mainly concerned with the *eros* between men and boys. But Foucault completely ignored the world of tragedy in his *History of Sexuality*, and drew exclusively on philosophical texts that presented a world in which, it is true, the interesting form of love was the one for boys. As we have seen, this corresponded to a sociological reality: the homoerotic exclusivity of aristocratic circles who frequented the palaestrae and banquets. This also explains the particular interest of philosophy in the question of controlling desire: a challenge to the male body, its caprices and its potential effeminacy. In the theatrical universe, even when detached from the present day of the audience, the sexes are both involved, instead, in *páthŏs* amongst *phíloĭ*. And the women are more interesting.

In the light of Aristotle's normative poetics we realise that it is true: Greek tragedy is a cruel reflection and a series of experiments on the forms of 'friendship' that emanate from relations between the sexes. But, to assess fully the insight of Aristotle's definition, we must appreciate its ethnographical relevance. Aristotle understood that the substance of the tragic in classical Athens was to be found in its cultural ingredients. In theorising about the tragic composition as a *mûthos* of which the essential element was violence between dear ones, he pinned down a logic that the Greeks found extremely powerful: the connections between kinship and myth, and between kinship and violence.

The mythical tradition tended to narrate stories of a genealogical nature, in which the plot traced the sequence of the generations. Theogonies, genealogies, metamorphoses: the mythographic genre, if one existed, remained faithful, from Hesiod to Pseudo-Apollodorus, to a narrative structure in which following the plot meant following the various lines of descent and branches of kinship from one sexual union to another. This was ready-made material whose intrigues playwrights could draw upon and reconfigure for their scenes about *phíloĭ*. As for the idea of identifying the tragic with a fusion between violence and kinship, Aristotle put his finger on what we have already characterised as 'kinship practice' in Greece, namely the omnipresent risk of litigation and the fragility of close relationships. The dramatic invention created a world which manifested, in the most varied permutations (almost) all the possible and imaginable forms of conflict that the rules governing inheritance, lines of descent and alliances attempted to avoid.

Let us now take a glimpse at a world in which one right pushes aside other rights, causing a series of catastrophic transgressions. Given that excessive emotion manifests itself in the characters' agency and in the words they speak when preparing, justifying and commenting upon their acts, it is in the plot, in the *mûthos* as a sequence of actions (and not simply events), that the emotions are to be found. We will therefore examine a few complex narratives: Clytemnestra's adultery and murder, Electra's vindictive virginity, Medea's conjugal passion and infanticide, Deianeira's unintentional murder of her husband. We are amongst friends who tear each other apart from one generation to the next. Our reading will have to be sensitive to the distinctive fabric of the tragic genre, which, we might say, regenerates itself in a particularly genealogical manner.

Indeed, the playwrights did not invent in the sense of producing an original story that had never been seen or heard before. Their invention was in finding and extracting, from the mythical repertoire, narrative segments available to be literally recycled, or rewritten in other cycles. There was an attempt to transform the *fabulae* which already existed in the oral, written or indeed theatrical traditions, in order to create new plots. They would be new in relation to the existing versions, and their fascination for the public depended on the subtlety with which they explored possible dramatic, psychological and legal variations that had been ignored, avoided or merely hinted at in the existing versions. Unthought-of elements appeared in place of those which the authors wanted to replace in the work of previous writers. It was a competition. Writers constantly had to come up with new palimpsests in order to compete for the prizes conferred on them by the public at the festivals in honour of Dionysus.

If we were to speculate on the kind of audience that would have found this style congenial, we would undoubtedly think of one that was attentive, extremely familiar with all the stories and interested in the work of rewriting, reorganising and redistributing the times, places, story-lines and characters. These were people eager for relative, not absolute, innovations – innovations which were not original, but intertextual, and suited the authors' competitive race to write the most intelligent version of the same story.

CLYTEMNESTRA: PENELOPE'S OPPOSITE

The setting is the home of a lord, from which the lord is absent. A woman, his wife, awaits his return, but is uncertain that it will ever take place. Nevertheless she is sure that he expects her to remain faithful. He, in the meantime, has naturally been unfaithful. We have heard this story before, or at least we know this situation very well as the starting point for at least three narrative variants, three stories of heroes who return to wives they left at home: Agamemnon, Ulysses and Heracles, who were awaited by Clytemnestra, Penelope and Deianeira. These were three very different stories, so different in fact that their shared point of departure might go unnoticed. But the intense compositional activity just referred to can be clearly seen in the way the plots and characters were constructed in relation to each other.

If we start with the most ancient text and start reading from the very beginning, we find that action in the *Odyssey* begins on the top of Mount Olympus, with a conversation amongst the gods. Talking in a very casual manner and expressing a thought that has just occurred to him, Zeus tells of his regret over the unhappy end of one of the protagonists in the *Iliad*, the lord of Mycenae, Agamemnon. His wife was at home, and was being courted by Agamemnon's cousin, Aegisthus. The gods, Zeus recalls, tried to dissuade Aegisthus from his plan to marry Clytemnestra and kill her husband, by warning him of the danger of a vendetta perpetrated by their son, Orestes. However, the suitor would not listen to the messenger of the gods, who had taken the trouble to bring the message (*Odyssey*, i, 32–43). He persisted in pestering and attempting to seduce the lonely wife, eventually overcoming her initial resistance and managing to take her away with her consent (iii, 272). He set a trap for the returning husband by inviting him to his house in Argos: this was the end of the naive and unhappy Agamemnon.

The lord of the gods – who would have been remembered by the *Odyssey*'s public as the god who cruelly deceived Agamemnon in the *Iliad* and made him pay a high price for his argument with Achilles – is not so much moved by the victim's fate as disapproving of human stupidity, particularly when humans are in the habit of blaming the gods for their misfortunes. Zeus is thinking of Aegisthus and his insane refusal to be persuaded by the god's messenger. Athena, however, takes the opportunity to bring the conversation around to a matter dear to her heart. And, talking about that, the bellicose young goddess more or less says, there is another warrior returning from Troy who is in a very similar situation to that of Agamemnon. Currently Ulysses is prisoner on an island; he is detained by a goddess who is in love with him and obstructed by Poseidon from any attempt to go to sea. On her own island, as the gods know, his wife is courted by men who are devouring all his stocks of food (i, 91–2). And, as though the shift in the argument appeared to him to be entirely relevant, Zeus responds in the affirmative to Athena's appeal, just as he did in the *Iliad* with Thetis' requests, and he decides to release the double paralysis that held Ulysses in Ogygia and Telemachus in Ithaca.

It has been said that both spouses are 'courted', and on different islands. It should be added that the young men's courtship of Penelope in Ithaca is mentioned for the first time during this dialogue, from which the entire course of events takes its cue. It is referred to as a state of siege similar to the one suffered by Clytemnestra, when she was still defending herself (iii, 265–6) and had not yet agreed to follow Aegisthus (iii, 272). Penelope finds herself in the same situation Clytemnestra was in some years earlier. The course of events will depend on her behaviour. Will Ulysses' return to Ithaca be a rerun of Agamemnon's return to Mycenae? No, the *Odyssey* will be a variant of the *Oresteia*, but one which develops by deviating from an identical fork in the narrative path.

At the beginning of the poem and at other key moments (xi, 405), the poet insists too much on the contrast between the two destinies for the reader not to realise that these are two alternative ramifications, two combinatory variants starting from a single situation. The *Odyssey*, as the text repeatedly suggests, tells the story of what could have happened to Agamemnon, had Clytemnestra behaved in a different manner. Vice versa, the *Oresteia* never disappears from the horizon of the Homeric narrative, as though it represented an immediate risk, a probable catastrophe, given the same point of departure: the exposed position of a wife who awaits her husband and is tempted by another man. The two stories mirror each other counterfactually: what if Penelope were to act like Clytemnestra; what if Clytemnestra had emulated Penelope?

The Homeric Clytemnestra is very close to Penelope; indeed she is, in a way, even more loyal: initially she *rejects* (*anaínĕtŏ*: xi, 265) her suitor, something which, after all, Penelope will never do. Later she gives in and follows Aegisthus to his home on Argos, just as Penelope will be invited to follow one of her wooers of her own free will (*ĕthĕloūsa*: xi, 272). This consent and this desire of hers are what the lads on Ithaca fail to obtain from Ulysses' wife, at least until they face the challenge to pull the string of the fatal bow. But by then Ulysses is already there, and joining the competition with them as a covert candidate at the wooing of his own wife. Penelope, as we have seen, plays for time and flirts in an ambiguous manner, which is neither rejection nor acceptance. Clytemnestra changed her mind and shifted from a 'no' to a 'yes' that took her to another house, and then fatally to murder.

It was this sudden change from resistance to abandonment that tragic rewriting would mostly concentrate upon. The time between her no and her yes, which was a vacuum in the *Odyssey*, would be filled with thoughts, intentions and passions. Why does Clytemnestra betray Agamemnon? The Homeric poet does not reply to this question. Aegisthus speaks to her, enchants her and seduces her (*thĕlghēīn*: iii, 264). Charm does not always work. Ulysses, for example, remains unmoved by Calypso's divine and captivating *thĕlghēīn* (i, 57–9). But its powers are not lost on Clytemnestra. Perhaps she has lost hope of her husband's survival, or has been overcome by Aphrodite or *eros*. The erotic logic of the Homeric world allows for speculations, but they are only speculations.

The tragedies, on the other hand, provide Clytemnestra's consent with psychological content. She has good reason to repudiate the absent husband: the fact that he has put Iphigenia to death to appease the goddess Artemis, who had demanded the sacrifice of a daughter. This episode, although related to the background story of the Trojan Wars, does not appear in the Homeric poems. It was a narrative complication that was added later. It was certainly not invented by Aeschylus, who did however turn it into a powerful and, in a way, paradoxical dramatic component. Clytemnestra is now an adulteress and a murderer because she is a grieving mother. The woman, who cheerfully knifes a husband she has already betrayed, does so in the name of the indissoluble bond with her own daughter, with the being to which she gave birth. He has put to death a girl whom she had brought into the world; now it is she who, taking advantage of a sacrifice, draws the assassin's blood. *Páthŏs* amongst *phĭloĭ*, and a chain reaction of violence. Aristotle was not mistaken.

Aeschylus' plot overturns the Homeric template as a result of this magnified 'detail' which creates the tragedy. The essential element in the plot of the *Agamemnon* (which for good reason is not entitled *Aegisthus*) is the tension between two *phĭloĭ* who are husband and wife, both guilty of having killed someone who was dear to them. The relationship between Clytemnestra and Aegisthus is not that of a married couple in this version: the woman has not followed her suitor to his home, but has taken him as a lover, while remaining in her husband's palace. The lover merely has a walk-on part in this cast. Clytemnestra has control of the action. With overly obsequious ceremony, she pretends to celebrate the return of her victorious husband by a sumptuous sacrifice, only to slay him during the ritual. If he were Ulysses rather than the thoughtless man he is, he would make the connection with the sacrificial killing of his daughter and expect trouble. But Agamemnon has forgotten the death of Iphigenia, seems oblivious to what might be the pain of his daughter's mother, and allows himself to be drawn into the trap. Later on the same spot, Aegisthus and Clytemnestra will in turn be slaughtered by Orestes, Agamemnon's son. But won't the avenger of his father one day have to face up to the rights of the mother or to some form of justice, if he has soiled his hands with the blood of one parent in order to pay for the death of the other?

The *Oresteia* thus becomes a drama of relations between parents and children and between spouses (in episodes, as it is made up of three moments: the *Agamemnon*, the *Choephoroe* (*The Libation Bearers*) and the *Eumenides*). It is no longer a miniature tale of human stupidity encapsulated in a more complex one on the same subject – almost a short story within a novel. Knowing what has to be avoided – thanks, in part, to help from the gods – and yet being unable to stop oneself from going after that one thing! And this is a common mistake in a world in which gods and humans live together and continuously interact, and in which Aegisthus, like Ulysses, Agamemnon or Achilles, must have, above all, a shrewd understanding of how to behave in response to, and in anticipation of, divine interventions. The world of tragedy is no more about altercations between mortals and immortals: it is a stage for the pathology of kinship. Questions of blood (spilt and handed down the generations) and of marital alliances, such as who is consanguineous or what is a spouse, are raised within the plot and resolved by the characters in an explicit, philosophical and scientific manner. There is antagonism between passions and personal interests in the competitive construct of the tragedy, but the protagonists in action also hold theories, think about what is happening and act accordingly. The playwright gives the gods the task of throwing a sudden and intermittent light on the criteria by which to make judgements that transcend the turbulent events.

Being the son of his father and mother, Orestes must of course avenge his father, but he cannot kill his mother, because by killing her he is shedding the blood of a close relation, of another parent. He therefore finds himself in the position of having to carry out a legitimate vendetta and thus be the author of an illegitimate act: the spilling of family blood. The vendetta he has performed calls for another vendetta, in which he will be the victim. All takes place within the family and presupposes two 'legal' principles: the idea that there are divine powers, the Erinyes (or Furies), making sure that the shedding of blood between blood relations does not escape punishment; and the idea that parentage is bilateral, that is, that both mother and father are parents of their children. These two premises correspond to the convictions held by the Erinyes themselves in the *Eumenides*, the tragedy which follows the *Choephoroe*. 'They pursue the murderous mortals whom folly has driven *against their blood relations* until everyone is beneath the earth, and even there they do not leave them in peace' (Aeschylus' *Eumenides*, 334–40). When there is murder of a consanguineous kin they hunt down the guilty party and blind him or her with more bloodshed, but they leave in peace those who kill a spouse, as though a matrimonial alliance could not produce a bond worthy of a vendetta (ibid., 143; 158). For the Erinyes, a mother is a parent with the same rights as a father. 'Am I supposed to have the same blood as my mother?' asks Orestes of the Erinyes who form the chorus in the *Eumenides*. And they reply, 'What iniquity! Who nourished you in her womb? Do you then repudiate the blood that is most yours, the blood of your mother?' (606–9).

These beliefs are precisely what Orestes' predicament challenges and questions in the *Oresteia*. When Orestes appears before the court which Athena sets up to judge him, the god Apollo, who has guided his actions and urged him to kill his mother, testifies that only a father can be considered a parent and therefore only a father can demand to be avenged, while a mother is nothing more than a receptacle that takes in and feeds a stranger in her body. By killing Clytemnestra, Orestes has at the very worst killed his hostess. Thus, once he has been ritually purified with a piglet's blood, there is no reason why the Erinyes, the guarantors of murdered blood relations, should trouble him. Moreover, Apollo argues with the Erinyes over the value of the marital pact. Why haven't they tormented Clytemnestra, who murdered her husband? Is a husband not a relation? 'You take away all honour and put no value on the nuptial pledge sacred to Hera and Zeus', Apollo accuses them. 'In this way, you even deprive Venus of all her worth – Venus who grants the mortals their dearest things. Indeed, the marital bed is more powerful than an oath, because it is watched over by justice. You are indulgent with those who kill their spouses and do not look at them in anger: I therefore argue that you unjustly drive Orestes into exile' (213–21).

Apollo attacked the Erinyes' argument that there are two lines of descent of equal value, the maternal and the paternal one, but no kinship between spouses, and hence vendetta concerns the father and mother, but not the husband. He then came up with an opposing medical and legal theory. There is only one line of descent, the paternal one. There is a *díkē* (justice) specific to marriage, which creates a bond between husband and wife. There are therefore no mitigating circumstances for Clytemnestra, who has killed the man who is both her husband and the father of Orestes, whereas there are for Orestes who, by killing his mother, has killed a person to whom he was neither related nor allied. As for Athena, the third authority on human law, she votes for Orestes because she belongs to her father Zeus, who brought her into the world from his own head, without the involvement of a female body, and she therefore does not give any weight to the death of a woman and mother guilty of having killed a man and father. For Athena, the thing that matters is not the violation of the justice of the marital bed, but the affront to a paternal figure, who is exclusively responsible for procreation.

However, Athena is to play an even more important role. Orestes is acquitted – on equal votes – and the city of Athens, thanks to Athena, has now invented a court for murders. In accordance with the goddess's will, legal judgement will now take the place of personal vendetta. Consanguineous conflict will be resolved in the public forum on grounds of wisdom and truth, and will no longer be fed by personal reprisals that risk repeating themselves forever. A further characteristic of tragedy is that where there is a bond, whether of kinship or an alliance, it triggers a mechanism of retaliation. Solidarity means violence. This is true of both the Erinyes and Apollo, when they argue over the type of relation which calls for an appropriate punishment and not over the principle of violence itself. Although she votes for Orestes and shares Apollo's ideas on the line of descent, Athena goes against this tradition and breaks the logic of the vendetta.

A father who has sacrificed his daughter, a wife who has cut her husband's throat and a son who has slaughtered his mother: fortunately this is where the deadly tit for tat comes to an end. The Erinyes, who have now become 'benign' Eumenides, will watch over the Athenian court of blood crimes, the Areopagus, where, historically, murderers were tried. A metamorphosis occurs during the course of the trilogy. It starts with Agamemnon, who acts as though Iphigenia were his property and he could dispose of her as he wishes. Clytemnestra's pain over the loss of her daughter opens up a deep wound, as she feels herself to be the mocked wife whose maternity is neither acknowledged nor treated with respect. By turning the line of descent into a wholly paternal affair, Agamemnon adopts Apollo's theory that the father is the only parent. In response, Clytemnestra imposes the belief held by the Erinyes, that a mother is a parent and marriage counts for nothing, and accordingly she takes revenge for the murder of her daughter. Consistent with his view of kinship, Apollo encourages Orestes to butcher his mother: she deserves it, and it does not matter. This competition could go on forever, but when Orestes' fate has to be decided, this gory conflict becomes a theoretical problem. The divine powers involved actually think about this, and the resulting compromise admits the priority of the paternal line of descent (here, Athena agrees with Apollo) but must incorporate the maternal Erinyes. The trilogy celebrates the recognition of the asymmetrical and bilateral nature of procreation: Orestes, who avenges his father, is acquitted of matricide, but the conclusion requires acknowledgement of maternal rights as argued for by the Erinyes, who now become the Eumenides. And the killing comes to an end.

DEIANEIRA: PENELOPE AND MORE SO

Sophocles' *Electra* reworks the tale in order to accentuate further the connection between the two murders: Agamemnon's murder of Iphigenia and Clytemnestra's murder of Agamemnon. The adulterous wife acts in this version solely as the slighted mother. This is a specific choice. In the *Oresteia*, Aeschylus had added another reason for Clytemnestra's resentment: her anger at Cassandra's inclusion in the booty from the Trojan War. Apollo's prophetess – the unwilling mistress of the king – remains on the scene as the drama unfolds. She is the one who reveals what is going to happen in the palace and what does in fact happen. She stands out as a dominant figure. Clytemnestra already has good reason to attack her husband, but the arrival of his young lover, whom he has brought with him with the intention of introducing her into the home, provides her with another motive for taking pleasure in what she is about to do. Cassandra is an unexpected seasoning for the sacrificial banquet. Jealousy adds flavour to the vendetta, and intensifies its enjoyment. The undervalued mother is also an offended wife in regard to the *díkē* of the marital bed, as with Medea.

Sophocles scraps this jealousy for Cassandra. The poet composed another play, *Trachinian Women*, entirely dedicated to the humiliation of the wife, who awaits her husband's return only to see him turn up with a slave lover. The plot stems from the same narrative matrix – a wife is waiting for a man gone to war – but Heracles takes the place of Ulysses or Agamemnon, Deianeira the place of Penelope or Clytemnestra, Iole the role of Cassandra, and the young Hyllus the place of Telemachus and Orestes. With these ingredients, so interlinked in the memories of the Athenian audience, Sophocles created a variation on the intertextual tradition.

Deianeira is the essential tragic character who kills a *phílŏs* without really intending it. After she has waited devotedly and loyally for her husband to return from the war, he finally comes back covered in glory and proud to show off Iole, a beautiful girl who has been taken into captivity, and indeed to offer her as a gift to his loving wife (*Trachinian Women*, 464). If marriage were solely a social phenomenon, there would be nothing strange about Deianeira greeting with indifference the women her husband enjoys sexually. What could possibly be wrong with a concubine who exists alongside the appointed wife? However, this is not how Greek women do business, even in fiction. Deianeira has the bad taste to care about her man and to desire his love. She incautiously starts to suffer when he imposes a rival under the same roof and under the same blanket, in the same bed (539–40). As, like all literary heroines, she is an active woman, she tries to do something about it.

A long time before, she had provoked the passion of a centaur, and Heracles, then jealous, had killed it with an arrow. However, the dying monster wished to give Deianeira a few drops of its blood, which he said had the powers of a love philtre. Heracles' young wife had not had occasion to use this artifice, but now that she had been betrayed, neglected and threatened by a rival in her own home, she naturally makes use of the drug. She spreads it on a tunic she then gives to her insensitive husband in order to regain his attentions. Loyal like Penelope, Deianeira becomes like Clytemnestra, an instrument in taking her husband's life. The philtre is in fact a poison, similar to the one Medea will use to eliminate her rival. Heracles dies, racked with pain, because of an error – because of his wife's amorous desire.

Deianeira embodies those aspects of the Aeschylean Clytemnestra that Sophocles expunged from his version of her character in *Electra*: the humiliation and grief experienced on the appearance of another woman who is to share her home. Deviating from the *Oresteia,* Sophocles spreads the two motives for killing Agamemnon – sacrifice of the daughter and infidelity – over two different characters in different plays. His Clytemnestra is only stirred by her maternal feelings for Iphigenia; his Deianira, only by her feelings as a spurned wife. As the use of this plot drifts in different directions, we encounter yet another Clytemnestra, primarily wounded in her erotic pride and violently motivated by her anger with her husband over Cassandra's intrusion. This Clytemnestra–Deianeira emerges in Euripides' *Electra*, who has an imperious sexuality that clearly contrasts her with the Sophoclean mother, and who conceals instead Deianeira's temperament.

ELECTRA: VIRGINITY AND VENDETTA

Electra's brooding greatness does not depend, as in the case of Oedipus or Antigone, on a single great and memorable text, but on three surviving tragedies in which she is the female protagonist, a rare event amongst extant classical texts. There is one for each of the playwrights of the fifth century BC: Aeschylus' *Choephoroe*, Euripides' *Electra* and Sophocles' *Electra*. The three plays were written very close to each other, and in the sequence of the three versions we can follow the transformations of a story whose plot was already available, in the epic tradition, as far back as Homer. It is the story of someone who was the antithesis of Ulysses. As far as we know, a significant role for Orestes' sister only appears when the plot is transferred to tragedy.

We need to examine the evolution of the three stories, and how the character is built up and modified. In the *Choephoroe*, Electra enters the stage and goes towards the tomb of her father, Agamemnon, the warrior hero who was killed by his treacherous wife together with her lover. Electra is followed by a chorus of women. They all wear crowns and carry precious liquids to be offered to the dead man. They have been sent by Clytemnestra, the murderous wife, and the women wonder about the strangeness of this ritual and the ambiguity of a ceremony which usually expresses devotion and due care, but is possibly inappropriate when a murderer has requested it for her victim. What are they to do? Electra is uncertain whether she should become the intermediary to her mother's gesture or hurriedly pour the libations, as though throwing them away. Should she make herself carry her mother's prayers for the dead, or keep her silence? The women of her retinue reply that she should ask for her father's protection against the murderers in the vendetta. Electra must call for the intervention of someone 'who can repay death with another death'.

This, then, is our first Electra. Inexpert, unsure of herself and in need of other people's advice before she wishes for a death she had previously not thought of. She was almost ready to obey her mother; only later would she realise that she hated her. The women who live with her need to remind her of the bond that ties her to her lost father and her absent brother, in whose names she now starts to plan the vendetta. The confused young woman enters into the rationale of the blood feud.

She calls for an avenger, but in reality the avenger is already there. Concealing his identity, he watches and spies on her. He is her brother, Orestes. Electra has difficulty in recognising him, and discovers that he already intends to act: this is his plan and his destiny. Orestes not only wants to kill his father's murderers; he considers it his duty. The god Apollo demands it. 'At all times, he loudly spurs me on, and threatens me with wild threats that freeze my feverish heart,' Orestes declares, 'unless I press for vengeance on my father's slayers and repay them with the same coin' (*Choephoroe*, 269–74). Apollo pushes Orestes to feed the vendetta. He, the god of Delphi, reminds Agamemnon's son that victims of murder who are not avenged and are of the same blood remain present, or rather they are represented by untiringly malevolent forces, the Erinyes. These foul and monstrous creatures 'feed and grow out of the blood of the murdered father; they are dark mysterious darts that the dead fire from beneath the earth and vendettas called for by murdered blood relations' (284–7).

Thus Orestes, like Electra, was requested and obliged to take on the role of avenger. Unlike Hamlet, Aeschylus' Orestes does not hesitate. Too many motives converge on the decision to act: the god's command, the father's suffering, and the misery to which his life would be reduced if he did not react against the intolerable oppression that his mother and her suitor have inflicted on him. If he were not to take on the task that falls to him, 'his father's hidden anger' would pursue him and turn him into a pariah, someone denied the company of his peers. The vendetta is the only means whereby Orestes can avoid dependency and persecution – the only act that will allow him to exist.

Orestes and Electra quickly agree on the deception required in order to enter the home of Clytemnestra and Aegisthus: Orestes will pretend to be a foreigner bearing a message. The message will be ironically pertinent: the false news of Orestes' own death. The neglected son is to experience the ultimate humiliation; he will witness his mother's joy on hearing of his death. Once the plan has been finalised, Electra enters the palace to oversee the sequence of events, and will never come back on stage. Orestes remains outside, plays the part of the foreigner, gets the doors to open and enters what was and will be his home. First Aegisthus and then Clytemnestra are slain. Murder and deceit are repaid with murder and deceit. Aegisthus is killed at exactly the same spot where he cut Agamemnon's throat, and in the same way. Although the debt has been paid with Aegisthus' death (he has killed and has been killed), blood still has to be spilt between Orestes and his mother. On the point of being struck down, Clytemnestra threatens Orestes with her furies, the Erinyes, who will attack him viciously. Orestes replies that his father's Erinyes are already pressing him. But no sooner have the paternal phantoms been placated than his mother's monsters appear and tear into him. The blood spilt on the other line of descent shouts out in turn against the avenging killer.

What is Electra's role in all these events? Electra, it has already been said, is presented as a confused and uncertain figure, who has to be reminded of the gravity of what has occurred in her own home. As Orestes' female *alter ego*, Electra behaves like Telemachus in his father's house, once it has been invaded by Penelope's suitors. She knows she has suffered an act of violence, but remains in a weak and cautious position. She awaits Orestes, just as the young Telemachus awaits Ulysses. She needs a push before starting to think seriously about the means of redress. When Orestes appears on the scene, she does, it is true, give him assistance, but only in a secondary manner: she is sent home to check that all is proceeding as expected. Electra is a witness to the injustice that reigns in Agamemnon's house, occupied as it is by his wife's lover, and, following the advice of the Choephoroe, she nurtures her thirst for revenge.

What happens instead in Sophocles' version? Why does this fragile girl find herself in the position of the protagonist, *prima donna* in the text which bears her name? First of all, the Sophoclean Electra imposes herself on the play from the very beginning, by taking control of her own sentiments and intentions. Electra waits for Orestes before carrying out the vendetta, but she always has a clear, unambiguous and intense desire for what she intends to achieve. From the moment she appears on the stage, the Sophoclean Electra is all hatred, sobbing and lamentations. The chorus, which in Aeschylus beseeched her not to forget her father, here suggests that the time has come for a little distance and a respite from tears and grief. She rejects it, asserting that she will never pause or abandon this lament. She has been entirely taken over by this one obsession, consisting of rancour, distress and crying out for revenge. This absorbs her days and her nights, and leaves no time for anything else (Sophocles, *Electra*, 121). But the chorus insists: incessant lamentation does not placate or dissolve the pain of one's misfortunes; it only leads to the repetition and the permanence of the wrong. What is the point of clinging to this suffering? Why cultivate this 'hyperalgesia', which is so excessive when compared with other members of the household? Why not accept the influence of time, and place oneself at an equal distance between forgetfulness and bitterness (177)? These are wise words of reconciliation but they have nothing to do with tragedy. If time were to heal and lead to prudent use of one's days, there would be no drama. Electra replies that time is for her a waste of life, dissipation and decay (187). This is an abandonment to the business of death, whose duration she wishes to be without limit. Electra will not renounce the comfort of her tears (286) and her resentment. The character is therefore presented within this dimension of total and absolute devotion to her dead father. Sick with memories, she is all regrets, recriminations and rapturous suffering. This obstinacy leads Orestes' sister to take action: she is his active partner, and, when she believes him to be dead, she thinks of taking the initiative herself. Should Chrysothemis, her cautious sister, refuse to get involved, she will carry the deed out on her own (1019).

Secondly, Sophocles' Electra broadens as a character and is enriched with aspects that in Aeschylus were distributed dramatically over other figures, such as the Erinyes and Athena. Sophocles' Electra brings together these disparate features and introduces a profound contradiction within the initial appearance of Electra as a monolith of hatred and grief. In the *Oresteia*, Athena and the Erinyes are antagonists: the political monopoly of violence on the one hand, and the free market of vendetta on the other. Athena rejects the free circulation of death within the sphere of alliances and consanguinity. She rationalises justice, and includes the Erinyes within the city's space. Now Sophocles' Electra inherits this antithesis from one text to another.

Electra gives a speech that Athena would probably approve of. When her mother acts as the champion of the logic of the vendetta and justifies the murder of her husband on the grounds that he had sacrificed their daughter, Electra gives her a lesson in law in the manner of Kant. If everyone thought like that, she says, then you should also become a victim, since you killed Agamemnon. Orestes and I should in turn murder you (589). By asking her mother to identify the law by which she can defend the legitimacy of the vendetta, Electra has put her finger on the inherent defect within the mechanism of reciprocal violence: the way it fatally rebounds on those who perpetuate it. Electra warns her mother that the perpetrator of a murder is automatically destined to become a victim (955). But does this lucidity over the way in which violence works mean that Electra will renounce her own desire for vengeance? No, and the tragedy consists in exactly this. Electra has a little of Athena about her, but she has a great deal of the Erinyes.

'Oh Erinyes, venerable daughters of the gods, who look after those who die unjustly and those whose marriages are stolen, come and assist me, avenge my father's death and send me my brother' (112–17). From the beginning, Electra invokes them in support of her desire for vengeance. She asks them to send Orestes, whom she saved from death, as though the Erinyes were prolonging her work and defending what she holds most dear. But, above all, she imitates them. By living in her mother's house and remaining attached, as an omnipresent slave, to this usurped space that should belong to her father, Electra prevents Clytemnestra from enjoying her new situation. Electra's unending lamentations keep the wound open. The wound is shifted to the body of the murderous mother. If Clytemnestra has spilt Agamemnon's blood, then Electra will suck hers. When Clytemnestra believes that Orestes is dead, she does in fact experience a great sense of relief: 'Today I will be freed of this scourge that lives in my house and continuously drinks the pure blood of my life' (783–6). Drinking blood is precisely the way in which the Erinyes usually make their presence felt (Aeschylus, *Coephoroe*, 146). Electra is like a tick, a parasite on her mother's body. Permanently. And with this obsession with the 'always' that becomes her way of life. Electra persecutes her mother just as the Erinyes would, as they are a demonstration of the incurable perpetuity of memory, in contrast with the will to purify and bring an end to hate. Neither the Erinyes nor Electra accept the idea of symbolic compensation.

Sophocles' Electra is explored more deeply as a female character. In the *Coephoroe*, Electra is treated as an auxiliary female kin, and simply sent home. With Sophocles, the sexual aspect of her femininity, her virginity, is brought to the fore and becomes her destiny (Sophocles, *Electra*, 960). It is a destiny imposed by Aegisthus, who does not allow Chrysothemis and Electra to marry, as they might produce an avenging son. This threat is not absurd. Let us remember that a man's daughters are always the potential mothers of his male grand-children, his proper heirs. As long as Orestes is away and perhaps dead, Electra finds herself in the position of the *ĕpíklērŏs* woman, whose marriage would bring a direct issue to her defunct father. Aegisthus, the opposite of a tutor, condemns her to remain a virgin and, moreover, intends to murder her. The only maternity to which Electra has access is a metaphoric one: she gives birth to conflicts (218–20) and generates curses (235). This is the point that Euripides uses to transform the story once again.

In Euripides' *Electra*, the scene opens in front of the house where Electra lives with her husband. The dangerous virgin has got married. Does Aegisthus still fear her? He does indeed, and more than before. This is why he has forced her to marry. But that marriage will perform the same function as her forced virginity: it will forestall the birth of a proper heir to Agamemnon. Aegisthus has chosen a man who can neutralise her power to generate an avenger. He has given her away in marriage to a peasant: a socially weak husband, who does not belong to the circle of those who have a right to revive the vendetta, a father of sons who will be socially inept and will never dare to rise up against him. The potential of the *ĕpíklērŏs* has been undermined not with chastity, but with a strategic coupling. But Electra is no fool.

In order to thwart Aegisthus' plan, here Electra uses virginity as a vendetta. She has been given away to a peasant, so that he could make her give birth to incompetent sons in the place of those she could have had by marrying a noble or, perhaps, in secret. Well then, Electra pretends to put up with the marriage meekly, but uses chastity to foil Aegisthus' plan. She refuses to conceive and to give birth to the peasant's sons, and remains therefore still capable of giving birth to sons who will take revenge. As for the husband, he ennobles himself by abstaining from sexual intercourse with a wife of whom he is not worthy (Euripides, *Electra*, 382). It is true that Electra does not produce an avenger and her husband does not take any initiative: they wait for Orestes. However, in this waiting game, her continuing virginity acts as an astute way of sabotaging Aegisthus' plan. It is also a way of remaining loyal to her father's memory: daughter and sister.

In Sophocles' plot, which is very similar to Aeschylus' narrative, Aegisthus uses Electra's virginity to avoid the vendetta; in Euripides' version, we encounter a variant that weaves together various elements to create a more intricate story and shrewder characters. Euripides' Aegisthus probably thinks he has behaved cunningly by using, not the woman's virginity, but its opposite – a fertile marriage – to achieve the same result. But it is Electra who now comes up with the idea of using her own sexual integrity to impede Aegisthus's intentions, and it is as though Euripides were criticising the logic of the myth: if Aegisthus wishes to prevent a vendetta, then he must impose on her an unworthy marriage, which removes forever the possibility of her being an effective mother. Virginity, Euripides claims with his version of the play, would make the young woman more dangerous, because it leaves the way open to a possible heroic line of descent. All she needs is the wrong marriage. We can imagine the pleasure of a cultured Athenian spectator and regular visitor to the theatre in discovering the inspired variants of these three playwrights.

Both Sophocles and Euripides, we said, elaborate on the femininity of Electra. But it is Euripides who makes her most aware of her resources as a woman. The non-marriage changes its value and its meaning is inverted, while the characters acquire a degree of cunning and dissembling which profoundly changes them. Electra is more mendacious than when she was simply her brother's accomplice. In order to make the fiction of her unconsummated marriage more convincing, she pretends to be pregnant and on the point of giving birth. The trick is to be used to entice her mother to come, so that she can be killed. Clytemnestra falls into the trap. We have said that Euripides' Clytemnestra is primarily a sensual woman, whose erotic pride has been offended. She has therefore avenged her husband's infidelity rather than the murder of her daughter Iphigenia. Her maternity appears atrophied and distorted to the point where she wants her daughter Electra to give birth solely in order to protect herself and her lover from a future vendetta. And it is this wish that is to prove fatal for her. In a typically Euripidean reversal, Clytemnestra's unmaternal nature blinds her to her daughter's deception – the daughter who pretends to be a mother and prepares to commit matricide.

Sophocles re-establishes Electra's integrity and her mother's dignity.

MEDEA: A MOTHER'S PASSION FOR HER HUSBAND

Medea invites us to wonder how far a husband's passion should go and to what degree love for the conjugal bed should allow a wife to obliterate the mother she also is. The question of sensual love in marriage is almost more interesting from a woman's point of view than when it is presented as a male dilemma, as in Tolstoy or Moravia. Of course, the drama is always in the jealousy – too much in *The Kreutzer Sonata* and too little in *Una passione coniugale*. In the case of Medea – a woman who loves passionately – we see that the conflicts caused by a rival rebound upon her children. The children become the thing that has to be destroyed. They have to pay for the affront, which is not so much against their mother as against their father's wife. Why? Who is Medea when she kills her children? Is she Jason's wife or the mother of her little ones? Who does she want to eliminate when she cuts their throats? Her children and herself, or her husband's children, and thus the husband himself, or even the couple they had once formed, with the children who were produced from it? The two plots of *Medea*, one by Euripides and one by Seneca, provide a dramatic reflection on procreation and alliance, while also revealing the tension between maternity and sensuality.

In order to make sense of Medea's actions, we need first to insert her story into the framework of Greek marriage as a community (*koīnōnía*). In the myth, Medea gave up everything. As we saw in the first chapter, she tore herself away from the family, betrayed her father, and cut her brother to pieces in order to leave a trail of his flesh for those who followed her. Her marriage to Jason, the

handsome foreigner who came in search of the Golden Fleece, was not celebrated as a contract to create friendships and solidarity, but was the scandalous
choice of a woman in love (Euripides, *Medea*, 8). Her marriage was an act of
rebellion that divided two cities and two families. Having treated her own
blood relations with cruelty, she viciously turned on her husband's family: she
planned the death and dismemberment of Pelias, Jason's uncle, whom Jason
wanted to eliminate. To please her husband, she did not hesitate to commit one
crime after another. Now tied to a man whom she has followed to a foreign
land, she finds herself so intimately attached to him that this fusion becomes
all-consuming (13 and 228). Her children came into this world to represent an
essential part of that whole.

Marriage is a social connection, but also a sexual bond: this is why the
importance Medea attaches to the children remains compatible with the erotic
nature of her love. It is only when the complicity of the marital bed falls apart
that the unfortunates become victims. It is at the moment when no more
pleasure is to be had in that bed, because Jason has deserted her in order to
contract a new marriage with the daughter of the King of Corinth, that Medea
decides to attack her own children. Suddenly there is no common space for
husband and wife – Jason leaves home to settle in the home of his father-in-
law – and therefore there will be no more shared ownership between them.
The things they have left to share are grief and misfortune (1361).

As has already been suggested, the idea that children are part of what is
always undivided in the marriage and that which constitutes a married couple
into a community and association (*koinōnía*) is explicitly argued in theoretical
texts on marriage, from Xenophon to Demosthenes to Plutarch. Children
belong to both the parents and favour concord between them (Demosthenes,
Against Boeotus, 1, 23; 11, 29). They are the ones that turn a married couple into
a genuine society (Xenophon, *Oeconomicus*, 7, 30). The indivisibility of everything as a model for marriage in general is put forward by Plutarch in *Conjugal
Precepts*. It is against this cultural background that we can understand why
Medea kills those who were born to her and Jason: they embody the destroyed
conjugality. Let nothing survive of that absolute *koinōnía* which was her
marriage: nothing, except the sorrow and tragedy of its loss; nothing, except
undivided agony.

This interpretation of the reasons why Medea murders her innocent children instead of committing suicide, for instance, or simply stabbing Jason, bases
itself on the value the Greeks put on 'community'. A tragedy, we said, offers a
highly operatic glimpse at the underpinnings of those theories of kinship
which have been accepted and put into practice. But it does so, we also said,
by unmasking the back-stage, so to speak. A tragedy plays out an anthropological meditation on the pathology of kinship rather than on kinship itself: it

shows either the chaotic past of current norms or their potential transgression. The simple logic of marital community is therefore too simple to account for the construction of this plot and these characters. Through its discontinuous storyline and Medea's contradictory agency, the play exposes the indeterminacy of cultural choices about marriage and parenthood. Habits and rights that seem obvious now could be highly uncertain, elsewhere and sometime ago. This is why bodies suffer and emotions erupt.

This perspective generates two other compatible and no less pertinent readings, which capture the tragic questioning of the anthropological context, not merely its relevance. On the one hand, Medea wishes to strike herself by striking the children of her own seed (Medea 816), but, on the other, she wishes to mutilate Jason by amputating him of his sons (817). To whom, then, do the sons butchered by Medea belong? Whose children are they? Are they hers, her husband's, or do they belong to both of them? All three options are true at different moments of the action. This multiplicity of competing viewpoints on the cultural norms of having children, and their final clash, is what creates the texture of the tragedy.

At the beginning of the play, Medea talks of them as though they were hers (112). She asks of Creon − the King of Corinth, who has become her ex-husband's father-in-law and has ordered her to leave the city − for a day of respite, in order to take care of her dearest children (342). The mother has been banished along with them, and is still wondering whether she should take them with her. She now intends to make use of the extra day to exterminate the other family, which has just been formed: her former husband, who has just married for the second time, his blissful young bride, Eurydice, and her ageing father Creon (288; 375). She and her offspring rise up against all of them − all to be murdered together. Medea and her children are the only *phíloï* and have remained as such in the face of the new alliance created by the traitor Jason, who is no longer one of his own people (467; 470). Jason is not a *phílŏs* any longer, but has become an enemy amongst other enemies (374). Between the two households, it is a complete break.

Suddenly, however, Jason upsets the plan. Incautiously attempting to soothe Medea's anger, he starts to claim that there is still friendship and *phílía* between him and his ex-wife and children (459). In this less trivial version, we still recognise the pathetic compromise of 'let's stay friends' after an irreparable split. Jason carelessly aggravates the situation by explaining to Medea that, in reality, the second marriage is nothing more than an extension of the first. If she thinks about it, he continues to blunder, he has only remarried in order to create useful and prestigious brothers for Medea's sons (563). Ever more clumsily, Jason appropriates these boys by treating their mother as their material cause, to use the language of Aristotle, or their uterine host, as Aeschylus'

Apollo claims. In other words, he posits them on a continuum that relates to him and, in so doing, he creates a distortion of the principle of bilateral descent: he actually excludes his former wife from their ancestry. His children born to Medea, he argues, are no more than the first in a series that other descendants, born to another woman, will finalise. With offensive thoughtlessness, Jason thinks of his *génōs* as a single line. He intends to put all *his* sons on the same plane, and wishes to consolidate *his* line of descent (564). He is concerned with *his* dynasty (562).

All these possessives, which he uses solely to refer to himself, cut the mother off from the generation and evidently produce a catastrophic effect on the person he is speaking to. Moreover, the whole argument presupposes an unflattering comparison between a first wife of barbarous origin, without any prestige in Corinth, and a second wife who is well born and daughter of the local king. Wholly concerned with his sons and their vulnerable status in a foreign city, Jason humiliates Medea by treating her as though she were a person of little standing, whose non-Greek birth could harm his unfortunate sons. On top of his refusal to acknowledge her contribution to the line of descent, he insults Medea by adding that she is an unworthy mother for a Greek's sons. This double gaffe is to be understood in its cultural significance, but at the same time − and this is the beauty of the tragedy − in its emotional impact on the character of Medea. Because she gets the point of Jason's contempt, she gets furiously angry. Because the man's intent is so blatantly significant in terms of social habits and rights, she now feels the most burning, unforgiving, passion. She has been undeservedly offended; she is hurting; she will take revenge. But the plan has now changed.

Jason chooses the most unsuitable rhetoric to placate Medea, who responds, on the one hand, by claiming to have royal and even divine ancestors, albeit not Hellenic ones, and, on the other, by insisting upon the irrevocable separation and undying hostility between her and his new family. The proud granddaughter of the Sun defends herself, but Jason's words have transformed her perception of her own children. Medea ends up cursing and decreeing the massacre of Jason's entire household (608). And, sadly, the young boys are now part of this household without knowing it. Following Jason's imprudent appropriation of the children, Medea changes her mind and modifies her strategy. She will not destroy Creon's family (Creon himself, his daughter Eurydice and his new son-in-law), as initially planned, but Jason's one (608), that *génōs*, that *oîkŏs* which the fool has said he wants to reassemble in his own fashion, by bringing together the children of two women.

Medea reacts to the insult with a calculating fury. Suddenly, she pretends to have resigned herself to her former husband's intentions. She starts to conceal her loathing. She appears to display understanding for, and even complicity with, this brilliant marriage, which will bring so many benefits to her little ones (884–8). She affects to approve enthusiastically of Jason's tactics (869), and even suggests that she should entrust him with the children, his children, so that they can settle in well in their father's new home (943). With treacherous docility, she asks if they could be received immediately into the young bride's apartments, so that Medea can ingratiate herself with her and pay her homage with some wonderful little presents, as a pledge of future friendship (969). Naively Jason is delighted and congratulates her on her submission to common sense. He foolishly has no suspicion of Medea's desire to use the innocent creatures as a weapon: she sends them, loaded with deadly and insidious gifts, to a place where she has no intention of letting them stay – a place she considers to be the cursed home of Jason and his new wife, who has become her 'mistress' (970). The gifts she sends to decorate the young woman's body and make it even more attractive will release a terrible contagious fire, which will consume Eurydice, disfigure her and inflict excruciating pain on her. As for the children, Jason's children, Medea will cut their throats once they have served their purpose.

Medea develops her plan with the aim of striking the target that improvident and witless Jason has pointed out to her: that patrilineal *génos*, of which he wishes to be the sole reference point. Being attached to this man in her anger as she was in her love, she wishes to attack, wound and annihilate him in his most sensitive spot, which he himself has revealed. That spot, clearly, is his children. But Medea's reversal would be too simple still, if she went from nurturing the boys, because they are her own issue, to taking their lives in anger, when they become Jason's property. Less thoughtless than Jason, Medea knows that there are always two parents; that, although paternity prevails socially, motherhood can never be erased. In the context of Athenian culture and law, let us remember, the father's words are not sufficient to undo the indissoluble maternal bond. That bond is indeed there – and she loves them still. Those children are also Medea's – indeed the things she holds most dear, hence she would never abandon them to the paternal home – she is also striking a blow against herself (816–18).

As Aristotle explicitly acknowledges, *Medea* is a tragedy about *philía*, because it involves a mother killing her own children, who are bound to her by love and proximity and are the only beings she can love now that Jason has become her adversary. Euripides' tragic version of the story of Medea and Jason has a very simple and short plot when compared with the convoluted, long story mentioned at the beginning of this book. Essentially, all that happens on stage is the conception of two different plans for a vendetta. The change of plan has to be considered the dramatic climax, when the narration takes a new direction: up to that moment we are expecting an aggression against outsiders and hated enemies – the other woman, the other home and the estranged husband. After that moment, we are directed towards the massacre of *phíloǐ*, and therefore to a tragic ending in the purest Aristotelian sense. This is why the element that Euripides enlarges upon is precisely the theme of whom the unlucky children belong to. In other words, Medea plots to kill others, all her rivals, for as long as she considers her children to be her own. As soon as Jason includes the little ones in his own extended family, Medea reacts by endorsing that inclusion, thus adding them to the outsiders she intends to kill: if they are not hers, then they shall meet the same fate as all the others. But Jason himself will have to survive in order to suffer the horror of that loss. By killing Jason's sons, Medea also kills her own seed and her most loved ones. Herein lies the tragedy.

More explicitly than other plays, *Medea* is a tragedy of sex and sensuality. Sex, we said, calls into play sexual difference, sexual relations, and their social formalisations: habits and rights. Here, in the competing arguments about marriage and descent, everything that has been discussed so far has been sexual in this sense. But then there are bodies and emotions. There is the everlasting *eros* that has inspired an entire life; there is the sensual attachment to the marital couch. There is love in the immense anger of the betrayed woman, whose husband has deserted their bed and who has been rejected for a girl. Eurydice is a rich princess. She will be a better deal for Jason and his offspring. But she is a body: a body which is to take pleasure with Medea's man in a new bed, a body which will burn away, instead, in the most atrocious pain.

If we fail to read Medea in her double dimension, that of sex and sensuality, we are in danger of committing Jason's mistake. It is precisely in his misunderstanding of this feminine *eros*, which manifests itself in so many different emotions, from prostration to pride, boldness and rage, that Jason reveals the coarseness of his feelings as well as his cultural insensitivity. Both of these will cost him dear. Let us look for a moment at this short-sightedness. Medea openly diagnoses the origin of her resentment: she asserts that a woman usually displays alarm just on seeing a weapon, but when she suffers an injustice which concerns the marital bed, there is no one as bloodthirsty as she is (263). Jason knows that this woman is suffering because she has had her man's bed taken from her (286). He has therefore been warned: the source of the pain is, as it were, localised to where the bodies touched and aroused each other, in the embrace of a long matrimonial intimacy. However, for Medea, this place of pleasure, physical contact, eroticism and procreation does not belong to a private and carnal world, separate from the one in which she lives. The marital bed – this highly material thing – is also a theatre of justice and honour: to deprive her of it is a wrong, an offence and a public humiliation. In other words, the destruction of that bed is a social act that has to be judged on the basis of moral criteria. This occurs in the dialogue between the woman and

King Aegeus of Athens, who immediately acknowledges her justifications and offers her assistance.

Now the connection between sex and justice – the famed *díkē* of the marital bed, which was also violated and discussed in the *Oresteia* – is precisely the thing that myopic Jason is incapable of understanding. He talks as though marriage were an entirely social affair: to settle down in Corinth, enlarge the family and consolidate the status of his sons. For him, *eros* is not part of being married. 'If you weren't so blinded by your obsession with our bed,' he essentially says to her, 'then you would understand that I am marrying someone else for your own good, just as it is for the good of the children' (568). He treats Medea as if her love for him were nothing more than an emotional whim, irrelevant to the social rationale of procreation and alliance. In this manner he fails to acknowledge all that she has done in the name of love to assist him in his various enterprises. He dismisses all that ardour as, simply, the effect of Aphrodite's influence (524) – a passive and passionate condition which does her no credit. Even worse, Jason starts to regret that paternity cannot occur independently of women and their obsession with the bedroom (569–75). If only procreation did not require sex! If only having children could be completely separated from women and their desire!

Jason talks as though sex and reproduction were two distinct things and should be such in nature, whereas they are one and the same for Medea (and for the Greeks). She perceives *eros* as something that motivates everything she has done in her life, from her flight into exile to the crimes she has committed for her husband and the children she has produced with him. The reckless husband's attack on her way of thinking, as though it were irritating and womanly, means denying her entire existence, which she has put at his service, and belittling the love on which their very marriage was based. The antagonism is so clear-cut and the refusal of one to acknowledge the other so obstinate that there is no common ground for reconciliation. If this is the case, if her love was meaningless and if her children do not embody something they share, but belong solely to the father (given that they should have been produced by him alone), then she can take no more.

Medea is a monster. There is a calculating relentlessness in her slaughter of the children, which ultimately goes beyond tragedy. Violence among dear ones constitutes the source of tragic *páthŏs*, according to Aristotle's *Poetics*. But voluntary crimes against family members cannot inspire pity and compassion, according to Aristotle's *Rhetoric*. In his judgement, then, these deliberate acts are not tragic, but simply horrifying. And Medea, with her two strategies, both of them elaborately thought through, is a champion of careful deliberation. The chorus, which we might interpret as an expression of a culturally plausible opinion, criticises Medea for wanting to kill her children because of sex (999), which brings so much suffering to women and so many wrongs to mortals (1291). The horror of Medea's infanticide follows the script of anger. Undeservedly offended, she decides to retaliate. There is no tragic – unintentional that is – error on her part. Jason, in contrast, commits a supreme injustice by refusing to acknowledge, even for a moment, the just demands of their relationship. He seems to be absent-minded, heedless and incapable of taking the measure of his own actions, their effects, their consequences. In this blindness, it is he who makes the tragic error.

JOCASTA: THE TIME OF INCEST

Oedipus' tragedy is not one of destiny. It is not a tragedy of knowledge, and still less a tragedy of sovereignty. Much has been written to play down the core both of the myth and the plot of Sophocles' play: the story of a man who, having killed his father, becomes his mother's husband is a sexual tragedy. Kinship is sexual, let it be stressed again, as it is the product of a relationship between two sexes. Sex is everywhere in the tragedy, precisely because the play deals with that 'pathology of kinship' of which we have spoken particularly in relation to the *Oresteia* and *Medea*. But *Oedipus King* is, more than anything else, a sexual tragedy.

The ban on incest, an unwritten law, prohibits marriage and sex between kin. More precisely, it prohibits that the sexual origin of consanguineous bonds be replicated in a new relationship, a contact between bodies. It is an attempt to protect the proximities generated by sex from a repetition of that union from which they derive. Every society delineates a boundary of varying comprehensiveness within which sexual contact between blood relations is considered unacceptable, 'incestuous' that is. The limits are therefore relative, but the idea, until proven otherwise, is universal. Incest, we could say, consists in the physical proximity of persons who are already genealogically in touch. Sophocles' play tells the story of marital contact between a mother and a son, who are unaware of their relationship.

Anthropology and psychoanalysis place incestuous transgression at the centre of their reflections. In every child of whatever society there is an erotic desire in relation to one of the parents, accompanied by an aggressive drive against the other. These are the infantile sexual theories that, according to Freud, manifest themselves with youthful vividness in the Sophoclean myth. The play impresses us because all spectators experience the reawakening of a thought that has become subconscious, a hope that had once been theirs, deep in the past and during the very first years of life, before the parents themselves imposed the prohibition. Myths and rituals which authorise unions between parents and children also express this dream – exceptions which confirm the rule of prohibition that is necessary to the healthy development of exogamous genital sexuality.

Claude Lévi-Strauss has replaced the universality of infantile desire with an ambitious anthropological theory based on a social imperative. Indeed, it is the quintessential social imperative, one that is indispensable to the existence of society. In order for a society (a *koïnōnía*, as the Greeks would have called it) to be formed, new bonds of solidarity have to be made artificially with others, outside consanguineous connections. These links have to be cultural and not natural. What is required in order to create these alliances? The exchange and circulation of goods: a movement of objects that optimises complementarity, creates the obligation to reciprocate and encourages the establishment of alliances. The exogamous marriage between men and women who belong to distinct family groups (the limits of otherness varying from one society to another) constitutes the fundamental strategy for bringing these bonds into existence. We have seen that a particular interpretation of this contrast between consanguinity and alliance was profoundly Greek. Kin, especially siblings, are always on the brink of competing for power or property, whereas relations by marriage, especially brothers-in-law, tend to get along. In philosophical theories which admit a natural origin of sociability, for instance for Aristotle, society is not the extension of a consanguineous group, but the result of the sexual union of a woman and a man.

More recently, the reflections of another French anthropologist, Françoise Héritier, have literally redefined the very notion of incest (1997). To understand the phenomenon, you have to go beyond marriage and sexual union to the idea of proximity, both in the sexual and in the genealogical sense. Consanguinity is a more or less immediate closeness between relations (*agchisteía* for the Greeks). Sexual intercourse is also a kind of closeness, one between bodies. Both these forms of proximity create further connections to subsequent relations with different partners. Sharing the same lover – or finding oneself under the same blanket, to use Sophocles' suggestive metaphor – means coming into contact. These different degrees of propinquity must not be superimposed. If this occurs, the delicate balance of kinship, society and nature is upset. Thus 'incest', for Françoise Héritier, refers to a general phenomenon, which is not limited to making love with a parent. It concerns the physical contact between persons who are already in contact with each other. Hence incest refers to sexual intercourse between relatives (because they are genealogically linked), but it also includes the indirect intimacy which is formed between simultaneous or successive lovers of the same person. Because one of the bodies involved in these acts is the same, it puts in touch potentially, so to speak, the bodies of all his/her partners. Should these actually 'get in touch' with each other, their sexual contact would replicate a previous one.

Françoise Héritier's theory is not incompatible with that of Claude Lévi-Strauss, nor does it deny the Freudian primacy of desire. Rather, it broadens the concept beyond marriage, which was central for Lévi-Strauss, and beyond direct contact between two sexual partners, which was the essential point for Freud. As far as social anthropology is concerned, this notion of proximity introduces the pertinence of the body and the symbolic value of contamination to the heart of the theory. As far as psychoanalysis is concerned, the emphasis on incestuous and therefore metaphoric contagion, which involves those who come into contact with the same body, does not correspond to the definition of the Oedipus complex, but does confirm another Freudian theory: the one that jealousy often entails a homosexual component, which intensifies its bitter taste and torment, and turns it into a persecutor. Rivalry can become intensely and insanely erotic, just as paranoia carries with it a nucleus of unavowable and therefore suppressed desire, which is transformed into hate and projected onto another. Jealousy is a painful sexual attachment.

The Greek story of Oedipus is, of course, an obligatory reference point for the more forceful theories on incest. We are not talking about Freud, who went so far as to perceive Sophocles's text as the literary prefiguration of what psychoanalysis would eventually say about infantile sexuality, partly because Freud was so struck by it that he never thought he should provide an interpretation. He was so stunned by the transparency, the immediacy and the frankness of the myth and its narration of parricide and incest that we never find him applying psychoanalysis to *Oedipus King*. For Freud, it was enough simply to read the text or watch a performance in order to experience the impact of the story on one's own repressed desire. Lévi-Strauss and Héritier, on the other hand, put forward two very different exegeses, both of them interesting and correct, especially in their grasp of the mythical and tragic content. At the risk of becoming tiresome, it should be stressed once again (given that there has been a rash of desexualised allegoric interpretations, however strange this might seem) that we are dealing here with violence between *phíloï*, with a dramatic reflection on kinship and alliance, thus sex.

Oedipus is the son of the King of Thebes, Laius, who had been advised by an oracle not to have children because a son would kill him. Laius makes his wife Jocasta pregnant by accident (in a state of drunkenness) and she produces a beautiful boy. The dangerous new-born baby is, of course, entrusted to a shepherd with orders that he should be abandoned on Mount Cithaeron. The plan goes wrong for the infanticidal parents: the shepherd becomes fond of the child and, instead of eliminating him, he hands him over to another servant, who visits the same pastureland in the employ of the King of Corinth. He takes the child and brings it to the king and queen, Polybus and Merope, who want a child but have been unable to produce one themselves. Oedipus therefore grows up in his adoptive home with no knowledge of his own story. When he was an adolescent, someone insulted him by insinuating that he was not the son of Merope and Polybus. Intrigued, he asks for explanations from those he believes to be his biological parents, and receives evasive answers in return. He now becomes troubled and decides to consult the oracle of Delphi. When he presents Pythia with a factual question, 'who are my parents and who therefore am I?', the prophetess does not reply, but only utters a disturbing warning. He must be careful, because he will kill his father and, she adds, will marry his mother. Oedipus is devastated. Suddenly the unsettled boy appears to forget the doubt surrounding the identity of his parents – the question which had brought him to Delphi. Acting as though he were now certain that the father and mother of whom the oracle speaks were Merope and Polybus, he decides never to return to Corinth, in order to avoid his appointed victims.

He goes down from Delphi along the path that leads, in the plain, to where three roads meet, and, instead of the road for Corinth, he takes the road for Thebes. At precisely that moment, Laius appears on his way to Delphi. He too wants to consult Apollo's priestess. The two meet and the oracle's prediction starts to fulfil itself. There is an argument over the right of precedence, and, while the old man is aggressive, the young man is easily offended. Oedipus strikes a mortal blow against a man he considers an arrogant stranger. On reaching Thebes, Oedipus discovers that the city is in a state of desperation. The monstrous Sphinx is torturing the inhabitants with an enigma no one can resolve, and devours those who challenge her and fail. Oedipus undertakes the challenge and gives the right answer: the being that has four, two and three legs is man, who crawls as a baby, walks on two legs as an adult, and leans on a stick in old age. To crown his achievement, they offer him the opportunity to marry the Queen of Thebes. Although astute enough to interpret the Sphinx's enigma, Oedipus is not sharp enough to associate the events of which he has just been the protagonist – his killing of an old man on the road for Thebes and his marriage to an older woman, who has just been widowed – with the words pronounced by the Pythia. He knows what a human being is, but he does not know himself. Forgetting his youthful doubts, he now insists on believing that his parents live in Corinth, sheltered from his dangerous proximity.

This is the story. The plot of Sophocles' play starts from the moment in which a deadly and mysterious plague strikes the city in which Oedipus has now reigned for years, in harmony with his wife, by whom he has had four children. The queen's brother, Creon, Oedipus' uncle and brother-in-law, goes on a pilgrimage to Delphi to ask the oracle what has to be done. The plague results from the presence of Laius' murderer amongst the Thebans: this is the diagnosis. He needs to be discovered and expelled from the city. Outraged by this revelation, Oedipus undertakes to discover the killer and swears to throw him out of the city.

As Freud correctly pointed out, Oedipus' clumsy attempts to hunt himself down and his resistance, in complete good faith, to evidence resemble psychoanalysis. On stage, the conflictual process of the enquiry ends with Oedipus blinding himself, so that he can no longer see anything, as nothing can now bring him pleasure. Jocasta, his mother and wife, who appears to have had no suspicion when she encountered this young man who so resembled her dead husband, hangs herself. In relation to the myth, Sophocles has chosen to dwell upon Oedipus' struggle against himself and eventual discovery of himself, upon the terrible ignorance of what should be so obvious and upon the tension between the human blindness and the enigmatic, ambiguous and misleading knowledge of the oracle. Neither Apollo nor his prophet Teiresias do anything to help Oedipus to understand. Instead of giving replies, they add further enigmas to the Sphynx's enigma.

Sophocles' play is therefore very selective in relation to the myth. This has favoured interpretations which play down the sexual nature of the affair and the scandal of incest. Lévi-Strauss, however, links the tragedy to the narrative material on which it is founded, and sees Oedipus' story as a transformation similar to the one we have discovered in the *Oresteia*. The events concerning Orestes, we said, start with the clash between two unilineal theories of descent, one supported by the Erinyes and the other by Apollo, and culminate in a fusion of the bilateral and the asymmetric. For Lévi-Strauss, *Oedipus King* tells the story of the conflict between one model of procreation, without parents – the Sphynx is a monster who was born out of the earth – and the opposing model, in which the parents are close relations. Procreation must find its place between these two extremes: no genealogical connection versus too much of it. Although far from intuitive, the structural analysis acknowledges the sexuality inherent in the tale, and indeed turns it into its essential argument.

As for Françoise Héritier, if we were to apply her expanded definition of incest to Oedipus, we would be led to detect incest within the incest. Oedipus appears to carry out the quintessential incestuous act by marrying, and making love to, his mother to the point of procreating children who are also his uterine brothers and sisters. If, however, we postulate that the truly problematic aspect of union between consanguineous relations consists in the sexual contamination of partners already related genealogically or sexually, we have to conclude that, by penetrating Jocasta's body, Oedipus meets up with Laius again – with Laius who had been there before him. Apart from the immediate sexual contact with his mother, he has entered into an indirect sexual relationship with his father. Does this sound far-fetched? Well, we can say that homosexuality is not absent from the myth, as Laius provided evidence of it in his youth, when he seduced the son of his guest, the King of Pisa. And, more to the point, Sophocles' text insists upon Oedipus' return to the furrow ploughed by his father. The fruitful intercourse of mother and son has produced genealogical chaos, where individuals occupy multiple positions in the web of relations. A son is also a half-brother; a daughter is a half-sister; a maternal uncle is also a brother-in-law. This confusion derives from that original superposition: the coming back of an adult body into a belly where he had lain as a growing foetus, and also where his own father had been.

On closer examination, it becomes clear that the plot of *Oedipus King* treats sex as an essential problem, even though the play unfolds as a tragedy of knowledge. Sex is there as much as Jocasta is there. In the timing of the action, the parricide makes itself felt through the mysterious plague, but the act itself belongs to the past. The incest, on the other hand, is still taking place. Oedipus lives with his mother, consummating his monstrous marriage before the spectators. While the protagonists busy themselves with unmasking the perpetrator of a murder that occurred years before, the other and more ignominious half of the prophecy is unfolding in real time. The dialogue between Oedipus and Jocasta presents the audience with a particularly tender relationship between a husband and a wife who are unaware that they are mother and son. This intercourse, in its blindness, is gripping. Laius and Oedipus met accidentally, got into a fight, then the young man killed his father in anger. There was no time for recognition. But Oedipus and Jocasta have been living together in the strictest intimacy for years: how could they fail to detect the signs of their kinship, the traces of their intertwined history?

What goes ostentatiously unnoticed by the characters would probably not have eluded even an audience with little education. Jocasta was better placed than anyone else to obtain the clues and open her eyes to the truth. How could a mother who had pierced the feet of the baby in order to expose him (Sophocles, *Oedipus King*, 1173–4) fail to associate that act of hers with the scars on her young husband's ankles, which she must have at least caught a glimpse of? It is those scars which cry out Oedipus' identity to the shepherd of Corinth (1032–6), who then speaks of them in the presence of Oedipus and Jocasta. Was this the first time she, the mother–wife, could see those scars? And what of the resemblance between Oedipus and his parents? Is there any? Well, Jocasta notices it. When describing Laius, she tells Oedipus that her first husband's shape (*mŏrphḗ*) was not unlike his own (743). Jocasta had seen Laius' features in Oedipus. She is aware.

Sophocles created an ambiguous Jocasta, who undoubtedly understands before anyone else and has perhaps always understood. From beginning to end, Jocasta does not help Oedipus. She opposes and impedes him. When her husband speaks for the first time of his terrible destiny, she minimises it and makes light of the fear of incest – making love to one's mother is simply an inconsequential dream (980–3). The fairly long exchange between the two characters, in which Oedipus' heroic search for the truth clashes with Jocasta's repeated and insistent pleading for him to remain in ignorance, reveals a wife who would do anything to keep her husband in the dark, as though she wants their situation to continue unaltered. There is a moment in which Jocasta clearly understands, and instead of expressing her surprise and outrage, she does all she can to keep this knowledge secret from Oedipus. Jocasta is willing to pretend that nothing has happened and to ignore the enormity of incest. It is Oedipus' obstinacy, together with the imminent arrival of the final revelation, that drives her to flee to her bedroom, where she hangs herself.

Let us focus on this turning-point. A messenger from Corinth comes to announce that King Polybus is dead: Oedipus can accede to the throne. Oedipus, however, fails to rejoice: he is reluctant to go back to Corinth, he claims, because he is afraid to end up married to his mother, as an oracle has threatened. Nonsense, replies the messenger, Merope was never his mother! He knows what he is saying, the messenger insists, because he is the servant who, in the past, delivered baby Oedipus to Merope and Polybus, after receiving him from the hands of a shepherd in the service of the King of Thebes, Laius. Because Oedipus has no memory of his infancy before Corinth, he can only grow more and more puzzled, but Jocasta's reaction to the Corinthian's tale is one of panic. And rightly so. She is the only one who can already draw the final conclusion. She has delivered her baby boy to a shepherd from her house, for him to be exposed on Mount Citheron. She knows that. If now this man from Corinth says that *that* baby is the same person as Oedipus, then her husband is her son.

Should Oedipus discover his history, *she* would be unmasked as the mother who maimed her child and condemned him to death, before taking him as her husband. Firstly infanticide, and then incest: what a mother! Jocasta has good reason to halt the enquiry. She implores Oedipus to let it go and to renounce his desire to know who he is (1060–72). But to no avail. Before the arrival of that Theban shepherd, to whom she had handed over the little child for elimination and who is capable of confirming this final detail that will make Oedipus' life history complete, she rushes from the scene to kill herself.

Jocasta's failure to recognise her son comes across as an error which is persistent to the point of self-deception or, perhaps, make-believe. It should be said in her favour that, in the version of the oracle's prophesy that was given to Laius (and then reported to her), there was only mention of the threat of parricide, and nothing about incest. Only Oedipus receives the complete revelation of the nightmare. Jocasta was therefore not expecting an incestuous marriage with her first husband's killer from the moment that she first heard the warning from Delphi. Moreover, she seemed absolutely certain that her child had been devoured by wild animals (856). But how could she not wonder about that young man with those tortured feet? How could she not reflect upon the striking resemblance between the stranger and Laius? And how could she defend the status quo at all costs?

This brief repertoire of tragic plots and characters proves – if proof were needed – that the theatre was a preferred space for theorising about sex – not normative discourse on the use of pleasure, but rather in a dramatic reflection on its desirous intensity. The theatrical space was not only full of all sorts of passions; it was also dominated by women and the complexity of their emotions. It is true that women occupy the stage primarily because tragedies deal with family stories. These stories reveal the uncertainty of norms and their transgression. But the manner in which the pathology of kinship is brought to light is related to the externalisation of what is inside women and would otherwise be invisible: thoughts, sensations, intentions and desires. The obsession with the marital bed – married life's centre of gravity and the source from which the family itself is generated, but also the place where women throw themselves down to die – provides an external projection of that inner space. The hidden polyphony of feminine sensuality contrasts with the simplicity of the male sexual urge, which is so showy and uncomplicated.

Dwelling on male desire would have meant hard core pornography, and this is what occurred in comedy, in which the phallus unashamedly triumphs, together with many other noisy and unseemly exhibitions of corporeal exuberance. On the other hand, it is never possible to examine the complications of female passion in sufficient depth, as its symptoms stubbornly retain their ambiguity. As has already been suggested, this too could be a form of pornography, if you consider that, for tragic women, all emotions, in their variety, are connected to *eros*. *Eros* is at work in full view of the audience and manifests itself in Jocasta's blindness, Deianeira's jealousy, Medea's anger, Electra's virginity, Clytemnestra's vendetta and Phaedra's shame. The bed, which is never put on view, is the real stage.

PART TWO

MOLLIS AMOR – UNMANLY LOVE

DIRA LIBIDO – 'INSANE LIBIDO'

'It is not the belly that is insatiable, as they would have it, but the false opinion concerning the belly's unbounded lust' (Epicurus, *Vatican Sayings*, 59). With this simple affirmation, the viewpoint that had dominated Greek philosophical reflections on desire was overturned. Epicurus put an end to the idea that appetites are unlimited and the pleasure of satisfaction therefore impossible. Quite the opposite, pleasure is what is most easily and copiously available to human beings, and it lies precisely in the satisfaction of their aspirations, as long as those aspirations are natural.

Lucretius' *On the Nature of Things* opens with pleasure, *voluptas*, which is Venus' effect upon mortals and gods alike. This is undoubtedly the best summary of Epicurean thought, a lesson offered to the wider public and more pleasing for its poetic style. The physics of atoms, the critique of religion and the relaxed attitude to death: these great themes of ancient materialism unfold within a magnificent framework, expressed in a language that is both elegant and raw. If it is true, as Cicero wrote, that Epicureanism was the most widespread philosophical tradition in Roman Italy, then this must have been largely due to Lucretius. And if it is true that belonging to Epicurus' flock did not only mean studying his text and ideas, but also practising a way of life (as is made clear by the more or less sarcastic remarks that appear in satiric poetry), then we can think of Lucretius' work as crucial not only to philosophy, but also to Roman culture.

'Delight of men and gods alike, life-giving Venus' (*Hominum divumque voluptas, alma Venus*) are the opening words of the poem and an invocation to the mother of Love, the fountain of all sensuousness. But when Lucretius starts to talk of human sexual pleasure, we read one of the cruellest pages in the history of eroticism. The Platonic abyss of insatiability opens up once more through this desire which is both natural and necessary, but, immediately, also illusory and pathological.

The desire is aroused at the time of puberty, when the seed spreads into the canals of the body. Images (*simulacra*) of a beautiful face or exquisite skin detach themselves from a body and move over to excite those places that are now inflated with an abundance of semen. In dreams, these images alone are so effective that they produce an immediate emission. And in reality? The semen originates in the whole of the body and, through the limbs and organs, it collects in certain oversensitive parts, where it stimulates the genital areas. Once

excited, these parts swell up with semen. The desire to expel it is produced, but
not to expel it in any direction, but towards a particular destination, which
attracts with an intense power. The body searches that point from which originates the wound – love's wound (*vulnus*) – inflicted on the soul. When a
weapon cuts the skin, the poet claims, blood gushes forth and lands on the
person who struck the blow; equally, Venus looks to those who have fired their
arrows, be they young men with womanly limbs or splendidly sensuous
women. The desire to come together and to eject fluids from one body into
another is the response to an arousing image. This dumb craving precedes
sensual pleasure.

Desire (*dira libido, muta cupido*) is therefore quite natural. It is the reaction of a
mature male body to another body, whose femininity strikes and stimulates
(whether or not that femininity belongs to a woman or a young man). The
analogy of the projectile that pierces the flesh and causes blood to squirt onto
the enemy's face could not express more clearly the idea of mechanical sequence
in this cause and effect: the impact and the specific response. The whole vocabulary of arousal insists on the physicality of the event: the image 'shakes violently
or excites' (*sollicitat*), puts in motion or shakes (*ciet*), provokes, enrages or inflames
(*inritat*), moves violently or shakes (*commovet*), and assails or excites (*lacessit*). The
will (*voluntas*) to ejaculate has nothing deliberate about it: it corresponds to what
Aristotle considered an involuntary movement. Even though it is so focused on
soiling the person who provoked the stimulation, the desire is aroused by itself
(*fit voluntas*), at the precise moment of the collision between the image and the
soul, simply because the body is ready, genital areas are full of semen, which in
turn is pressing to be released (*ciet*). Desire is made up of food and representation, Aristotle claimed, and Lucretius shared the idea of this combination of
causes. He considered it a particular case of physics, founded on the encounter
between two bodies which either join together or reject each other. It happens
that a particular face appears before us and 'makes an impression'; what follows
is automatic. The erection is nothing more than a wound from which the vital
fluid must spring. The desire (*voluntas*) is a wound (*vulnus*).

We have suddenly returned, in Roman culture, to the theme with which we
started, Homeric eroticism. Male desire is a paradoxical passivity, a physiological vulnerability in the face of female beauty, which is a more provocative
object when it is immobile and inactive. This paradoxical vulnerability involves
the experience of desire, which is all the more intense for being involuntary,
because in the presence of beauty there is an immediate reaction in the agent
whom Alberto Moravia comically immortalised as 'him' (and which remains
nameless in Lucretius' *On the Nature of Things*): the penis. The plentiful male
matter that presses on the genitalia responds to the female image. *Haec Venus est
nobis*: this is what Venus is for us, concludes Lucretius.

And what is love? Love is the transformation of a physiological response into a pathological one. The wound, which is spurting fresh blood, can become inflamed and gangrenous. Thus an incurable abscess is formed – one that will always hurt, and which every subsequent impact of the image aggravates and reopens. Falling in love is this persistent desire of the *libido* to direct its semen into a specific body, the one that has emanated the excruciating image, the sight of which inflames the sore. Lucretius' poem offers two remedies for the patient who ignores the cause, and these involve acting upon both the representation and the food. The patients need, first, to avoid meetings, find distractions and force themselves to think of other things, and, second, to offload the semen that has been accumulating dangerously, and do so with any body at all. Venus *volgivaga*, who is promiscuous and of the people (*pándēmŏs*), as Pausanias argues in Plato's *Symposium*, offers a radical cure: the first sores should be replaced by new wounds deflecting the desirous impulse towards multiple and different objects. This introduces the deliberate will to expose oneself to further arrows and to seek out actively other encounters, which are no longer casual ones. We have entered the terrain of the art of love.

Or rather we should say an art of *not* loving, of actively avoiding love (*amorem vitare*). It is better to enjoy Venus, the Venus *volgivaga*, than to suffer the illusion of love. The passion for a single person, for an individual whose sight upsets the soul and excites the body, reveals the very nature of loving desire. It shows that it is insatiable and that the sensuality of the sexual act is destined to remain impure (*non est pura voluptas*, *On the Nature of Things*, iv, 1081), mixed (*admixta*, 1085), because it is contaminated by suffering. Erotic craving is different from other appetites that can be satisfied naturally and easily. When we are hungry or thirsty, we can satisfy our hunger and quench our thirst with very little. When we are in love, the more we possess the more our crazed desire burns in our heart (1089–90). At the moment of greatest intimacy, when bodies embrace, intertwine and are bound to one another, and kisses turn into bites as though in a wish to devour the loved one, we discover the impossibility of fusion. Making love – with panting breath and mixed saliva – is the fight of two bodies to penetrate and tear shreds off each other. It is a paradoxical fray in which, while wrestling, we attempt to tighten the bonds of Venus and, while experiencing the failure to become one, we fail to pull apart. It is a collision, in which yearning turns into cruelty: inflicting pain is the only way, albeit a vain one, to reduce the distance that physically separates. Emptiness triumphs: we cannot incorporate the other, who ultimately remains a faint image incapable of bringing satisfaction (1101–20). The orgasm does not bring a paroxysm in which one blends into the other; it merely introduces a pause and a truce. Instead of satisfaction, even temporary satisfaction, it does nothing more than momentarily interrupt a thirst that could not be extinguished even in the middle of a river in flood. And then the frenzy resumes.

This poem produces a first theory of eroticism as cruelty. As pleasure is always undermined by desire, the other body has to be grasped, bitten and torn apart in order to get inside it or inhale and absorb it into oneself. Sade seems to appear on the horizon. However, you can also hear Platonic background music. Firstly, the most pernicious love is the one that fixatedly admires a single individual, according to Diotima in the *Symposium*, because this prevents us from understanding that qualities exist independently from the particular individual to which we attribute them. The woman we adore is very beautiful, but so are others, Lucretius asserts (1173). In the *Philebus*, sensuousness is miscellaneous and impure, precisely because it is always mixed with the suffering of dissatisfaction. 'Sensuousness is not pure' (*Non est pura voluptas*) is echoed in *On the Nature of Things*. Whereas Epicurus systematically overturns the Platonic ethics of pleasure by denying that appetites are insatiable, Lucretius appears to recover Plato's adverse arguments on the nature of love. This appetite alone is the inexhaustible one.

The ideas that *Venus* is the remedy for love (*remedium amoris*) and that sex, in its hedonistic naturalness, should be given free rein in a libertine manner mean that we do not delude ourselves or despair over our inability to join with the other in a single and complete body, fulfilling the yearning to merge with the other suggested in the myth of the hermaphrodite in Plato's *Symposium*. As in Jacques Lacan's paradoxical maxim, *il n'y a pas de rapport sexuel*, there is no sexual relationship – and in sex there is no relationship. There are salutary moments of joyful and relaxing expulsion of one's own semen – when the body is aroused – into another body. Or else there is conjugal intercourse – if possible, from behind, 'in the manner of beasts' (*more ferarum*), in order that the semen enters the womb directly, without the useless deviations provoked by the languorous and sensuous movements of the hips typical of prostitutes, to do the blunt and brutal business of procreation (1260–77).

ARTE REGENDUS AMOR – 'LOVE MUST BE RULED THROUGH ART'

Ovid's *Art of Love* came as a response to Epicurean art, in the very first year of the Christian era. Yet another poem, a *carmen* which transforms a lesson into something pleasing: whereas Lucretius' *On the Nature of Things* is based on reason (*ratio*), Ovid more modestly uses art (*ars*) to put his case. The poet enters the scene with a specific purpose, that of handing on his experience as a lover: he has been struck many times by Love's arrows and has been burnt by his flaming torches, but he will eventually take his revenge by bringing Love, this elusive and ill-disciplined god, under his control, because Love is also a malleable being and no more than a child (*The Art of Love*, i, 7–30). Ovid starts with the thought that passion can and should be educated, 'love must be ruled through art' (*arte regendus amor*, i, 4), that *érōs* is not a *túrannŏs* because Love is a *puer*, whose tender age is suited to being kept under control and disciplined: *aetas mollis et apta regi* (i, 10).

Love, who, being a child, is a diminutive and capricious god, loses the aura of fatality and menace that made him so devastatingly cruel in *On the Nature of Things*. First of all, an amorous encounter is not the casual result of an image detaching itself from a body, travelling through space, striking the soul and arousing the body. The young woman who can truly awake your passion, Ovid warns, will not come towards you slipping through the insubstantial air (*haec tibi non tenues veniet delapsa per auras*; i, 43). In other words: beware! A girl is *not* a Lucretian simulacrum. The object of love has to be sought out with one's own eyes, deliberately and carefully (44). To start with, therefore, you must force yourself to go out and find what you want to love (*quod amare velis reperire labora*; 35). The suitor is a soldier who prepares for battle but will not be taken by surprise, or rather he is a recruit who must go and laboriously search for his battlefield. The desire is not an event: it is a strategy that depends on the will.

The second labour that falls to the erotic hero is the contact with the girl he likes. The young woman must be persuaded and conquered (37). An effort is required to make happen what, in Lucretius' view, just occurs – and tragically: that attachment which the Epicurean philosopher dramatically characterises as yearning, illusion and delusion, and therefore as a disaster to be prevented. The third task is that of making love last (38). Nothing could be further from Lucretius' lesson in anti-erotic materialism: his idea that falling in love automatically degenerates into a chronic disorder for which countermeasures must be taken before it becomes 'an inoperable love', as Marcel Proust defined it. For Ovid, constancy becomes a delicate operation, whose success depends on a thousand precautions and stratagems. Duration is the ultimate achievement of the art of love.

Ovid teaches us to put into use all that Lucretius demands that we avoid, because the former believes it to be a question of will, talent and competence, whereas the latter believes it to be something involuntary, physical and fatal. Ovid puts his ironic *ars* in place of Lucretius' *ratio* – a theory of nature which imposes automatic responses and pathologies on the body – and he does this in a manner which is too systematic and precise to be considered casual. *The Art of Love* is a parody of the genre of handbooks in vogue in Roman culture, but it is also a philosophical statement on the nature of desire. By turning it into an exercise that requires technique and savoir-faire, Ovid implies that there is nothing spontaneous, irrational, irresistible or insatiable about love. At the opposite pole to the Platonic anguish in the face of 'crazed libido' (*dira libido*), Ovid reassures us that the problem is not avoidance, but rather helping the savage child into this world and teaching him good manners. Love? 'He is but a child' (*Sed puer est!*).

COSÌ FAN TUTTE

The apprentice lover must therefore follow the trail. No longer a vulnerable prey, he has become a hunter, well equipped with weapons and wiles. He has to learn which are the places favourable to encounters and to frequent them at the right time. He has to acquire knowledge of how to make the first approach, pay compliments, comply with the other's desires, make himself useful, and give presents – or, in other words, how to court a woman. This advice does not apply to a court, but to a city, the city of Rome with its theatres, temples, roads, fountains, banquets and spas. In this cityscape, the poets invented a kind of 'urban love', a forerunner of courtly love. The hunter–warrior creates the character-type for the discrete, patient and yearning lover, who is unstinting in his doggedness and self-sacrifice. He has to excel in procrastination and in the postponement of pleasure. Emaciated, melancholic and pallid in every sense of the word, he has to parade his suffering from frustrated but constant and assiduous desire. This is, however, playacting, because in reality he knows he cannot fail. 'Put out your nets,' the poet reminds him, 'you will find that you will catch something.' The crucial point of the art of love is in fact the acquisition of self-confidence: the certainty that all women can be captured.

Male desire depends entirely on the libido that women are supposed to have. All the scheming, the traps and the encirclements men are advised to deploy in the first two books of the *Art of Love* presuppose that all women ('as a whole', *cunctae*) carry within them an intense and hidden sexual desire. Indeed, it is more intense and more hidden than male desire. The male libido is more moderate and less crazed (281 and 341–2). *Puellae* enjoy furtive loves as much as men, but, whereas men are not good at dissembling, women know well how to protect the secrecy of their passions (275–6). The most important secret to be learnt is the existence of this sexual energy in all women, a potential consent to male desire that must never be doubted (343), even when they appear to say no. Even the one who appears not to want it wants it (274). Women adore being desired and courted (345), and birds will cease to sing before women cease to give in to a young man who tempts them gently (273).

This is why the suitor has to be persistent. This is why it is worth pursuing closely, and above all waiting for, the particular woman who attracts him more than any of the others and to whom he can make up his mind to say, ' You're the one I love, and only you' (42). The suitor has faith in himself, because he knows the secret sensuality of all women, which gives him hope that this one will capitulate sooner or later. Out of a kind of physical necessity, water, which is the softer substance, eventually ends up wearing down the stone, which is harder (473–4). They will all fall for it, if the virile young man is willing to behave in a tender and refined manner, burst into tears and refrain from imposing his harshness. Above all, the first kisses must be delicate and must not inflict aggression on soft lips. The young woman must not be able to complain of finding her suitor rough (665–6). Made up of softness and malleability (*mollitia*) and delay (*mora*), art protects the suitor from the impatience of cruelty.

The supreme adroitness of the artist of love can be measured by the dosage of violence over time. He is a soldier, a hunter, but not an ignorant peasant (*rusticus*). He knows that he can count on the libido of all women, but he also knows that modesty (*pudor*) is what basically defines a woman's social role. This modesty consists specifically in the imperative to avoid manifesting one's own desire, not taking the first steps, never asking and never surrendering to the suitor immediately. Unlike female animals, women hide their extreme and crazed sensuality because this is what morality imposes on them. Ovid insists on the fact that the young women of whom he speaks are not married women (*matronae*); they are free women (*libertae*), who are socially and sexually more accessible. They are not, however, prostitutes, with whom there would obviously be no need to play the waiting game. These are women who have dignity, and the suitor must therefore respect the hesitation, the resistance and the initial rejections, while at the same time confidently aiming at eventual success. Time is his secret weapon in response to the secrecy of female desire, which has to make itself desired.

It all comes down to being aware that there is, on the one hand, a general consent that is bound to manifest itself – the sensuous availability of women as such – and, on the other, a personal 'yes' in these particular circumstances, which has to be extorted from this particular individual woman, who has her own time frame and her own sense of modesty. She cannot take the initiative, but is thankful to the person who does. It is up to the man to ask, beg and implore, if he wishes to take her, in the knowledge that she wants to receive his request anyway. To keep him waiting is the only way in which she is allowed to enter the erotic game (704–14). She has to put herself in a passive position, as though she expects to be courted, and the sophisticated suitor has to avoid imposing himself on her too forcefully, thus always keeping the correct distance. He even masks his real intentions and pretends to be solely interested in friendship (717–21). In a way, he makes his behaviour appear similar to that of his intended lover, by adopting female mannerisms such as blandishments, tears, a sickly pallor and a semblance of her libido.

However, *vis* (vigour, power or energy), which is the violent root of the word 'virility', always lurks in the background, ready to pounce. The Roman lover always counted on the fact that young women are pleased by force (*grata est vis puellis*, 671). In the amorous exchange, they love to concede against their will that which gives them pleasure. They love to be suddenly violated and consider that offence to be a gift (672–4).

In Rome, the matrimonial rite itself – the form of sexuality most desirable for a woman – celebrated a collective rape which had a crucial role in the city's foundation story. The primitive community created by Romulus was in fact a gang of rough and vicious soldiers incapable of reproducing itself. They decided to kidnap the daughters of their civilised neighbours, the Sabines, in order to acquire women, set up families and have children. Rape (*stuprum*) was therefore part of the founding violence, which survived in the heart of the institution. It was in memory of the Sabine women that the Roman bridegroom lifted his bride in his arms to carry her to the bedroom, as though he had dragged her bodily, and then divided her hair with a spear. The ritual celebrated force and resistance.

It makes cultural sense to admit a 'crazed libido' in all women and then to put forth the idea that this socially unacceptable desire – remember the entrepreneurial initiatives of the Athenian women in Aristophanes, or the catastrophic attachments of Phaedra, Deianeira, Medea or Jocasta – remains secretly available and always ready to manifest itself in the only permissible manner, that of an apparent refusal, a reluctant consent and a 'no' that means 'yes'. Like marriage itself, seduction is played out with sexual violence never far away: it is the staging of a pretended misunderstanding, which conceals a true desire. But everyone must play their part: the young woman (*puella*), clearly, with her modesty, but also the expert lover (*sapiens*), who must limit his force (*vis*) to a particular dosage and know how to plan it. Impetuousness, *Veneris subita rapina*, must take the woman by surprise at exactly the right moment, when she can no longer defend herself and can achieve her desire with impunity.

Ovid sketches the portraits, almost caricatures, of the inexpert lover and the learned lover. The former is so impetuous that he kisses too avidly and bites. The kiss is, in fact, a transition phase, during which the young woman struggles because of her modesty, but at the same time wishes to be overcome (664). If a lover uses force at this stage, he will be rejected and she will stop him from going any further. He will not have achieved his aims because of his coarseness (*rusticitas*), and not because of his respect (*pudor*). Moreover, the woman will be mortified and disappointed precisely because of her desire, her 'crazed libido' which has not been satisfied. In contrast, Achilles is an example of the cunning lover in a particularly revealing circumstance (679–702). The hero hides himself on the island of Scyrus to escape having to fight in the

Trojan war. He is dressed up as a woman and passes his days with the girls of the royal palace. One night he finds himself in bed with Deidamia, the daughter of King Lycomedes. She discovers that Achilles is a man (*vir*) as the result of a rape (*stuprum*). The poet insists, however, that she wanted to be overcome by force (*sed voluit vinci viribus illa tamen*, 698). Deidamia is indeed raped, but at the same time she wants the rapist to stay and invites him to do so with her soft voice. Where does that violence come from (*Vis ubi nunc illa est*)? The violence derives from a shudder of virility, which makes Achilles rebel against the cowardly disguise imposed by his mother in order to protect him. The violence is to be found in an act that took place in the right place at the right time: in bed, at night, in such a manner that the virgin of royal blood could be forced and made to want this without having to struggle and without dishonour.

The Achilles who divests himself of his female clothes for a well timed rape, an event that allows everyone to save face and obtain pleasure, represents a model of the erotic hero and expert lover. He is a warrior capable of disguising himself as a woman, and this self-fashioning enables him to gain a position of such proximity and such favourable circumstances that the final and impetuous outcome is a foregone conclusion. The cross-dressed warrior behaves like an actor, and owes the triumph of his virility to the flexibility of his gender identity. The height of seductive expertise is the ability to conceal this very expertise, when an air of incompetence could prove advantageous.

But there is more: Ovid claims that the ideal image of the suitor is that of a Greek god, Proteus, who was the master of shape-shifting. Ovid is the greatest poet of mythological metamorphosis, and a theorist of change as a vulnerability of human beings to the power of the gods, but also as a process of open-ended cosmogony. His *Art of Love* is consistent with this vision of the world in flux: like everything else, love is transformation, for the beloved who is to be mollified through courtship; for the poet and lover, whom the art softens just right; for the discourse of love which, from flattery, will turn into sincere praise.

SAPER MENTIRE – 'KNOWING HOW TO LIE'

The fundamental lesson of the *Art of Love* is that love means suspicion and jealousy, betrayal and duplicity. It is a fiction and a theatrical exercise. The first reason for this is that everyone knows that the libido exists, but no one must display it, because this only occurs in the realm of prostitution and sexual exploitation, which is reserved for slaves. Women and men disguise their desire: the former, out of modesty, and the latter, in order to overcome that modesty. The second reason is that the final aim of the erotic chase is love – the lasting love for a single person, to whom you can say 'You're the one I love, and only

you' (*tu mihi sola places*). It means attracting a lover and maintaining that relationship for as long as possible. Now, this entails a certain amount of deceit,
because a privileged attachment should not compromise the possibility of
other pleasurable affairs with other *puellae* and other friends. The stability of
the permanent couple, full of seduction, surprises and erotic variety is still
compatible with, or indeed complementary to, a certain kind of libertine
licence. The art, therefore, is essentially one of reconciling duration and infidelity. These amatory somersaults obviously require both men and women to
engage in a great deal of flirtation and dissimulation or *saper mentire*, 'knowing
how to lie', in the words of Despina, the artful maid in *Così fan tutte*.

Good nature, perseverance, generosity, devotion and boundless admiration
are as indispensable as discretion to the man who wishes to maintain a relationship that has been constructed at the cost of great effort. 'Enjoy yourselves by
all means', *Ludite!* the poet invites the reader, but all misdoings must be
concealed in a seemingly unaffected and furtive manner (ii 389). Do without
vanity and boasting of manly exploits! Women who discover a rival to their bed
explode with wild and vengeful jealousy, and inflict the same suffering on
the guilty party. And this is well deserved (397), as the art of love is based on
the absolute imperative of elegant deceit, which aims at sparing one's loved one
from such unforgivable humiliations, which can devastate even the most stable
unions (385).

Ovid evokes the great figures of Greek tragedy in order to illustrate situations and emotions with exemplary portraits. He draws an important lesson
on female sensuality from such violent figures as Clytemnestra and Medea.
That more intense libido of women (*acrior libido*) entails erotic pride. The
cause of all women's fundamental availability is also the cause of their
susceptibility. The bed is a territory, and its exclusive possession a precious
privilege. It is this aspect of dignity that turns passion into something crazed
(*furiosa*). Desire is not just intense; it has a potential for fury (*furor*), for the
rage that is inevitably unleashed by an affront (*iniuria*) or injury (*laesio*)
(450–61; 550; 489). The language used in Ovid's analysis and description of
what we call jealousy insists upon the offence caused by the preference for
another woman and upon the resulting desire for revenge, rather than upon
the concepts of betrayal, broken promises and disloyalty. Within the framework of ancient emotions, jealousy is anger. It is therefore an essentially
narcissistic passion: a surge of self-love in the face of the insulting defection
of the other's love. As love is idealising admiration, superlative praise, attri-
bution of a supreme, even absolute, power to please – *tu mihi sola places* is the
lover's motto – anyone who sees it fade to another's advantage feels dimin-
ished and at the same time challenged. Uniqueness is so intrinsic to love
that any threat to it is an upheaval, and the negation of love itself.

This is why betrayal is more unbearable when the slight is undeniable. Clytemnestra heard that, during the siege of Troy, her husband had taken Chryseis to his bed, but she decided to let the matter rest. However, the reaction is very different when, on Agamemnon's return from the war, she sees before her Cassandra, who has been brought home as a prisoner but to whom the victorious king has made himself a prisoner. Deeply offended by the ignominy, Clytemnestra takes a lover into her heart and into her bed (399–408). There is a gulf between a vague piece of news that reaches your ears from afar and unmistakable visual evidence, which you are unable to take your eyes off. Transparency has to be avoided at all costs and, in the event of being caught *in flagrante*, one must always and in any event deny everything (410). Deny and then make love immediately and as much as possible, because only the bed can resolve these crises. Conversely, it pays to stir up the jealousy of a very possessive lover: get her to believe that there is a rival and let her explode with anger, make a scene and then faint, so that you can reassure and console her, once again, in bed. While it is important to hide infidelity from sight by lying and denying the evidence, it is equally important to suggest things to the hearing (435–60). This is good use of the other person's erotic pride: provoke her with words sufficiently to titillate a false rivalry, without however creating a visual comparison, on her own territory, whose certainty would cause lasting offence.

Women, too, need to know how to lie. Firstly, they have to compose a theatrical identity, unlike men, who must retain their naturalness. Echoing the archaic Greek theme of artificial femininity, Ovid reminds women that they must not stop at beautifying themselves by constructing a mask of cosmetics, hair dyes, wigs and accessories that make up for physical defects; they also have to dress up for the stage and conceal the very fact of doing it. Only the result must appear before the eyes of the lover, who is both partner and audience. The artifice is a deceit (iii, 209–50). Secondly, women are no less unfaithful than men (i, 328). In spite of social pressure, even married women have difficulty staying faithful (ii, 388). Women desire to be desired, we said. If courted with persistence and patience, Penelope herself could be seduced (i, 475). Clytemnestra takes a lover to exact revenge. Helen betrays her husband simply because he goes away and leaves her under the same roof with a guest who is not a boor, even though he knows she detests sleeping on her own. She is not the one who sins, nor is Paris, who has simply done what any other man would do. Menelaus forced them into adultery, by providing them with the time and the place (ii, 359–67).

Women are slightly less deceitful and are sometimes bad at lying, so their lovers soon find out. In embarrassing situations, men should learn to reject the evidence of their own eyes (ii, 522), to ignore furtive looks of recognition, and

to resist the temptation to intercept suspect letters. They should become prac-
tised in the use of patience: tolerance of a rival and pretence that nothing is
happening is the best method for eliminating that rival. On the whole, it is
worth letting partners believe they have got away with their deceit (520–60).
On the other hand, women must learn to send messages without raising suspicion, to cultivate cunningly their partners' jealousy and to pretend to be
jealous themselves. It is important to make men think they are loved: they are
so in love with themselves that they are easy to deceive (iii, 673). Like men in
a similar situation, women must learn to put up with infidelity without excessive anxiety, and they should not lose their heads on hearing news of a rival
(673–84). Above all, they should not give immediate credence to gossip, which
can be fatal – as in the case of Procris, who ends up getting killed while stalking
her husband, whom she incorrectly believes to be unfaithful. We should not
forget that the poet has just advised men to create false suspicions in order
to excite attacks of jealousy in their beloved, which she will interpret as an
infallible sign of true love.

The dance of mutual deceit culminates in the use of the door and window.
When faced with a locked door, a lover must show his zeal by climbing the
wall, lifting himself onto the roof and sliding through a window. Women adore
these acts of gallantry and take them for pledges of true love (ii, 243–8). For
her part, the young woman should lock the door to oblige her lover to climb
through the window. Men enjoy experiencing a sense of danger once in a
while, and they adore the thrill of furtiveness (iii, 605–7).

With his advice to each party, Ovid orchestrates a paradoxical complicity,
based not on trust (*fides*) but rather on the understanding that sincerity is cruel,
mendacity a necessity and truth elusive. The art of love (*ars amatoria*) is a form
of scepticism, a mixture of suspension of belief and suspension of disbelief.
There is an imperative to believe, to pretend to believe and to allow oneself to
be deceived. There is a fundamental reason for all this; it is the discrepancy
between what love should be if it were left to nature and chance, and what love
becomes when one learns how to love. Love has a winged body, and is a boy
who, unbidden, wanders the world and flies from place to place (ii, 17–21).
Only art can educate butterfly-like cupid and teach him to stay still for at least
as long as decorum requires. Without a sentimental education, men would
follow their promiscuous and casual urges, and women would unrestrainedly
display their intense libido, like female animals. The art of love consists entirely
of measuredness and deception, in the sure knowledge that Love could never
settle for very long on the same object, if left to chance and nature.

The purely fortuitous occurrence of erotic encounters can be progressively
corrected by strategies of approach and courtship, and then by the techniques
for navigating the high seas once a couple has been formed. Nothing is down

to chance if love is to last (ii, 14), because chance is always offering up more opportunities for new affairs. It is obvious that adultery will be the end result, if chance brings together a not uncivilised guest (*non rusticus*), a lady who does not like to sleep on her own and a dim-witted husband. By seizing the chance, a man and a woman follow their libido and all its natural and indiscriminate recalcitrance. Paris only does what any other man (including Menelaus himself) would have done in his place, because desire is a question of nature and circumstance: being in the right place at the right time with the right body. Simply because she is a woman, Helen harbours sensuality and an inability to remain faithful, something that a sensible husband should acknowledge and foresee, if he wishes to remain in charge.

Consequently, a lasting and constant relationship must be consciously wished for, and then carefully built, maintained and protected. In the first place, it is essential to keep desire alive and rekindle it from time to time. For this reason, a well tempered infidelity is one of a couple's essential allies, along with the various displays of kindness and lovingness. In the context of this urban – and urbane – lovemaking, the most difficult balance is between presence and absence and between availability and distance. 'Delay always spurs lovers on' (*Mora semper amantes incitat*, iii, 473–4). A properly judged waiting period and the ability to make the other wait and therefore to make oneself more desirable is also a source of arousal. 'Delay is the best go-between' (*Maxima lena mora est*, 752). This is why wives, who are always accessible, find it difficult to make themselves desired (579–85). In accordance with this same logic, the feeling that there might be someone else on the horizon prevents love from growing tired and reignites the dying embers (592–600). To make someone jealous means to make oneself passionately desirable. A terrible scene, with its sickly pallor, its weeping, its insults, its scratching and its swooning, is nothing but an explosion of competitive libido; thus it always means a return of an earlier enthusiasm. This is true for both men and women (ii, 435–60). The poet warns that, without these techniques, love will grow old (iii, 594). If you fail to make use of these devices, you will find that the erotic flame is irretrievably extinguished and the *puer* cupid has become a dotard. Or else he has flown elsewhere.

As we have said, Ovid reverses Lucretius' physics of love. Firstly, he demonstrates that it is possible, and necessary, to tame chance (*casus*) using art: 'Do not expect to see a girl slide through the air towards you: go and get her!' Secondly, he deflates the threat of an erotic attachment to a single person. For Lucretius, this is an unrelenting and overpowering disease; for Ovid, it is the opposite. Constant love is not a fatal infatuation to be avoided; it is a deliberate choice, which is arduously cultivated and is compatible with other pleasures. According to the *Art of Love*, passion does not become an addiction over the long term; it becomes just senile. Consequently, libertinism could never be used as a remedy for the folly of monogamy, but rather it becomes a collateral aspect of expert eroticism, which knows how to reconcile a relationship based on 'You're the one I love, and only you' with occasional flings that are enjoyed tactfully and discretely. In the knowledge that an unmentionable libido burns in all women, it is easy to move on to another love interest, if the first one says 'no' or if one wants to play the field (*ludere*).

As far as jealousy is concerned, it is clearly foolish to get angry over a sexual affront (*iniuria*), because of the nature of love. As love has wings, infidelity is spontaneous, one might say physiological. Volatility can never be eliminated from either male or female sexual life: on this Lucretius and Ovid are in agreement, but they draw completely different conclusions. Lucretius' terror of the subterfuges that torment lovers – the understanding looks, sideways glances, furtive smiles (*On the Nature of Things*, iv, 1135–40) – is replaced by Ovid's techniques of effective make-believe, pretence that nothing has happened in an embarrassing situation, and arousal of suspicion solely for the purpose of awakening one's partner's fury and therefore libido, but only in small doses. The lover who is persuaded by Lucretius' reasoning will be convinced that love is unhappy. The sophisticated lover, however, knows that desire is agonistic and thus stimulated and revived by rivalry: the anger of those who feel hurt (*laesi*) is just as inevitable as unfaithfulness, and simply expresses the vitality of amorous excitement. In this sentimental education, erotic pride is of supreme value: if properly tuned, it becomes the masterpiece of the art of love. The art consists of well dosed emotion.

In the name of truth and nature, Lucretius puts us on our guard against the inherent falsity of love: the unreality of the image, the mendacity of the beloved, and the pathetic self-deception that blurs the vision of the man who becomes enamoured. To fall in love is a process which transforms the object's actual flaws into superlative and much sought-after qualities in the eyes of the beholder (iv, 1160–70). In the name of the art of love, Ovid demonstrates that a theatrical game with one's partner and with oneself is the only possible truth when it comes to love. He recommends precisely the things that Lucretius warns against: the rhetoric of euphemistic praise, which enlarges upon an unfortunate distinctive feature and turns it into an exaggerated compliment. It is acceptable, the poet declares, to use your vocabulary in order to soften any defects (*nominibus mollire licet mala, Art of Love*, ii, 657). Do not skimp on admiration and flattering remarks, call the small woman agile and the fat one fulsome . . . *e la grande maestosa, la piccina ancor vezzosa* ('and the large one majestic, and again the tiny one cute'), as Don Giovanni would echo. Try to find the right words – just right because completely wrong – in order to depict a beauty that, in time, will become credible even for you. Love is not blind; it is painter, sculptor and poet.

Just as it is permissible for men to transform female shortcomings into some-thing charming, so women should correct their imperfections. Above all, they do this with clothes and makeup and by moving in a manner that highlights their best features, and conceals their blemishes. But the ultimate art consists of showing themselves off in the best possible light during sexual intercourse. Lucretius' language is particularly crude when he describes the positions that make sex more or less conform to nature. The range is limited: there are useful movements of the thighs, which carry the risk of diverting the trajectory of the semen on its way to the uterus, and there is a fixed position – the woman on all fours and taken from behind – which makes it possible to hit the target. The encounter between two bodies can be either pleasurable for the man or useful for procreation: that is all there is. Ovid concludes his *Art of Love* with the famous lines on the various positions advised for women, which could be read as a kind of rudimentary *Kamasutra*.

The bed is the stage on which the partner–spectator takes up a position from which he can perceive the woman's image in a certain light – close-up, from above, from the front or from the back – and obtain a general impression of her body, which depends on a particular viewpoint. Even in intimacy, there is a game of distances and therefore of perspective. A woman must know herself and choose the *figura*, the final visible posture, that flatters her most. She then displays it to the man, who looks on (*spectat*). Lucretius' tumultuous bed, on which lovers bite and tear at each other's hair, in the desperate attempt to turn the other's image into reality, is replaced by a studio in which lovemaking is about showing off and making a great impression. The notorious position behind, which the Athenians considered hurried and lascivious (Davidson, 1997) and Lucretius prudishly calls *more ferarum*, becomes not so much natural as aesthetically risky: to be adopted only if one has an elegant silhouette when seen from the side.

The young woman (*puella*) with an intelligent understanding of love knows that beds are sceptical devices, where whatever she is capable of making her lover see and believe will be the truth. She plays the admiration game: she assists in the lover's task of playing down her defects through his words by attempting to minimise them herself. Thus the small woman, to whom the lover attributes the corresponding compliment (*habilis*, agile, rather than short), takes up the challenge and returns the courtesy by adopting the erotic position that shows off her diminutive size in the best possible light. She sits astride the lover, who is lying on his back and thus can contemplate her torso, breasts and shoulders from below: she really does become *habilis*. The objective truth of her short stature disappears, as though her figure had actually adapted itself to the euphemism. Under the half-light of the bedroom, whatever is seen and believed becomes the truth.

NON NISI LAESUS AMO – 'I CAN ONLY LOVE WHEN I AM WRONGED'

Within the vicious circle of love's bad faith, both men and women are concentrating on the same end: pleasure. Are they, however, using the same means? Ovid teaches men that all women desire to be desired, which is a revelation, because they conceal their libido and keep their suitors waiting. As women already know that men want to make love, because male lustfulness is no secret, the poet teaches women how to make themselves loved individually – and how to make themselves loved for a long time.

In the first two books, Ovid speaks to his most obvious readership – young men (*iuvenes*) – in the capacity of a counsellor who has learnt this art the hard way. In the third book, he offers advice to young women (*puellae*), as though they were enemies to whom he is treacherously revealing confidential information. The mentor, who supports his own sex and has shared its experiences, becomes a spy and a deserter to the feminine world. This splitting of the poetic 'I' into solidarity and betrayal confirms the ironic and indeed triangular complicity that unites men, women and the poet in the theatre of urbane love. If everyone learns to deceive, and from the same manual, then no one will really be deceived. The *iuvenes* cannot fail to read further and discover the tips given to the *puellae*; the latter have already read the first two books. The model reader is bound to be surreptitiously curious and to pretend that nothing happened – as a shrewd lover should do.

But there is more to the cunning of this game: the designated reader is not the only lover. The poet himself is a model lover. Only literature can turn a suitor into an ideal master of *eros*. The poet of the *Ars*, we said, is a professor (*magister*) of pretence, but one who does not deceive his own audience; he teaches everyone the truth of deceit. The inventor of the art of reciting love invites his readers to learn how to lie (*fallere*), but at the same time he claims to be the most trustworthy and loyal suitor. 'We poets', he proclaims, 'do not offer presents like the rich or words like the lawyers. Our Chorus can only offer the gift of our songs' (*carmina*). Yet this is what counts most in love: it is the word which commends the beauty of the woman loved and keeps alive her memory. It is the poetic word that offers the ultimate, enhancing, flattering praise. The young women (*puellae*) whose suitor is a poet are the most fortunate: they can escape anonymity and become heroines. If Cynthia is famous (*Cynthia nomen habet*), then this is down to Propertius (iii, 536). 'This is why', continues Ovid's voice, 'we are more suited to love than all the others. By spurning the forum and wealth, we only seek the couch and its shade. Prone to passion, we burn with a strong and lasting (*validus*) ardour. And we are capable of loving with a fidelity that is almost too reliable' (533–46). Transformed by his art, the master of praise and therefore of courtship has the right degree of sweetness and devotion (540; 545). There is a god in us, the poet concludes.

Ars amatoria is the art of admiring, paying compliments and idealising. Given that poetry does these things in the most refined and sophisticated manner, it becomes the supreme form of the art of love. As both master of pretence and exemplar of sincerity, Ovid invents a textual flirtation: he teaches young men to seduce young women, and then 'secretly' suggests to the young women how to seduce the young men, without either party being aware of it; and he does all this in the same *carmen*, so that the secret is no longer a secret for anyone. He becomes the champion of faithfulness (*fides*) in his role as a poet – both as composer of *carmina* which exalt the false idealisation of the loved one, and in a *carmen* which is a handbook of trompe l'oeil and infidelity.

Counterintuitive as this might sound, it is the truth that wins in this frank and unsparing theoretical analysis of mendacity. The poet asserts that true love will be born precisely out of the staging of courtship (i, 613–14). He himself knows that he has been cheated, and he makes the supreme confession that the erotic insult only strengthened his love: 'I confess that I can only love, when wronged' (*en ego confiteor: non nisi laesus amo*, iii, 598). The poet is aware that, when it comes to the strategies of seduction, the hunter becomes the prey, the liar ends up making his own words come true, and deceit is self-deceit. With this recantation of fiction, Ovid responds to Lucretius' rationalism (*ratio*), which denies the possibility of true sexual relations because the other person is merely a misleading, treacherous image, by claiming what ultimately is the playfulness of the art of love: any hope of escaping pretence is vanity.

Thus the landscape of urban love gave rise to the urbane suitor who, quite unlike Penelope's admirers – those rustic and speechless islanders – puts poetry to use in the idealisation of his lady (*domina*). This figure would be revived in the French courts of the twelfth century.

OH DOLCI BACI E MORBIDE CAREZZE – 'SWEET KISSES AND SOFT CARESSES'

'What's happened to you, Nevolus? Why this sad face, this wild and matted hair, this uncared-for skin and these hirsute legs, invaded by forest hair? You, who like every good Roman, is always brilliant and full of spirit: what is up?'

Juvenal's *Satire* ix opens with a dialogue between the poet and a character whose mood is one of unusual sadness. Nevolus has the reputation of a pleasure-seeking kept man who is always elegant and fastidious about his hair-style and body hair. This famous adulterer is capable of seducing not only other men's wives but also those men themselves; it is difficult to understand why he doesn't continue to enjoy himself and he is in a foul temper. The reason, poor

Nevolus replies, is that a man who keeps him for his erotic services has suddenly become incredibly mean and, what is more, he has taken on other 'biped donkeys' for his own pleasure. Nevolus is fearful for his future and his future finances. 'My way of life', he laments, 'is useful to many, but not to me. There is, in fact, a destiny for our sexual organs as well. If the stars do not favour you, it is no use having a very long or even enormous one. It may be that Virro, dribbling at the mouth, saw you naked and at this very moment is untiringly writing his sweet and dense little letters – and it is well known that the *cinaedus* voluntarily attracts his male lover. But this doesn't take away the fact that the profit is negligible. The unmanly man who is miserly is such a monster!' (Juvenal, *Satires*, ix, 32–8).

Nevolus groans. Having an exceptionally large penis, he allows himself to be used for the desires of his master (*dominus*), a man who loves to be penetrated, an act that is not very pleasurable for Nevolus. 'It is not an insignificant thing to have to insert a penis worthy of that name into some guy's guts, where it comes across last night's supper. The slave who fucks the land is less unhappy than he who fucks his employer' (43–6). Moreover, the *cinaedus*, who is also the boss hands over his wife; for this effeminate man is incapable of fertilising the woman he has married. Nevolus also took this on, and provided an impotent man with a line of descent and a reputation for virility. And, after all this, Virro dares to show himself ungrateful. 'He is calculating and wiggles his hips' (*computat et ceuet*, 40).

Nevolus and Virro are an obscene couple, in which the master (*dominus*) uses his powerful social position to inflict his desires upon another man. Being an effeminate *cinaedus* who adores being sodomised, he uses his power to seek out actively the largest possible penis. On the other hand, the man who satisfies him with his outsize male member agrees to be the instrument of other people's pleasure and dignity in exchange for money. His hyper-phallic and intrusive sexuality represents a service and a servitude, whereas the receptivity of the effeminate (*mollis*) dictates the law and imposes submission.

The phallus, at the moment of its proud and aggressive use, constituted one of the most visible elements of Roman sexuality. The imaginary figure of Priapus was triumphant in Rome, and this little god with a monumental erect penis challenged and threatened passers-by with short epigrammatic poems (Richlin, 1992a; Veyne, 1982; Olender, 1986). The phallus actually belonged to the city's foundation myth. One of the stories of the origins of Rome and its names starts with the miraculous apparition of a male sex organ which becomes erect in the fireplace of Tarchetius, the King of the Albani. The king consults the oracle of Thetis in Tyrrhenia to discover the meaning of this portent. The response is that a young woman must have sexual intercourse with this prodigious phallus, and the result of this union will be the birth of an illustrious son, who will be excellent in virtue, fortune and vigour, in Greek *rhōmē*. The king then orders one of his daughters to proceed with the union, but she disobeys and sends a slave in her place. Tarchetius discovers the deceit and wants to kill both women, but the virgin goddess Vesta appears to him in a dream and prohibits it. The obstinate king shuts them both up in a prison with the promise of letting them marry when they have finished weaving a cloth. They pass their days making the cloth, but during the night other women come on the king's orders to undo their work. As in Ithaca, time passes. The slave reaches the end of her fateful pregnancy, and the twins Romulus and Remus are born (Plutarch, *Romolus*, 2, 4–8).

Hence the father of the nation, after whose vigour (*rhōmē*) Rome was named, was indeed nothing more than a faceless, erect penis in a fireplace under the protection of a virgin goddess, whose religious and political cult was organised around a sacred fire and thus represented the city's symbolic hearth. Vesta and the phallus, or virginity and virility, come together in this culturally significant myth. Firstly, the myth anchors the history of Rome to the history of sexuality. Secondly, it vividly expresses the bond between the value of the pure and intact female body (pure like the sacred fire in the care of the Vestal Virgins) and the value of the erect male organ, which triumphs over the uncertainties of desire and is ready to carry out the work of procreation. Like the Greek *parthĕnŏs* but in a more essential manner, the Latin *virgo* (maiden or virgin) is there for the *vir* (man). The invention of the hymen, which, as we have seen, was mentioned for the first time in medical literature, occurred in Rome within the context of a society obsessed with the language of sexual potency. Surely no one could think it coincidence that the Temple of Vesta and the Temple of Fortuna Virilis were built side by side.

From Catullus to Martial and Juvenal, satires have abounded with sexual challenges, directed at very different targets. One of the most famous, an invective by Catullus, demonstrates the competitive and defensive nature of male aggression: 'I will bugger you and make you suck my prick' (*Pedicabo ego vos et inrumabo*, Catullus, *Poems*, 16, 1). He is addressing Aurelius and Furius, one, a *pathicus* (man who likes to be sodomised), the other, a *cinaedus*. These two friends have accused Catullus of composing 'somewhat tender' verses (*molliculi*, 4). 'My poems,' the offended party replies, 'may be lascivious and lacking in modesty, and they certainly titillate erotic prurience, but this does not mean that I am not a real man.' Catullus ends the poem with his defiant threat: 'Do you think I am not manly? I will bugger you and make you suck my prick' (*Male me marem putatis? Pedicabo ego vos et inrumabo*, 13–14).

Catullus reacts angrily when he is accused of a softness (*mollitia*) which goes far beyond the urbane Ovid's proclaimed seductive gentleness of which the urbane poet boasts in his *Art of Love*. To describe him as a little soft thing, *molliculus*, simply because his amorous language, directed at Lesbia and at various delicate boys (*pueri delicati*), is full of sweet kisses and suave blandishments is to misunderstand his rhetorical mimetism and to doubt his virility. In order to reassert that virility, the poet has to trumpet his power to penetrate other men's bodies in all possible ways. In other words, the tenderness of his poetry has nothing to do with the hardness of his penis. Catullus considers himself to be the opposite of Thallus, whom he pitilessly belittles. 'Thallus, you, *cinaedus* softer than the rabbit's fur, a goose's down, an earlobe, a spider's web or an old man's limp penis' (25, 1–3). He never tires of repeating that his poetry may be supple, but his sexual organ is rigid (28, 32, 37 and 56).

The phallus was a Roman obsession, and it was so in a crude as well as complicated manner. Taken at face value, virility is power, penetration is domination – and even more so if the receiving body is also male. Libido is competitive in all sorts of ways. Social power, however, could be disconnected from sexual penetration and provide, on the contrary, the means to pursue a different kind of pleasure: the enjoyment of a sensuousness which was welcoming rather than intruding. As in the case of Virro and Nevolus, or indeed, on a much grander scale, in the case of the emperors, from Caesar to Caligula, it appears that there is not a simple association between political status or financial supremacy and sexual aggressiveness. Wealth does not make you more of a male. Quite the contrary. A soft man (*mollis*), one who would love to be sodomised, could use his money to hire a super-male and keep him at his disposal; a regular penis (*penis legitimus*) could find itself reduced to being the servile instrument of an employer's pleasures. Virility had less to do with power than with a psychosomatic firmness – the very opposite of *mollitia* – which concerned both character and the whole body, including the erect penis. Virility describes the identity of the man who becomes an adult both in his anatomy and his behaviour, and spurns his infantile (and feminine) *mollitia* – perhaps – forever. Roman culture was obsessed with the phallus, we said: it was terrified of the softness that threatens a man (*vir*), just as it was dominated by the celebration of the triumphant erect penis.

In order to understand this concept, *mollitia*, which was the fundamental category in Roman sexuality and anthropology, let me sketch a definition and a taxonomy. Softness refers to a range of characteristics, which are material as well as existential. Primarily it means physical malleability. It is the moist and yielding consistency of the flesh that causes what we call 'softness'. In the medical tradition this was the distinguishing feature of women and children, and thus it provided the basis for the biological analogy between childishness and femininity, in opposition to adult masculinity. For Aristotle, women are incomplete men, as though their physiological development was arrested in childhood. Like women, children are humid and not warm enough to perform the digestive concoction required in order to transform blood into sperm (Aristotle, *On the Generation of Animals*, 728^{a}17–25; Sissa, 1983). At the other end of the age range, *mollitia* describes the old man with a penis that is 'flaccid like the stem of a tender Sicilian beet' (Catullus, *Poems*, 67, 21). All these forms of softness are natural. But there are different kinds of soft male. The *cinaedus*, a male adult, is the archetype of the *mollis* and his desire is fixated on the bottom (*culus*). In extreme cases, the *cinaedus* is unable to make love to his wife, not even very occasionally in order to make her pregnant. Finally, there is the eunuch, who finds himself in an ambivalent position, having lost his testicles; because he is sterile and lacks prickly hair, he is capable of infinitely soft kisses (*mollia semper oscula*). If, however, he has undergone the operation after puberty, he is still capable of priapic erections and can provide endless pleasure without complications (Juvenal, *Satires*, vi, 366–76).

This taxonomy depends on a number of binary distinctions – soft/hard; humid/dry; cold/warm – but, above all, it is organised around a transformation: puberty. According to ancient medicine, from the *Corpus Hippocraticum* to Galen, the child's hairless, smooth, perfumed and pliable body, being saturated with its own humidity, is naturally similar to the female body, which is forever tender and downy. However, the softness of boys is temporary: as teenagers, they are destined to dry out and achieve the solidity of their tissues and the character which distinguishes the virile adult. The commencement of love-making involves losing moisture through ejaculation. This results in the growth of thick hair and the emission of bad smells (Pseudo-Aristotle, *Problems,* vi, 4; vi, 24). The adolescent finds himself in a period of transition, in which he has only just become hard: *iam durus* (Juvenal, *Satires*, vi, 377).

The *Problems*, this fundamental text of the Aristotelian school, explains in clear medical terms ideas which we find, scattered and incomplete, throughout the literature and historiography of Greece and Rome; and it, too, deals with this critical transition. The soft body of the *païs* and *puer delicatus* can be made definitively (although not exclusively) effeminate by the practices of a receptive sexuality. The repetition of invasive acts during puberty and not before, as the Aristotelian problem specifies, causes desire and pleasure, which are only awakening at this time, when the semen is travelling towards the genitals, to settle in places other than the penis. Should the semen, with its accompanying erotic sensations, be channelled into the anal area, it would then create an insatiable and feminine sensuality. Why? Because of a mechanical shortcoming. From the anus it is impossible to expel the fluid with the necessary force and therefore completely, as in the case of ejaculation. There the semen cools and accumulates in the tissues, maintaining constant arousal. This, the text claims, is against nature, even though it occurs within the body. It is wrong for the *païs* or *puer* (youth), at the moment of his maturity, to take the path of femininity instead of that of virility – and it is wrong even if he doesn't do so in an exclusive manner. It is not quite right.

The complex attitude towards pederasty can be explained by this physiological consideration: the failure of the boy to become an adult *and* virile man. We shall have to return to this point. For the moment, let us observe that the Roman obsession with *mollitia*, which enlarges upon the Greek contempt for *malakía*, partly depended on the ambiguity of softness. Even before its sexual incarnation in the infantile, feminine, effeminate, castrated or senile body, *mollitia* was associated more deeply with the very idea of culture, civility and urbanity. Whereas the growth of the individual is from soft to hard, the evolution of societies goes in the opposite direction – from hard to soft. *Mollescere* constitutes, literally, the essential element in cultural development. Precisely for this reason, progress appeared disturbing. It is maturity, but it can turn into decadence. It is the nightmare of a sophistication that could veer towards the feminine.

In the Roman versions of the process of civilisation, the social contract appears in the form of a sexual contract. Primitive human beings start to form a society, not so much between men bonding together in order to defend themselves from nature as between women and men, in the very first sexual encounters, as desired by Venus and nature. Originally, humankind was much harder (*durus*) than us, Lucretius writes (*On the Nature of Things*, v, 925–30). This hardness meant strength, and, above all, solidity and robustness of the bones and tendons (*nervi*). A higher degree of resistance to heat, cold and food resulted from this density of the tissues and rigidity of the articulations. The process of civilisation involves a progressive physical softening up. Humankind started to become soft (*tum genus humanum primum mollescere coepit*, 1014) – with the use of houses, skins and fire for protection against changes in the weather and difficulties in digesting raw food, but above all with the invention of marriage. Venus herself gave the initial impetus towards this transformation. When humans were still living in the forest, Venus set about joining their bodies together through mutual attraction, male violence, or rudimentary forms of gifts (962–5). It was therefore sexual pleasure that started to weaken humans, particularly men (1017): this process of enfeeblement culminated in a taste for good food and for visiting spas, and resulted in the triumph of luxury.

Erotic indulgence, comfortable living and culinary refinement revealed to men the pleasures of the senses – what we call sensuality – and therefore contributed to establishing a variety of customs and habits that ranged from the use of squashy mattresses (*mollia strata*, iv, 849) to the movement of supple limbs (*mollia membra*, iv, 980). Loosing the stiffness of their joints, humans became increasingly flexible and delicate: now there were new bodies, made for reclining gently, with bent knees, in the Greek manner, on yielding couches

designed for resting, dining and making love. A tone similar to this anthropological poetry was adopted by Celsus, a doctor who confirmed the story of
human fragility: it was *luxuria* that had left the human race undefended against
natural adversities (Celsus, *On Medicine*, i).

According to Ovid, who quotes from sources which he does not disclose, it
was, again, tender sensuality that softened up the savage spirits (*blanda truces
animos fertur mollisse voluptas*, *Art of Love*, ii, 467–88). Here, too, social life starts
with the erotic encounter between man and woman, before the art of love. But
what for Lucretius was a fatal deviation from the state of nature becomes for
Ovid the development of an increasing complexity and elegance of manners,
of which love in a city is the crowning achievement. Human sociability is the
creation of Venus. And the history of human beings is the history of how their
sexuality became sensuality.

We could add that the history of the Romans is the history of how their
sexuality became sensuality. In his memorable comparison between the origins
of Sparta and the origins of Rome, Plutarch insists on the difference between
Lycurgus' mission and Numa's. Whereas the Spartan lawgiver had to remedy
the rakishness of a population already enervated by *malakía* (the Greek equivalent of *mollitia*), the first king of Rome faced the opposite challenge. The
Romans of the first rudimentary community founded by Romulus were
soldiers, and overly harsh, coarse and violent: he had to soften them up, to
make them more *malakoí* (*Numa*, 8, 1 and 23, 6). Following the events of the
mythical phallus that fathered Romulus and Remus (or, in a different version,
the seduction of a Vestal Virgin) and then the belligerent abduction of the
Sabine women, Numa started the psychosomatic re-fashioning of the Romans,
who were to learn how to enjoy many pleasures, from eroticism to cuisine.

Mollitia or *malakía*, therefore, meant culture, and, above all, culture of the
body. When compared with the rude, robust and rustic body of the original
Roman, the Augustean citizen's sober, athletic and elegant body, distinguished
by a tan, impeccable hygiene and careful but not excessive attention, corresponds to a degree of softening which is still compatible with health, good
looks and, above all, masculinity. As we shall see in a minute, Ovid is almost
pedantic about the fine line of gender demarcation. But *mollitia* or *malakía* also
meant culture of the soul, or, as I would prefer to say, education and domesti-
cation of the whole person, which is made of body and habits. For Ovid, as we
have seen, tender voluptuousness acts on the ferocious souls of the natural men,
transforming not merely their physical fitness, but also their life (*Art of Love*, ii,
467–88, quoted above). In Lucretius' narrative, the discovery of sex affects
men's entire existence, because by feeling new, attractive sensations they will
change their habits, and those new mores will in turn modify their bodies. By
getting used to even temperatures, more digestible food and erotic delights,

they will acquire different desires and grow accustomed to a higher threshold of pleasure and pain. Numa's reworking of the Roman character, again, starts with the corporeal experience of pleasurable sensations, an experience which is repetitive and thus apt to fashion the character. In this materialistic and cultural vision of human evolution, men do not adapt to a competitive environment: quite the opposite. They find out how to adjust that inhospitable milieu to their changing self – their habits, their bodies. And this *trouvaille* occurs thanks to women and their contagious softness.

Mollitia means culture, but it also means femininity. The commencement of *mollescere*, we have said, is what women bring to history through sexual contact, which for men is indeed predatory, but also voluptuous – a *blanda voluptas* in Ovid's words. The softening up of thick skin, hard muscles and rigid joints comes with the cosiness of heated homes and cooked dinners. Females like comfort and create it, introduce men to the pleasures of the senses and are, indeed, juicy, mushy and pulpy, in their own exemplary bodies. As we have seen, boys with their womanly limbs are warm and humid, and old men with their limp penises are unmanly; women, it goes without saying, are the archetype of moisture and sponginess. Following the *Ars*, a *vir* must therefore be moderate in the care (*cultus*) of his appearance and leave young women to the more extreme forms of ornament, which on a man's body would take the civilising work of Venus to the wrong side of the border between the male and the female. Girls should be aware: a suitor with an overly groomed hairstyle and an entirely perfumed body is displaying an exuberant and therefore feminine sensuality, and – the poet warns his feminine readership – he undoubtedly has more lovers than you. The *Art of Love* is, amongst other things, a handbook for the identification and definition of gender. One might say that the *vir* must be like pasta: *al dente* and never soggy.

Is there a model for manliness that would be just right? Yes: it is the poet. When in love, a poet becomes the most cultured suitor, and a perfect example of the carefully measured softness on the spectrum of civilisation and, therefore, of gender. His placid art makes him tender to the right degree (*Art of Love*, iii, 545). Venus, the softest (*mollis*) divinity of them all (ii, 565) and Cupid himself, that soft and chubby little boy (*mollis Amor*), represent the extreme of the *cultus* which has slowly amended the rugged simplicity of the primitive Romans (iii, 113–32). Although he is languorous enough to create the misunderstanding against which Catullus rebels with such vehemence, the poet is still very much a *vir*. He is the type of man who approaches femininity to the point where he borders on adopting its manners in order to seduce women, but he never imitates them entirely.

We can compare the learned lover to two opposite extremes. On the one hand, let us remember the boys from Ithaca, the suitors of Penelope who spend days eating and drinking at Odysseus' expense (not to mention their sex with the servants) while waiting for their beloved to make a decision. This is not a rape like that of the Sabine women, but we are not very far from it. There is no poetry here, no praise and self-effacement. Gifts are still cattle, not tender verses. The young men feel only the most primitive sensation of softness: in the presence of Penelope their knees go limp. Their desire for that woman, who is not an interchangeable mate, is physical and yet it is seen (by the poet) as an attack of flexibility, so to speak, to their joints. Poetry is not pornography. On the other hand, let us think of the *cinaedus*. This man is effeminate in every sense, from the immaculate skin to the flamboyant and transparent tunics, from the artful hairstyle to the affectation of his gestures. He is the most sensual man there is, and his boundless and indiscriminate lasciviousness makes him desire both women and men, as though he has absorbed both the feminine *mollitia* of Venus and the infantile *mollitia* of Cupid. The mimicry of a *mollis* appears to be the culmination of a woman's *dira libido*, that sensuality which a permanently humid, and thus insatiable, body can feel as infinite pleasure and inexhaustible desire.

The *cinaedus* is an extreme expression of Roman cultural history. It is also a paradoxical expression, because its model is Greek (Dupont and Eloi, 2001), and the *cinaedus* – using all of his person, habits and body – subverts the very values that made Rome great. The violent, virile and hirsute warrior of Romulus' time has had to come to terms with femininity, eroticism, conviviality and pleasure. He has had to accept a degree of gentrification and become a little more polished and cultured. But just look where this fatal *mollescere* ends up: in languor and depilation. The traditional narrative of the increasingly decadent behaviour of the Republic and of its resulting decline (a way of telling the history of Rome that can be found in Sallust, Livy and, later, St Augustine) implies the idea of a loss of virility. We shall not be surprised to find unbridled and theatrically transsexual hedonism at the heart of biographies and portraits of the emperors.

To start with, Julius Caesar features in Suetonius with a reputation for having been, as a boy, the lover of King Nicomedes of Bithynia. Nicknamed 'the Queen', he is pictured in a parody of a wedding feast as the young bride, dressed up for the part and reclining languorously next to the king on the banquet couch. Apart from this story, in which the boy lost his virginity, adult Caesar was also famous as a dandy and seducer of famous women. Always very fastidious about his person, he wore a toga with long fringed sleeves, which was his own creation. He combed his few surviving hairs meticulously, and, rather pathetically, drew them towards the front of his head. Troubled by his baldness in Suetonius' account, he particularly prized, among the honours the Senate had voted for him – and which were to prove fatal – the right to wear a crown of laurels. Finally, like every other *cinaedus*, Julius Caesar removed all the hair from his skin (Suetonius, *Julius Caesar*, 45, 52).

'How could you distrust a man who parts his hair with one finger', Cicero asked himself, 'and think that he could overturn a republic?' (Plutarch, *Life of Caesar*, 4). Caesar could deceive with his air of *mollis*; political ambitions require tenacity and aggression, unlike personal wealth, which is clearly associated with lasciviousness. But Cicero failed to notice what is clear in Suetonius' shrewd portrayal of Caesar: the challenge of a new form of power. Caesar offered the image of frightening harshness, strenuous physical resistance and an iron discipline, but these traits of character were now compatible with an equally exemplary sensuality. An untiring adulterer, he came under the category of vain and promiscuous man. Without fear of corrupting them, he granted his very loyal and vigorous soldiers moments of absolute sexual licence, arguing that they could fight with the same vigour even when covered with perfume. The Roman legionaries under the orders of a leader obsessed with the myth of Alexander the Great no longer had any fear of femininity.

PAEDERASTY AND PUBERTY

In the Greek and Roman world, men chased after both women and boys, for the experience of an optional *vel* (choice) rather than of a puritanical *aut aut* (either/or). As Kenneth Dover has shown in his now classic work, *Greek Homosexuality* (1978), the reality of this practice and, above all, the value attributed to it must be seen within specific social contexts. It is nevertheless the case that a wide variety of sources demonstrate its obvious and widespread presence. The possibility and the plausibility of a desire unrestricted by gender characterised ancient sexuality, from the characters in Plato's dialogues to Lucretius, who considered the female body and the feminine body of boys to be alternatives, and from the versatile Catullus to Ovid himself. This can be interpreted as a cultural and ideological indifference to the specificity of gender, as though female and male were not relevant criteria in the choice of an object of erotic desire. This is the position taken by David Halperin (1994) when he refuses to apply the notion of homosexuality to the ancient world.

What some historians call bisexuality (Cantarella, 1988) while others actually refuse to identify as a type of sexuality (Dupont and Eloi, 2001) proves to be a paradoxical extension of sexual dimorphism. Women and boys could be considered interchangeable because of their similarity and because of the extraordinary difference between the sexes, when females and males reach their maturity. This difference affected all aspects of biological and social life, even the various phases in the development of a 'man'. A boy was analogous to a woman, and therefore pederasty was not so different from heterosexuality. For this reason it was paradoxically acceptable. We shall examine why.

For a boy under the age of puberty and thus lacking semen and, for the ancients, erotic sensations, it was not a serious matter to be courted. Such boys, according to Ovid, do not feel pleasure (and this is the reason why he says he prefers women, who are sensuous lovers). Being sexually inert, they risk nothing. Adolescents, on the other hand, by becoming capable of making love, acquire a sensibility that makes them vulnerable. The newly discovered desire and pleasure enable them to take part erotically in the sexual act; but, because they respond, they can also be changed by that act. They learn what, how and where to feel, they train their bodies and acquire habits. Sexually alive, they now run the risk of becoming effeminate – which also means remaining infantile.

Once the boy has become a man – hairy, malodorous and easily aroused, producing semen and ejaculating it into another person's body – it is normal for him to desire women or boys with womanly limbs. To desire a *vir*, on the other hand, as if he continued to find pleasure in a receptive sensuality, learnt during puberty, can only mean that the boy has failed to become a proper man. He has become a *male maris*, as Catullus put it (*Poems*, 16, 5). Indeed, only a *male vir* can desire to possess a *vir* (Ovid, *Art of Love*, i, 521–2), and he will do it with the feminine and proverbially insatiable appetite which Aristotle's *Problem* associates with the movement of semen to the rectum and Catullus expresses poetically in the image of voracious buttocks (*culus vorax*; *Poems*, 29; see also 33). Eroticism can take the form of cross-dressing, as in a scene from *La Cage aux folles*: one of the partners takes the part of the woman and even of the bride, relaxing on the bridegroom's lap with a saffron-coloured veil, in a parody of marriage – a parody both exhilarating and monstrous, to which nature refuses the fruits of procreation (Juvenal, *Satires*, ii, 117–40).

There was nothing wrong with an adult male courting boys, as long as those acts – carried out on womanly and sexually malleable limbs – did not compromise development in accordance with nature and future masculinity, by creating the scandalous desire of a *mollis* for a *vir*. This is the sense in which we should interpret the poetic entreaties not to penetrate boys. 'My love and I are yours to command, Aurelius – with the following humble request: if you have ever loved something that has to stay chaste and pure, keep this boy of mine in a like state. I do not fear those who wander about the squares dealing with their own business; it is you I fear, and your punitive penis – a threat to all boys, good and bad' (Catullus, *Poems*, 15, lines 1–10). *Infestus* (hostile, unsafe, dangerous) is the penis that harms the chastity and modesty of Iuventius, a young boy who defends himself even against Catullus' kisses (99). During the extremely sensitive period of adolescence, when the boy becomes hard (*durus*), it is appropriate to protect him even from eunuchs, whom some incorrectly believe to be impotent, but who in fact remain capable of powerful erections if they are operated on after puberty (Juvenal, *Satires*, vi, 376–8).

The fundamental problem is posed by the fact that the transitional process of puberty does not occur instantly but lasts for some years – from the ages of twelve to seventeen (Richlin, 1992a: 37), with progressive and partial transformations. It is during this long period of development that the adolescent finds himself exposed to the danger of becoming effeminate. One of Juvenal's satires portrays a boy who is experiencing problems in getting through this period, because, in hesitating between childhood and incipient virility, he starts to become effeminate: he timidly enters the baths, with his voice broken and his testicles now as large as a fist, but also with his armpits smooth and holding an oil jar in front of his groin, in a vain attempt to hide his already enormous penis (*Satires*, xi, 155–8). The attempt to prolong childhood and resist the relentless change is a theme of classical erotic paederastic literature in Greece and Rome (Richlin, 1992a: 34–44, and 289). The full development of adult males physical characteristics marks the end of paederastic attraction. Careful, boys! Now there are hairs! Once this sign has appeared, a boy becomes a hirsute *vir* or a smooth *mollis*. However, that process of slow and multiple transformation is exactly what makes boys increasingly attractive. The eroticisation of the child's body excites the paederast precisely because that body, still soft, is becoming sensitive and capable of reaction.

These acts, which we would define as sexual abuse, are supposed to contribute to pubertal development. According to Aristotle, girls who are introduced to sex during adolescence become sensual women. One of Martial's epigrams berates his hard-mouthed lover for stealing the soft kisses of Ganymedes. The lover should at least refrain from arousing his penis with his hand. Fingers can do more damage to an organ: they accelerate puberty (*praecipitant virum*). The point of view is that of an admirer of pre-pubescent and pubescent boys, who dreads the final appearance of a beard, body hair and the smell of goat. A medical theory accompanies this advice: 'Nature has divided the male into two parts. One is made for women and the other for men. Take your one.' A seducer, by stimulating a boy's penis, develops the part destined for women and therefore precipitates the appearance of the *vir*. Whereas if he restricts himself to the other part, he preserves the boy's childhood (Martial, xi, 22). Penetration of a boy contributes to keeping him a boy for as long as possible. Conversely, a lover who, like the miserly *mollis*, Virro, enjoys being penetrated, attempts to manipulate the onset of sexual maturity in the opposite direction: he cultivates the childish appearance of a young slave in public and in the dining room, but he uses his now virile body in the bedroom: *et in cubiculo vir, in convivio puer est* (Seneca, *Epistles*, 47, 7).

On reading these various texts, literary as well as medical, one thing becomes clear: the idea that one is homosexual or heterosexual according to whom one finds attractive is not only modern but historically misleading. You have to change perspective and shift your attention from the identity of the body and the other person's gender to your own desire, and from the homo/hetero dilemma to the ancient belief that a boy was 'other' in relation to a man, because of his temperament, warm and very humid, analogous to that of the female.

The ancients agreed that there is a sexual identity – a body and its habits – but they connected it, not with the person who is desired, but with the area in which their own desire was localised in their own bodies. A person who is aroused in his penis with an erection that aims at penetrating a woman or a boy is a virile man. Those who experience an erotic sensation elsewhere, because their semen has gone elsewhere or, more specifically, to places designed for reception – the vagina, the anus – are either women or effeminate men. There was therefore a strong identity, delineated by the anatomy and constructed by habit, but it was an identity centred on what one feels and, to be precise, on what one has learned to feel, physically. The fact that a man is aroused in parts other than the penis, in a non-exclusive manner, does not mean that sexual orientation is only a question of socially constructed gender. It means that sexual habits mature with time and that the body has a history. The fact that this history depends not only on nature, but also, and very much so, on sexual education, that is, on acts experienced at a tender age and repeated, implies that those who feel pleasure in penetrating boys are still virile and perhaps boast about it, but also have to face up to their paedagogic responsibilities.

The relationship of the adult with the *paîs* or *puer* should be seen in the perspective of that complicated development called puberty. Puberty is a more delicate affair for boys than for girls. The male body effectively finds itself exposed to a real dilemma, because of its form. The fact that it has two distinct parts (much more distinct than the female body) provides the realistic possibility of two different developments. Incipient erotic sensitivity can concentrate on the parts around the penis or shift to the receptive parts, creating the various types of sexual pleasure and desire Aristotle speaks of: those who wish to penetrate, those who want to be penetrated and those who are aroused in both places and want both things. Precisely for this reason, men have a responsibility towards the boys they seduce. Their own virility can be shown off with pride and arrogance, but this does not release them from their duty to be aware of what is happening in the relationship and of what are the consequences for the boy. In other words, unless they are unscrupulous cads, they have to care for the boy.

The various ways of morally assessing pederasty and judging it depended on these attitudes. We should recall here the contempt for Timarchus and his succession of partners which Aeschines' speech wishes to instil in the public. Ancient ethics was dominated by the question of the corruption of youth: to ruin the future of an adolescent – whether male or female – by affecting their malleable incipient sexuality constituted an offensive act. Just as a man behaved badly if he seduced another man's daughter or wife (the punishment for which was a symbolic sodomisation that cruelly derided virility used in an abusive fashion), the seducer of boys had to conform to a series of duties and obligations. He could court and love a boy, but he could not affect the physical desire of a *paîs* with impunity. He was supposed to know that pederasty is a sentimental education of the body: it leaves a mark and gives form to a body's pleasures.

A full erotic response by a boy to an adult's love, under the sign of the Celestial Aphrodite, only received unreserved approval in the Athenian aristocratic circles of the palaestra and symposium. But this was the world that developed an art of love – or, rather, an art of mutual loving – between men and boys – an ethics of reciprocity. We should recall that one of Pausanias' arguments in Plato's *Symposium* was the insistence on the moral and intellectual advantage that a lasting relationship can and should provide for the boy who accepts it, and that the latter should only accept it if he does in fact receive that advantage. A casual adult, in search of his own pleasure and indifferent to the good or evil he is causing the object of his attentions, was seen as a vulgar *ĕrastḗs* and had to be rejected. In paederastic interaction 'of high quality', the adult must love the boy and look after his best interests over the long term.

In the Athens of common people who are addressed by orators and appear in comedy, and in the Rome of Catullus and Juvenal, seduction was perceived as corruption from which boys and adolescents of free birth had to be protected. In Athens, there were the restrictions on adult access to schools, of which Aeschines speaks at length in *Against Timarchus*, and in Rome there was the *lex Scantinia* (Dupont and Eloi, 2001: 24–5). The fact that the same type of protection was extended to women was consistent with the system of values, medical theories and preoccupations we have discussed. Puberty had to be treated with respect as it evolved towards two clearly defined sexual identities, *both* threatened by an excess of insatiable feminine desire. Apart from avoiding the obvious disaster of a premarital pregnancy, action was needed to prevent a girl from being transformed into a lascivious woman by precocious sex, whose memory fuels sensuality. In order to avoid these dangers, Numa established the marriage of prepubescent girls who, being intact and pure, would be exclusively moulded sexually and morally by their husbands (Plutarch, *Numa*, 26, 2–3).

A young male cannot successfully get through adolescence and enter adulthood if he takes with him an effeminate body and a female eroticism. He is no longer a boy, who is deliciously *mollis* like Cupid himself, because he is becoming hard (*iam durus*; Juvenal, *Satires*, vi, 377). He no longer resembles a woman, unless he makes improper use of the instruments of *cultus* – makeup, perfumes, combs, transparent tunics and the indispensable pumice stone that makes skin smooth and soft, particularly the skin of the buttocks. The adult *cinaedus* fights the physiological virilisation of his body by wiggling his bottom, cross-dressing and, above all, removing body hair. It is a struggle against time and against the loss of childhood's femininity. Body hair proliferates, the skin dries out and the mature penis is now ready to fill itself up with semen and eject it with pleasure into the other person's welcoming body. If he prefers to remain that welcoming body, as if a boy or a woman, the transformation has not succeeded: he has turned out badly, a *male vir*, a man who desires another man.

We can conclude by asserting without exaggeration that for the ancients puberty produces a transsexual change – a change of gender. It is not, as in Freud's theories of child sexuality, the phallic girl who becomes feminine; it is the boy with the womanly limbs (*puer membris muliebribus*) who transforms into a male. Any attempt to obstruct this metamorphosis and therefore prolong the natural femininity of childhood through an artificial effeminacy would mean going against nature. This is why the language of passivity, which is also ancient, should be used with caution. 'Passive' can suggest something inert, inactive and static. But the man who wishes to be sodomised (*pathicus*) or desires to submit (*ĕpithumeî páscheīn*) is nothing of the kind. He is avid, voracious and quintessentially insatiable. This is what he has become. The relationship between the *ĕrastĕs* and the *ĕrŏmĕnŏs*, or between the *vir* and the *puer,* is not simply asymmetrical; it is powerfully paedagogic. The *paîs* is led in a certain direction. The object of love and desire, he becomes through this experience the agent of a particular kind of love and a particular kind of desire. His activity, sensitivity and sexual intentions are therefore the ones that are selected and cultivated: he learns to love and desire with the part of his body that informs his love and desire. Will he love as a man or as a woman? The more feminine his erotic body, the more imperious and inexhaustible his eroticism.

PART THREE

PERVERSA VOLUNTAS – DEVIANT INCLINATION

CHRISTIAN WATERSHED

It all started with St Paul's letters, particularly the First Letter to the Corinthians. Most of the texts the Church Fathers would write in the coming centuries (particularly in the fourth century, when monasticism developed, with its associated obsession with chastity and virginity) comment on, and prolong, the brief sentences which the apostle addressed to Greeks – namely the Greeks of Corinth – around the first century of the Christian era.

The first crystallisation of a Christian discourse on sexuality occurred on Greek soil, and not in just any city of the Roman Empire, nor indeed in one of its most Hellenised places, but at Ephesus and Corinth, two of the most archaic *póleīs*. Moreover, it occurred not only in the language, but also in the idiom of ancient ethics. Paul of Tarsus, a Jew who spoke and wrote in Greek, travelled around the empire to places where the first Christian communities were being created. In 54 he was in Ephesus. There was a particularly active group at Corinth, and it was riven by disagreements and conflicts. Its members sent him a series of letters posing the question: is it appropriate to get married? Or, to be more precise, is it appropriate for a Christian to get married? This was associated with other questions: is it appropriate to remain married, if one is already married at the time of conversion? Is it appropriate to give one's daughters in marriage?

Now we can imagine this very question being formulated, in Platonic language, as the well known expression, *ei gamĕtĕŏn* ('if one must marry'), since the matrimonial dilemma had a long tradition in classical ethics. In the cultural memory of these converted gentiles, who anxiously questioned the apostle, the choice between an active life or a contemplative one was always of fundamental importance. Domestic responsibilities had always seemed to be in conflict with intellectual asceticism. Philosophy and family were two orders of incompatible commitments. It was therefore quite natural that they reformulated that doubt in their own religious context.

St Paul wrote back from Ephesus in oracular mode, with short and antithetical sentences. Marriage is a good; virginity is better. Those who marry occupy themselves with things of the world, and those who don't marry occupy themselves with the matters of the Lord, 'for it is better to marry than to burn' (I Corinthians, 7: 9).

The essential message of the reply is contained in three concepts. The first is that there is a model of heroic existence for Christians, in which time is entirely devoted to God. The second is that desires and pleasures of the flesh, which include those of sex, come into conflict with this devotion and distract those who give in to them from the uninterrupted attention that God merits and demands. Therefore, ideally, devotion to God should be exclusive. The third is that the ardour of desire, which is the fruit of original sin, constitutes a permanent threat to the attention that must be paid to God. This is why God Himself invented marriage in order to restrict promiscuity and provide a dedicated space and time for sex. This is a less heroic life, but still basically a good one.

The founding words of the Christian discourse on sexuality emerged in the form of a reply to a Greek question. However, the reply created a complete break with the past, an immense shift. Firstly this was because Paul was Jewish, secondly because he was concerned with founding a community, and thirdly because Christ had never attributed great importance to sex, except in a paradoxical manner and as part of what might be called a counterculture. The reply of the Hellenised Judaism which we call Christianity to the question of the appropriateness of marriage created a new ethical landscape (Boyarin, 1993).

A GREEK QUESTION AND A CHRISTIAN REPLY

It was marriage that posed the fundamental problem for Christians of the first generation in the years around AD 60, and especially for converted gentiles. They were not so much concerned about sex itself or lust, but rather about the long-term relationship between a man and woman, which creates the space and time for a family and domestic life in all its social, sexual, economic and emotional aspects. The uncertainty of the Christians of Corinth over marriage was, above all, a doubt over the compatibility between living their new religion to the full and living in the world in accordance with norms and values which, for them, were traditionally embodied in the family, as we have seen in the previous chapters. Sex was a component of the marital state, a moment in that life-project which consisted of forming a couple so as to have children, creating a community and managing its assets. The children, in turn, would marry, and other houses and economies would multiply. Marriage was a genealogical operation, a projection of oneself into the future.

The householders – men who principally belonged to the cultured and rich elite of Greek cities – were the ones who posed the question of how they should live their new identity. Did it still make sense for them to maintain that life-project, which was such a commitment, involved such attention to external assets and required such trust in the future of this world, when Jesus had asked his first followers in Palestine to abandon everything and follow him? Was it rational to procreate and therefore invest in a future to be lived in contemporary society, when they were awaiting the imminent return of the Messiah and the advent of the Kingdom of Heaven? It is not easy to imagine the mood of these impatient men, in the exaltation of their new faith. These men were in a hurry, now that they had been converted to a subversive religion that actually promised them regeneration and an eternal life of absolute beatitude in a heavenly kingdom at the antipodes of human society. Having just made such a radical decision, they were ready for anything.

There were cultural reasons for this impatience. Two heterogeneous universes and two orders of arguments and emotions converged in the conversion of gentiles to Christian doctrine. On the one hand, they were fascinated by an experience which came from the desert and distant villages between the River Jordan and the Dead Sea, and, on the other, they adopted a philosophical language at the heart of their own cherished tradition.

As reflected in the first drafts of the various lives of the founder which would later become the gospels, Christ's words invited the first communities to think – and to live – by overturning the values of their own morality and abandoning their own customs. Jesus preached that we must forgive our enemies, that the last shall be first and that it will be easier for a camel to pass through the eye of a needle than for a rich man to enter the Kingdom of Heaven. With its parables, hyperboles, subversion and paradoxes, the language of Jesus of Nazareth shattered the whole way of being in the world and the way people related to time, to the body and to things. However, example was even more imposing than the words. This was particularly true of sexual matters, which he referred to in his preaching in passing, without attributing great prominence to them. Jesus, a man, abstained from marriage and sex, but, in the name of love, he pardoned a woman's adultery. The gospel broke with Jewish culture and posed a radical challenge to the world of late antiquity. We are talking here of the *traditional* Greek custom, which was characterised by the great store it set by procreation in the city and wealth in this world, and by a merciless intolerance of female extramarital sex.

The men of whom we are speaking were not just citizens who, within that cultural context, were simply immersed in a collective social imaginary. They belonged to the elite of Corinth and Ephesus, and it is therefore reasonable to suppose that they had a knowledge of philosophy. A certain familiarity, even just a superficial one, with Plato, the Stoics or Diogenes Laertius' *Lives of the Philosophers* would inevitably have taught them to despise ordinary forms of life and to consider marriage and the 'universe of pots and pans' to be a highly unpropitious condition for authentic devotion to a sublime ideal. As has already been noted, the question of whether it is appropriate to marry had a long pedigree. It arose from a fundamental and clearly male diffidence towards domesticity, with its toing and froing and its responsibilities, which are so harmful to the *schŏlē*, intellectual *otium*. This is what might be called the preliminary question in ancient ethics: what kind of life should one choose, and how should one use one's time, that is, oneself? We have returned to the category of ideas we explored in the first part of this book: human desire for external goods and physical pleasure tends towards constant repetition, because it is insatiable, and you therefore need to take a radical, *a priori* decision to avoid being carried away on its flood. You need to choose another existence, that of spiritual goods and intellectual pleasures.

This is what gave rise to an improbable encounter. A model of eccentric existential experimentation originated from the fishing villages of the Middle East and spread around the Roman Empire, and in the Greek cities it encountered a highly developed ethical system with which it could resonate and from which it could draw strength, which led to an immediate reform of daily life. Spurred on by Christ's exotic example and their own more demanding morality, the gentiles who converted to Christianity found themselves in an unprecedented situation of ethical and psychological hybridisation. The anxiety was entirely theirs. 'You ask me . . .', Paul wrote to the Corinthians. From the very beginning, the Corinthians' questions brought up the cultural and behavioural pattern which, in the centuries to come, pagans would find so striking: the passion for asceticism. When it came to choosing between their current vexed existence in an earthly city and a radiant and joyful future in the city of God, the converts had no doubts and wished to lose no time. The apostle reacted calmly to this anxious impatience. St Paul held to an extraordinarily strategic argument in the face of their ascetic haste and double fundamentalism.

The Christian shall leave his mother and father, and join with his wife to become one flesh. This intimacy mysteriously prefigures the union between Christ and the Church (Ephesians, 5: 31–2). Marriage is therefore a good. The Christian, as the apostle stated in the First Letter to the Corinthians, can choose freely between taking a wife and remaining celibate, and between marrying off his daughters or keeping them virgins. However, anyone who marries undertakes a commitment to a lasting and monogamous relationship, made up of a mutual sexual availability. Those who marry agree to offer their bodies for their partner's desire. The categorical condemnation of adultery, divorce and homosexuality defines a single legitimate space for sex. And, once entered into, this contract becomes binding both for the woman *and for the man*. Marriage is therefore a good in as much as it excludes both those forms of sexual promiscuity, which St Paul associated with the gentiles, and those practices of separation and second marriages which the Jews also accepted. Christian marriage does not allow for *pŏrneía* (prostitution) and *akrasía* (incontinence). It offers an alternative to lasciviousness, excess, physicality and incontinence. It reduces sexual commerce to an exchange between two persons. However, marriage is a costly and compromising option, because, once marital responsibility has been taken on, the married person is duty-bound to deal with the consequences. According to St Paul, family life is full of anxieties, predicaments and anguish. Chastity is better, because it avoids them.

St Paul's rhetorical strategy responded to two aims. On the one hand, just twenty years after the crucifixion of the religion's founder and in a state of uncertainty over the date of his return, it was necessary to protect the early communities of converts from the inevitable demographic extinction that would be caused by an excess of ascetic zeal. Virginity and perfect chastity could have destroyed the Christian movement before it was properly born. It was therefore a 'yes' to the Christian family and the procreation of Christians: marriage is a good. On the other hand, the apostle had to allow for the neophyte's desire to forge for himself a strong identity in the likeness of the son of God. Christians can accede to the supreme success of imitating Christ and to achieving perfect happiness through the heroic relinquishment of pleasures which appear derisory when compared with those that will be gained. Hence a 'yes' also to an aristocratic ideal of virtue, which is open to everyone and for which everyone can compete: virginity is best.

The most striking aspect of St Paul's position is its moderation. To understand this, we need to consider the culture in which he was brought up: Hellenised Judaism. It is well known that Jewish thought remained generously open to the experience of marriage and procreation. The thought of the rabbis, who were developing their ideas at the same time as the Church Fathers, acknowledged the unarguable value of conjugal love. St Paul himself identified a 'carnal Israel', when distancing himself from that world in order to theorise the Christian breakaway. 'Carnal Israel' remained loyal to the Old Testament, and a 'spiritual Israel' embraced Christ's message and started to change. This distinction was taken up by St Augustine, who added a moral significance and accused the Jews of being entangled in matters of the flesh.

St Paul was the decisive interpreter of the Christian innovation. He was the one who irreversibly consolidated the idea that the teachings of Jesus of Nazareth broke with the Law, the Temple and the chosen people. He was the one who gave a voice to Christian cosmopolitanism and to the unrestricted and boundless extension of the privileged identity of the children of God. The foundation of a spiritual and not carnal Israel meant rejecting all the indicators and specific characteristics that tie an individual to a community and to a particular culture. The spirit is transcultural and universal. It is in the context of this project that we have to interpret the refusal to observe the proscriptions relating to food and to the Sabbath, as well as the general rejection of the literal truth of the Old Testament. Christians are citizens of the city of God. Now 'flesh' means that being-in-the-world which defines an individual's immersion in his or her own environment. Flesh means contingency, accepted and experienced: social status, gender, the more immediate relationships, conventional norms, the mother tongue and the daily humdrum. Flesh is the body which lives that entanglement, complies with it and even desires it. Flesh is marriage, which can be defined as a blanket 'yes' to the world of the here and now. If the Christian spirit, with its universalistic ambitions, yearns for an absolute transcendence, it is only logical that virginity really is the most favoured choice.

Yet St Paul asserts that marriage is a good. He refuses to go along with the frenzied zeal of Greek converts. They are the ones who are concerned about whether one should marry (*ei gamĕtĕŏn*). They are the ones who wish to follow Christ's message to the letter, and St Paul replies in the manner of Jesus: render unto your wives that which is theirs. If you have chosen the flesh, you must be carnal. Return to making love after periods of abstinence. Give in to your spouse's desire. And this applies to you, women, naturally subject to your men, but also to you, men, who have chosen to be married. Of course, St Paul understood the Greek question of choosing how to live, and he responded with the Jewish concept of the 'undivided heart', a concept that came close to the classical idea of an uninterrupted contemplative life (Brown 1988). But he also responded with fundamental respect, if not wholehearted sympathy, for the passion for married life. More than anything else, this ambivalence reflects his cultural complexity.

If we accept this historical sketch of the meeting between Christian teachings and the converted Greek elites, we see how this process of dissemination around the Roman Empire, which we generally call 'Christianisation', owed a great deal to ideas about sex – the terrain on which it engendered the initial enthusiasm. St Paul's proselytism had to confront the ambitions and expectations created both by the evangelical paradigm and the classical education typical of the upper classes of the period. The fervour of the Corinthians and Ephesians was nourished by the unexpected resonance between various forms of asceticism born in completely different contexts: the daily life of Palestine and the philosophical reflections of classical Athens. This fervour could have relegated early Christianity to the marginality of a fundamentalist sect incapable of regeneration. He needed all his rhetorical skills to channel that ardour in the right direction without extinguishing it.

The sexual metaphor of the relationship with God was already emerging in St Paul's eschatological language: that eroticisation of eternal beatitude, which would soon culminate in the mystical marriage between the soul and Christ, a dominant theme for the Church Fathers. This way of talking about the renunciation of the pleasures of the world in positive, even rousing and erotic terms was profoundly similar to the Platonic metaphor of spiritual procreation and intellectual pleasure, which was the only truly intense and pure one. From the very beginning, we can detect the emergence of a language of divine love that is infinitely preferable to the sorry loves of the flesh; and this language was undoubtedly familiar to educated pagans, given the popularity of vivid Platonic images. Indeed, we can imagine how St Paul was able to address the Greeks, whose way of thinking was permeated by such metaphors, when he evoked the sexualisation of abstinence as a promise of happiness, which created formidable hopes and passionate faith. The apostle appropriated the extraordinary conceptual somersault whereby chastity is not the most virtuous choice but rather the most sensuous. The enjoyment of God is erotic: this was the power of Christ's message.

Precisely because it was such an attractive desire for those he engaged with, St Paul could not inflame it; he had to contain and redefine it. Thus he accompanied his measured evocation of the mystical marriage constituted by the perfection of virginity with praise for carnal marriage, which is imperfect and restless, but nevertheless indispensable to the survival of the church (*ĕkklēsía*). In other words, the enthusiasm for renouncing the flesh constituted an excessive and potentially suicidal passion for the gentiles who converted to Christianity and therefore became the protagonists of Christianisation. It was probably the most profound reason for Christianity's success and the greatest threat to its existence.

St Paul's words to the Corinthians would have an unchallenged theological influence, right up to the encyclicals on virginity of the twentieth century. Any reconstruction of the history of Christian thought on sexuality involves following the destiny of those words in an uninterrupted tradition of comment and interpretation.

'HE THAT IS MARRIED CARETH FOR THE THINGS THAT ARE OF THE WORLD' (I CORINTHIANS 8: 33)

We cannot find the slightest allusion to a kind of intrinsic negativity towards sex in St Paul's arguments. Sex is not an absolute evil, as though the body, or matter, were inherently impure: this would become the view of the Encratites and of the Manicheans, which the Church Fathers, from Tertullian to St Augustine, would have to resist. For St Paul, sex is a relative good, and it is only relative in that it interferes with the superlative good of thinking always and only of God. Paradoxically, sex is an ill – in spite of being a good – only in the sense that it is an inferior good. Ultimately, sex is time, and time wasted on the flesh, which means, on the world and on oneself rather than on being immersed in the consideration of God. Sex is another concern.

Saying this does not involve minimising the importance of sensuality in Christian morality – through diseroticisation of the sexual, one might say. Quite the contrary, a dialectics develops, from the creation of man in the image and likeness of God, through the 'fall', which is simply the destruction of the privileged relationship with the Father and the loss of likeness, to culminate in redemption – the recovery of the human in a new sacredness, made possible by the incarnation of the Son. Christ is the second Adam, who reconciles sinful humanity with its creator in his double nature of word become flesh. This reconciliation consists of the attempt to conduct an angelic life in the world, in other words, a life that strives to rediscover and bring back the lost intimacy with God through almost uninterrupted prayer, persistent reading of the sacred texts, and charitable works. It is no longer the earthly paradise and it is not yet the Kingdom of Heaven, but it is a state of beatitude and the highest, albeit imprecise, state of beatitude granted to man for his pilgrimage on earth, since the original sin. This is the design, taking form within the history of the world, in which sexuality acquires its perennially troublesome value for Christians.

It is not that the original sin was a sin of lust; it is rather that sexual desire was the symbolic *punishment* that God inflicted on human beings for their first wrongdoing, which was one of arrogance. Sex is the cursed destiny of creatures who have decided that they want to be the ones who choose between good and evil by repudiating their affinity and contiguity with God and therefore their obedience and submission to his will. The libido is the 'corresponding punishment' (*poena reciproca*), as St Augustine called it, the corporeal and illusory preference for the world and for oneself. That rebellious decision in favour of oneself (distinguishing between good and evil, instead of obeying the Father) is repeated with persistent hostility and irony in sexual desire, in other words in the indiscipline of the passions and of certain parts of the body with regard to the only just will, the one that makes us turn to God. Every arousal is a distraction from that which is God. Sex is therefore a symbolic torment in the manner of Ovid's metamorphoses and Dante's talionic or like-for-like punishments for the original betrayal that first Eve, and then Adam, dared to perpetrate against their creator.

So 'flesh' is a synonym for 'world'. The body is understood not just as a thing or receptacle for sensations, but rather as a vehicle of self-interest and a way of using time as though it were one's own. The body is therefore open to the world itself through acts, thoughts and interactions which are alternatives to exclusive attention to God. It is understandable how chastity and virginity become the most effective method for binding to the Lord the sinner who has at last been delivered from his sins, the Adam redeemed in Christ. Those who do not marry can attend to the Lord's business (*měrimna tà toũ kuríoũ, de deo cogitant*). Those who do not marry can maintain their whole selves – body, soul and time – in a constant and intense relationship with the Lord. They can pray, invoke, praise, give thanks, fast, sing, meditate, read, interpret, teach, preach and suffer martyrdom. St Paul did not say, 'those who do not marry avoid touching, kissing and penetrating dirty and impure bodies; those who do not marry abstain from an excessive pleasure or insatiable desire'. He defined virginity and chastity in existential and positive terms – in terms of what is made possible by the renunciation of a certain type of care, looking after the affairs of a husband or wife. All the time that is gained goes into concentrating on the affairs of the Lord, from prayers to sacrifice. Chastity is a form of daily life – a routine that revolves around a single centre of attention. The monastery, convent or coenobium (which comes from the Greek for 'shared life', *koīnŏs bĭŏs*) would become the ideal place, being designed to make such an existence possible.

The Christian discourse on sexuality dwells with a cruel abundance of detail on the comparison between family life and a life devoted to the Lord.

St Gregory of Nyssa, one of the Greek Church Fathers who contributed most to these reflections, provided a memorable depiction of domestic cares in his treatise *On Virginity* (*c.* AD 371). The only way in which this tiresome, oppressive, anxiety-ridden life can be described is by borrowing the language of tragedy, the language of that theatrical genre which has always dealt with the probability of misfortune and the imminence of death. The only way to represent the figures of man – and especially woman – in a family is as tragic characters obliged to experience an incurable restlessness. Marital life will never bring happiness, even in its most promising version, with a young couple which has health, beauty, wealth, prestige and children. The young husband sensuously and admiringly contemplates the face and flowing locks of the splendid girl he has married. He enjoys her presence, but then a terrible thought suddenly insinuates itself into his mind and destroys his pleasure. These cheeks, these lips, these eyelids will one day be repellent bones. This beauty will pass and end in nothing. This very presence cannot last, and already the thought predicts the absence and loss; it contaminates the current wellbeing with the suffering of a future death. Death does not announce itself with specific signs, but quite the opposite, it is always to be feared as imminent, given the uncertainty of the future (*On Virginity*, iii, 3). Family life is a mixed existence, which is ambivalent and full of contradictory experiences that become confused. Tears and laughter, sadness and joy are inseparable, given that approaching death leaves its mark on all pleasures (3, 20–4). Who could ever relax and enjoy and trustingly savour the delights of this life, when fear of change keeps us in a state of continuous unease (4, 15–18)?

Fear of death and of seeing one's loved ones die dominates family life. The marital bed can suddenly transform itself into a funeral bed. Giving birth often becomes a dramatic event. Even if the mother and new-born baby survive, we are immediately troubled with concerns over the child's growth, health and future. A married woman lives in a state of terror and anguish over everything that could happen to her little ones and, what is more, over anything that might deprive her of her husband. As she is not mistress of herself, but by nature dependent on the man who dominates her and is responsible for her, as St Paul asserted, a wife trembles at the idea of losing the centre and support of her existence. Hence she stares constantly at the entrance to their home, as she fretfully awaits his return. Alert to the slightest murmur, her heart stops in fright at hearing an almost imperceptible rustling: is it bad news?

A wife's condition makes her highly vulnerable and exposes her to the risk of solitude, which isolates her socially as well as emotionally. All this can be so extreme that she is not able to control her fears, and she lives in permanent expectation of the worst. According to the Stoic tradition, fear is an excessive and overhasty evaluation of a future evil, whereas courage is the ability to correct that overevaluation and reduce the impact of the danger.

In this portrayal provided by St Gregory, a married woman is presented as a deeply apprehensive figure, prey to the incessant and overly rapid movements of her heart and thoughts: she is always afraid of the possibility of an imminent disaster, even when there is no good reason. This obsessive foreboding, usually based on error, is inherent in her condition. The primary cause is her body. Gregory held a theory of procreation by which pieces of a mother's heart are detached and go to each of her children; this is why she empathises with everything her children feel, whether it is pleasure or suffering. A mother shares all their sensations and therefore finds herself with a multiple sensitivity, a kind of chorus of emotions. Apart from the physiology, there is also the choice of family life, with its many demands and inevitable consequences (varying from the dependency of one's life on the husband to a myriad daily concerns), which causes the debilitating anxiety that only a fool could define as happiness.

Domestic life, this wellbeing made up of loving relationships, calm and security, proves to be a drama at whose core the woman is endlessly torn by competing demands, just like a tragic character. Whom does the wife depicted by Gregory remind us of? As she awaits her husband's return with her heart in her mouth, it must be Deianeira. In her awareness of the void into which she will fall if her man, who for her is everything, were to abandon her, she evokes Medea's desperation. The devastating pain of losing a child echoes Clytemnestra's calculating fury. The subversion of marriage, which transforms itself into a funeral, awakens our memory of Greek culture, and indeed the memory of Gregory and his readers; it reminds us of the scenes of sacrifice and murder that turned the wedding feast upside down, as in the death of Iphigenia.

Gregory uses the sensational drama of the tragic style with expressive intent, but, as a considerable expert on Platonism and Aristotle, he also develops an ethical argument. Marriage creates, as we have said, a bond and a network of relationships made up of the responsibilities, commitments, tasks and concerns in which we find ourselves entangled day after day. Marriage creates a life in which the external goods of health, wealth, beauty and reputation, amongst others, acquire a predominant importance for us, for our own peace of mind. In other words, marriage creates dependency and anxiety. If we consider the wife and mother, we find that everything escapes her control; everything that concerns her is in the hands of what the ancient poets and philosophers called *túchē*, the set of events on which our happiness depends but over which we have no control. In conclusion, domesticity culminates in alienation from the world and in insecurity. In the home, women experience the most extreme subordination and loss of freedom.

Gregory of Nyssa appears only to see the distressing and oppressive aspects of the domestic universe. There is no charity in his conjugal tragedy, and there is no appreciation of the 'labour of love' and the cherishing and beneficial care, much to the enduring embarrassment of Christian scholars of his thought. In this context, a woman's renunciation of sex and maternity is the intelligent pursuit of ataraxy (a state of serene calmness). The emotional, generous and gratifying aspects of looking after others are entirely shifted towards God.

HE THAT IS UNMARRIED CARETH FOR THE THINGS THAT BELONG TO THE LORD (I CORINTHIANS 8: 32)

The virgin is free, happy and serene. Without children who risk becoming orphaned, sick or delinquent, without a mortal husband who might never pass through that doorway again and leave her a widow, and without a home that could be ruined at any moment, a virgin can savour the true happiness of this world. She is serene because, being independent and not subject to a spouse, she has nothing to lose and nothing to fear. And this has nothing to do with her being in a state of destitution; quite the contrary, she can truly possess forever the presence of an immortal spouse, who is never absent and shall never abandon her. Virginity achieves what human marriage pathetically claims to be (Gregory of Nyssa, *On Virginity*, iii, 8, 13–25).

Perceiving sex in terms of self-orientation, one's use of time or, to put it another way, 'commitment', does not mean forgetting one's erotic nature. All this 'thinking of God' unfolds within a state which is not only physical and mental, but also emotional. This 'caring for God' is love and seduction: those who do not marry in effect attempt to *please* the Father. The most paradoxical language of Christian ethics can already be found in the writings of St Paul: the rhetoric of the mystical marriage between the individual soul and the godhead. In his Fifth Letter to the Ephesians, St Paul interprets the joining together of a man and a woman in one flesh (*una caro*) as an allegory that prefigures the relationship between the Church and Christ: an impenetrable mystery. A collective person, the Church, is a spouse, who is indissolubly bound by an intimate, physical and sexual relationship to the youngest member of the Trinity.

In the third century, Origen attributed an allusive meaning to the biblical text, particularly in his *Comment on the Song of Songs*. The language of love and the sensual celebration of the bride prefigure the relationship between the soul and God after the arrival of Christ. This is a relationship based on desire, admiration and sensuousness.

Methodius of Olympus and Gregory of Nyssa would enlarge upon this theme with a profusion of variations. They borrowed from the traditions of the Bible, St Paul and Origen, but also from the language of Plato and Neoplatonism. In this metaphoric representation of subjectivity, the soul, Psyche, is a paradoxical female body ready to be inseminated and to generate thoughts and discourse. Diotima's speech in the *Symposium* discloses the similarity between knowledge and love, basing its arguments precisely on this perception of the soul as an incorporeal body, capable of procreating living beings of an intellectual nature. The very famous maieutic scene in *Theaetetus* is based on the same analogy. Socratic midwifery works with male souls rather than with feminine bodies. Through his questioning Socrates helps young men bring into the world the beliefs that they have conceived and now carry.

At the same time as St Paul was theorising the Christian revolution while travelling between Ephesus and Corinth, in Egypt another great Jewish philosopher was commenting on the Old Testament from within it. Philo of Alexandria read and wrote in Greek. He rethought the Scriptures in Plato's language and idiom. He was also, perhaps, one of those who most fervently enlarged upon the maternal metaphor. The entire dynamics of the relationship between the individual and God, and all the mystery of prophecy (fundamental themes in the Jewish religion) were for Philo part of a kind of erotic and fertile attraction between the soul and the divine. The wombs of the soul receive the divine insemination resulting in prophecy. It is as though the Platonic oxymoron of the soul/body and the flesh of Psyche served to express a dualism that attempted to lessen the distance between its various components. The immeasurable distance between the human and the divine is both admitted and denied precisely in the mystical metaphor of the bringing together, the contact and the penetration that sexual intercourse expresses better than any other image.

Returning to the Platonic tradition in the allegorical interpretation of the Canticle, the Greek Church Fathers used sensual love as the dominant metaphor for devotion to God. The parable of the virgins in the Gospel according to Luke (12: 35–8) was also read as an allusion to the loving trepidation of the soul awaiting the adored betrothed who is Christ. Those who do not marry concern themselves with the matters of the Lord and not with those of the husband or wife. Those who do not marry concern themselves solely with things that fully give satisfaction and do not create anxiety. Those who do not marry think about God, as though God were a spouse. Attention to God is erotic time. Virginity is a passion.

MARRIAGE IS GOOD, VIRGINITY IS BETTER

The question to which the apostle replies in the First Letter to the Corinthians with those formulas on which the religion was founded concerned the appropriateness of *getting married* (*ei gamĕtĕŏn*). Marriage is good, but virginity is better. The complexity of the arguments we find in the works of the Church Fathers arises from this initial ambivalence. For a long time, the recognition of an uncontroversial value of marriage as a sacrament remained alien to their reflections. Before St Ambrose and St Augustine brought about a dramatic change in the history of Christian sexuality at the end of the fourth century, the arguments in defence of this choice and its reproductive end were laboriously defensive: marriage is good in the absence of something better.

As in the case of Gregory of Nyssa, some of those arguments appear to have been inspired by a veritable utilitarianism. Beyond good and evil, the question of whether or not one should marry became one of intelligent hedonistic calculations. 'I do not dissuade you from marrying on the grounds that this would be a wrong' – St Paul had claimed – 'but in order to spare you a life full of boredom and torments.' The Church Fathers' dramatic descriptions of the horrors ensuing from sexual union derive from this allusion to the tribulations of domestic life. But how can we reconcile a paradoxically utilitarian asceticism (as though 'for your good' meant 'in your own interests') with the celebration, even in the case of St Paul, of the marital bond as a model for the relationship between the Church and Christ? How can you square the contempt for fertile sexuality between husband and wife with the command in Genesis, 'Be fruitful and multiply'? We should examine a rigorist version of this contradiction.

Marriage is a good, but only second choice when compared with chastity. If it is compared with the ardour of the flesh (*fervor carnis*), marriage is again a good, but should be interpreted as a lesser evil. When he asserted that marriage is a good but virginity is better, St Paul was doing no more than tolerating, permitting and acquiescing to a form of contained sexuality. He did it out of necessity, simply because we are weak and the flesh is stronger. In his advice to the Ephesians and the Corinthians, monogamous marriage only appears desirable as a means 'to work off the ardour of the flesh' (*fervorem carnis despumare*). It is not a good in itself, since such a good is defined as an absolute value, irrespective of any comparison; marriage is better when compared with a torment (*poena*) and as an alternative to the greatest of evils (*pessimum*). It is better to lose one eye than two: this was the logic behind St Paul's indulgence. 'Better' obviously meant 'lesser evil'.

Marriage is a good; virginity is better: these two assertions should be separated, because they derive from two different voices. The first expresses a human opinion, the product of a grudging concession (*invitus indulsit*) to human frailty, whereas the second reflects the word of the Lord and the model the apostle chose for his own life, which invites us to experience marriage as though we were not married and to be like him, a 'eunuch' for God. How can we explain the symbolic association, in the Fifth Letter to the Ephesians, between human marriage and the union of Christ and the Church?

If we put the sexual question into the perspective of human history, we can understand this idea, that Christ became flesh in order to be a second Adam. Christ returns us to our primitive perfection through this 'restitution of the beginning' – of our original state, which was lost as a result of the original sin. With the New Testament we return to the origins, before the events that led to our being driven from the earthly paradise – before the events narrated in the Old Testament. This is why we free ourselves from Jewish culinary taboos and rediscover the freedom to eat what we like, except for blood; this is why we abandon circumcision and restore the wholeness of the flesh. This is why we restore the model of the monogamous heterosexual couple – Adam and Eve – and reject the polygamy permitted at the time of Abraham. Although Adam is a paradigm to be followed because of his monogamy, which mysteriously prefigures the (no less monogamous) union between Christ and his Church, his example is still imperfect when compared with that of his successor. The second Adam is better than the first: not for nothing does the second one come into the world to correct the primordial error committed by the first; it is not without significance that he is celibate, chaste and pure. Christ's virginity represents the absolute perfection, which is to be preferred to the marital union of the earliest progenitors – which was still the lesser evil compared with Jewish promiscuity or polygamy and which prefigured the mutual fidelity of Christ and his Church.

It is Tertullian who offers us this complex commentary on the Pauline texts in his short treatise *On Monogamy* (*c.* AD 214). The striking feature of these arguments, which has been bitterly criticised, is the ambivalence towards sex: marriage is a lesser evil or second-choice good, of course, but also the most powerful metaphor for something that will always be so important to Christianity, the fervent and exclusive union with the divine. The prefiguration of the relationship between Christ and his Church in the Fifth Letter to the Ephesians will always be an obstacle to the absolute belittlement of the sexual union. As an example of a loyal and loving bond, marriage remains a positive model. But we have to insist upon the narrow margin of manoeuvre that makes it possible to assert that marriage is a good, *with a few provisos.*

IT IS BETTER TO MARRY THAN TO BURN

It is better to care for God than it is to care for oneself or one's family. The care of a husband or a wife is, however, preferable to leaving sexual desire to its own devices. Outside marriage, sex is not care; it is fire. It is burning, ardour and flames: the variations on the theme of erotic passion develop all the nuances of the metaphor of fire.

God is like an infinitely wise and infallible doctor. Just as human doctors who care for the body decide upon the dosage of medicines and the extent and method of their operations in relation to the gravity of the illness and its development over time, so the most able of therapists cares for our souls. At the beginning of our life as sinners, immediately after the original sin, God began to cure the disease which consists in the disorder of the passions. In that particular and most critical moment, when human nature was prey to folly and unable to contain the impetus of passion, God instructed the two first sinners: 'Be fruitful and multiply!' At that time there would have been no other remedy for this incandescence. If God had ordered them to abstain purely and simply from lust, his command would have been without effect and would only have aggravated the inflammation. A drastic intervention would have made the fall even more ruinous and would have rekindled the embers of desire. It was not the opportune moment to preach about virginity. But later, when humanity entered a less acute phase, the radical remedy became reasonable.

In this discourse, marriage appears not as a lesser evil, but as emergency aid. Human beings are falling and burning. God, in his infinite intelligence and goodness, catches them and throws them a parachute – or is it a fire extinguisher? 'Be fruitful and multiply.' Marriage, the use of sex for procreation, is nothing more than the instrument God provides for halting the fall and for bringing the fire under control. Marriage was therefore given to us in order to have children, but *much more (pŏllôi dè plĕŏn)* in order to put out the fire of desire, which derives from our nature. St Paul demonstrates this when he advises 'let every man have his own wife', but, instead of justifying this choice in terms of procreation, he specifically states the reason: 'to avoid fornication' (I Corinthians, 7, 2). When he invites the couple to return to their shared life after a period of chastity, it is not in order to have children, but so 'that Satan tempt you not' (I Corinthians 7: 5). Let them marry, the apostle concedes, not so they can multiply, but because they might not be able to maintain their continence.

God allowed humans to put their passion to the work of populating the world. It would, however, be a serious error to think that this end justifies the means to the point of making it valid and admirable. In the first place, the fact that the first progenitors came into this world without sexual intercourse having taken place proves that the creator had no need of sex to achieve his purpose. Sex is not inherently necessary to the appearance and spread of life, and therefore should not be considered its precondition. In the second place, times have changed. Now the earth has been populated and, knowing that this could have been done without sexual procreation, the only reason for agreeing to marriage remains the one that originally was the most important: to eradicate incontinence, debauchery and shamelessness. Sex offers relief to those who wallow in and relish passion, and wish only to live like pigs and destroy themselves in brothels. Marital union liberates us from the baseness and compulsion of sex.

These were the ideas of St John Chrysostom. In his treatise *On Virginity* (*c.* AD 382), this great promoter of asceticism and monastic life reconstructed the history of humanity, which developed from an original virginal condition, fell through sinful event and finally rediscovered the ideal model for a paradisiac life in the perfect chastity of a few heroic individuals. God created man, the creature for whom he had formed the world. He provided man with a helper. Woman should have been this and only this: a presence of support, but certainly not a wife or a lover. Life in the Garden of Eden was a blessed life. As they enjoyed familiarity with God, the happy days flowed smoothly by, like a stream of crystal-clear water. There was no sexual desire, there was no pregnancy, there was no painful childbirth and there was no marriage. There were no cities, houses or work. There were no worries, which we call 'cares'. It was an existence far superior to our own. It was a virginal existence. But they committed sin, and sin has deprived humans of their closeness to God and their uncontaminated virginity, at the same time. As long as they remained insensible to the temptations of the devil and obeyed the Lord, Adam and Eve enjoyed an incomparable luxury, a gift which was like being clothed in gold, like an extremely precious jewel. But, at the moment of the Fall, when they lost everything and found themselves victims of death, malediction, suffering and a life of tribulations, the sinners also lost those clothes and magnificent ornaments. Together with all their other misadventures came marriage, this shabby little mortal garment worthy of a slave. Marriage is the result of disobedience, male-diction and death. Where there is death, there is marriage (St John Chrysostom, *On Virginity*, xiv, 3–6).

IT IS BETTER TO BURN THAN TO MARRY

These texts, which commented upon, returned to and developed St Paul's letters to the Ephesians and the Corinthians, demonstrate the coherence and continuing relevance of those commands. When we read Tertullian, St Gregory, St John Chrysostom and St Methodius, we see how those precepts were linked one to another, and how the apostle's arguments always related back to a conceptual nucleus: perfect chastity is a way of life, and virginity is to care for the Lord. We can also observe that, beyond the question which the Greeks addressed to the apostle – is it appropriate to marry? – Christian philosophers touched upon another question, which is the one that interests us. What is wrong with sex? If we follow our authors word by word, we run through what is effectively an exegesis that remains within the limits of the conjugal dilemma. Yet we perceive a persistent underlying problem, which is more or less explicit. The original sin is not a sexual fault, but sex is sinful. Marriage is a good, and virginity is better, but sex is always misplaced, whether it is marital or extramarital.

We realise that some interpretations of the letters, although referring at all times to the Pauline arguments, misleadingly insist upon abstention from sex even within marriage. St Paul had made it clear that marital sex was a duty, and that both members of the couple are required to concede their bodies to the other's desire. He had also stated how important it is to return to lovemaking after a period of chastity, if this is what either of them wants. For St Paul, that 'burning' which marriage remedies is the suffering resulting from an unsatis-fied desire, the obsessive intensity of the sexual drive. Marriage makes it possible 'not to burn', exactly to the extent that the couple's sexual activity *appeases* their mutual desire. In the Christian writers, however, the 'fire' becomes the promiscuity into which lust would fall, if marriage did not *extin-guish* it, as St John Chrysostom wrote. And, to be consistent, if married life is designed to extinguish desire, it is recommended that, as far as it is possible, married life should involve the renunciation of erotic pleasure.

At the end of the fourth century, Tertullian's rigorist violence could be heard in the words of St John Chysostom. That fire, that ardour from which marriage frees us is nothing more than the craving of the flesh, the ephemeral and volatile desires of beauty and youth (Tertullian, *To a Wife*, 1, 5) and the insa-tiable covetousness of the flesh (Tertullian, *Exhortation to Chastity*, xii, 1). It is the danger of incontinence that justifies marriage as the lesser evil: *quia propter incontinentiae periculum permittitur nubere* (viii, 2). As we have seen, St John Chysostom is not sparing when it comes to displaying his sarcastic contempt for the vulgarity of dirty, bestial and incontinent sexual desire. The Latin *stuprum* and *incontinentia* or the Greek *pŏrnĭa* and *akrasía* describe sex in its crudity, spontaneous brutality and avidity. We should not be surprised, then, that the fervent ascetic from Antioch, who during the same period wrote his treatise *Against the Adversaries of Monastic Life*, should interpret St Paul's writings in such a profoundly anti-marital way. That which is freely available does not excite a strong desire. According to St John, this proverb expresses the truth about marriage. Satisfaction (*apŏlausis*) creates what we call boredom; it weakens ardour to the point that it ebbs away. If, by some chance, the flame of lust is reawakened, then a sexual union can quickly placate it (*On Virginity*, xxxiv, 3–4). Marital sex therefore has a purely anti-aphrodisiacal function. It is designed so as to cool off and enervate desire. The benefit that St Paul attributes to marriage, with his 'it is better to marry than to burn', becomes a benefit exclusively for the ascetic. But this is still not enough. What if, by some chance, the married couple ends up enjoying that daily eroticism which availability and satiety should have cooled off, and achieves a state of lasting incandescence? This would mean that incontinence (*akrasía*), the vice that marriage is supposed to combat, has perversely insinuated itself into marriage itself. When there is an inability to avoid fornication except by continuously making love with one's wife and finding enjoyment in it, then this is a case of incontinence (xxxiv, 6). St John goes as far as distorting St Paul's text, and has him say that returning to making love with one's wife means being a slave to *pleasures* (ibid.).

It is important to see how the containment of sexual excess within marriage changes meaning in this kind of interpretation of the First Letter to the Corinthians. What had been understood as the realisation of a *reciprocal* desire within the continuity of a faithful and intense relationship, in which husband and wife love each other passionately, becomes simply an outlet for the erratic and impersonal urge towards the pleasure of one's own body. The obligation to consent to the spouse's desire in a relationship of exchange and bilateral availability becomes slavery to one's own hedonism or, at the most, slavery to one's own wife. St John Chrysostom cannot accept that St Paul attributed a positive and emotional content to marital sex. The apostle's words seem to him to be a warning against 'enslavement' to one's own enjoyment or another person's desire (xxviii).

For rigorists like Tertullian and St John Chrysostom, desire is always adulterous; lust, or the fervour of one's own flesh, is always egotistical and, when excessive, it scatters here and there, but usually it diminishes within a routine. If habit does not make one frigid, this does not mean that marriage, as a mutual attachment to a single person, is working. Quite the contrary, this means that one of the spouses – the husband – is so excessive in his incontinence that he has to turn to his wife continuously. A marital passion has nothing to do with love – an exceptionally lasting love between two people – but is a kind of monogamous promiscuity in the home. Following this same logic, one would expect a sensuous man to be constantly unfaithful, if not in his deeds, then undoubtedly in his thoughts, given that the Gospel according to Matthew (5: 28) claims that anyone who looks at a woman with longing commits adultery in his heart.

The rigorist distortion of the apostle's words leads, then, to a reversal of his intended meaning. That fire is perhaps preferable to its extinguishment. If getting control of the flames means making love, if one must use pleasure in order to kill the desire, then it is better 'to burn than to marry'. The widow who refuses to take a second husband makes precisely this choice: she prefers 'to burn rather than marry' (*uri quam nubere*, Tertullian, *Exhortation to Chastity*, xiii, 3). Virgins, who are unable to use sexual intercourse to dampen down the flames rising up in their souls, undergo an almost miraculous experience: they have to fight the flames without burning, and they have to contain a fire within themselves without allowing themselves to be consumed by it, as though they were walking on hot coals. No one can survive their clothes catching fire, but virgins actually survive a fire that rages inside them. They contain it and suffer it (St John Chrysostom, *On Virginity*, xxxiv, 4). The greatness of perfect chastity is measured in the heroism and torment of an incandescence for which there is no remedy. He who is unmarried burns.

Christian rhetoric follows a thread of argument that denies any fundamental disgust for sex. Occasionally, however, the network of explanations rips apart and there emerges an incontrovertible repulsion for the thing in itself. But this thing in itself – this very particular desire – is not necessarily analysed, nor is any explanation given for its origin, nature and therefore quality. In St Augustine's thought we find an attempt at a systematic understanding of sexuality, which goes as far as developing a genuine theory of desire.

SENSUALITY AND WILL

In the *City of God*, St Augustine reflects upon the problem of rape suffered by Christian virgins during the persecutions (*City of God*, i, 16, 18–22). He asks what we should think of these women. Are they intact or corrupt? Should they do penance? Does the loss of material virginity interfere with the chance of salvation? Given that Christian thought turns virginity into a question of the soul and not of the body, and of intention rather than unalterable fact, an unde-sired sexual act imposed by violence presents a delicate problem. In the face of carnal violence, which was violence against the Christian identity, primacy has to be given to will and to virtue. However, it has to be asked whether something doesn't really happen within the virgin's soul when the body undergoes aggression which is also a sexual manipulation.

We have already seen the importance the ancients attributed to the idea that sex acts upon the desire of the person who experiences it. This occurs during the development of puberty and, in particular but not exclusively, it threatens the virilisation of boys. Lysias clearly demonstrated this when he reminded his Athenian public of the distinction between violence and adultery: seduction is more serious than rape, because the latter induces the victim to hate its perpetrator, whereas the former corrupts the victim's soul and entraps the victim's desire (*On the Murder of Eratosthenes*, 32–3). The problem that faces St Augustine is the corruption of the soul not only in a complicit relationship, but even in an act imposed by force. Carnal violence seems offensive to him not so much because it degrades the body as because it ensnares the will. Its degree of violence is reflected in the risk of arousal. Almost adopting as a presupposition the widely held Roman belief in the latent sensuality of all women and in their underlying consent to manly impetuousness in spite of any apparent modesty, St Augustine perceived an undesired sexual act as something dangerously desirable. At the very moment in which the body suffers this type of contact, consent might be produced: a sensuality that could be will, and is therefore a sin. The offence is in inducing temptation and creating an immediately pleasurable desire in the victim.

The coexistence of desire and pleasure, in a movement of consent, is the fundamental problem of Christian sexual morality. We can see this in various interpretations of the well-known passage from the Gospel according to Matthew (5: 28): 'whosoever looketh on a woman to lust after her hath committed adultery with her already in his heart' (see also Sissa, 1997). But the fact is particularly evident in the works of St Augustine.

The sexual event takes place in the heart, where desire is satisfied at the very moment in which it appears. This implies a realist conception of phantasms. Placing the act in the inner self, where intention manifests itself, means acknowledging a concrete and effective presence of the psychic representation of the desired object. For Christians, sexual fantasy acquires a new importance. Dreams and imagination become authentic realisations of desire. According to St Augustine, life is all temptation (*tota temptatio*), and an erotic dream allows a man to experience his own impotence in the face of the performative power of desire which declares itself within him. The sex urge is unstoppable in a dream: when it is dreamt, it quickly finds satisfaction – an emission of sperm in response to a visual stimulus. The body does not act on its own. For, if particular visions present themselves to our soul, they do this solely because we allow them to. To dream means to give consent (*consensio*) to images that remain alive in the memory and permit the fulfilment of a pleasure (*delectatio*) and almost an act (*factum simillimum*). The soul perpetrates the turpitudes that images suggest to it up to the emission of the flesh (*usque ad carnis fluxum*), because it approves them in the dream (*Confessions*, x, 30, 41–2). Although unconscious and involuntary, desire that is realised in dreams comes under the category of paradoxical consent, according to St Augustine. The fact that it is realised demonstrates the existence of complicity, a 'yes' that the soul of the sleeping person utters to an object it considers present and real. Because the will, paralysed by sleep, is unable to obstruct the efficacy of the desire, that 'yes' immediately transforms itself into coitus.

The experience of dreams demonstrates how good will is unable to control the representation. This is because sexual desire is deviant will (*perversa voluntas*). In the earthly paradise before the Fall, the penis acted like a finger, and its owner could move it about and keep it still as and when he wanted. The procreative act was not accompanied by any pleasure, and therefore there was no reason to have a 'marvellous and unspeakable desire' for it. It was a friendly, deliberate, useful and rational act. After the original sin, however, the human being became an animal to whom the body was no longer obedient. The phallus was transformed into this rebellious organ, over which fallen man could no longer exercise any authority as a result of his imprudent arrogance. Because he had disobeyed God, he now had a limb that no longer obeyed him. Because he had disregarded divine instructions, he was now mocked and thrown out of control by a capricious and impulsive soul that gives in too easily to pleasure. While the penis starts to swell, it is already rushing towards the image of any desirable object, in the hope of immediately possessing it. Grappling with sensuality, the mind can no longer command itself and loses control of the body. Man, who has separated himself from God, is now divided from himself.

Sexual pleasure, a sign of this division, would become his sin and his punishment: as a result of the first sin, he is now condemned to sin and be attracted by his own insidious sensations. It is the libido that moves the penis. But this power, which prevails over any other form of volition, does not emanate from a specific part of the soul, as for instance Plato believed. The erotic urge is nothing other than the *voluntas*, the will consenting to a particular object. 'What is desire or enjoyment, if not the will that consents to what we want? . . . When this consent makes us propend towards that which we like, it takes the name of desire; when it gives us pleasure, we speak of joy' (St Augustine, *City of God*, xiv, 6). Desire is want – impetuous, forceful and impatient want. Given that want is consent, desire is the equivalent of launching oneself into an enthusiastic 'yes!' Enjoyment is also want and therefore consent. The difference is a temporal one: I desire if I say 'yes' to an object that is not yet present, and I enjoy it if I find it here before me. The desirous consent, however, becomes advance and phantasmal enjoyment when its intensity and rapidity are such that the object appears to be already here. Precisely because it is desire that something or someone be present, eager desire (*cupido*) conjures up the presence of people and things. Desire is already pleasure. This is what we are taught by dreams, in which the consent (*consensio*) is accompanied by an emission of semen. It is the distressing legacy of original sin, which is reactivated with every movement of the penis: a movement that is always 'involuntary', but only because it is wanted by a deviant will (*perversa voluntas*).

What are the philosophical premises for this complete reappraisal of the object that appears in a dream or a visual perception? How can an image impose itself on the soul with a presence that is so vivid and realistic that it causes enjoyment? After Plato and before the Church Fathers, there are the Stoics. It is they who were responsible for developing a theory of knowledge whose principles were used by Christians to define their concept of sexuality. The emergence of a Christian ethic based on *phantasía* (manifestation, appearance) and our consent to its images actually drew upon Stoic epistemology rather than upon Stoic morality, which Christians found intransigent and inhuman.

'In the first place,' Cicero wrote, 'Zeno [of Citium] formulated some new opinions on the senses, which he believed to be linked to something that struck them from the outside, and he gave this thing the name of *phantasía*' (Cicero, *Academica*, i, 11). These apparitions are independent from the intentions of the subject who receives them passively. In order to be able to dominate them, a human being has to be able to give or deny them his own consent. This consent (*assensio*) depends entirely upon ourselves. It is voluntary and amounts to an exercise of the will in the cognitive process. We can always delay, reject or suspend our adherence to that which strikes us from the outside. Knowledge is therefore an intentional activity and the progressive acceptance of an impression created through the senses, to the point that it becomes our own. 'Once we have received the appearance and have given consent, we have an understanding, as defined by analogy with objects that can be picked up.' Using a metaphor we now take for granted, Cicero insists on the meaning of 'to understand' as 'to get', 'to grasp' or 'to get a handle on'. Perception is impossible without the soul's agreement: it is like having something in an open, outstretched hand. Precise understanding means deciding to close the fist firmly around it. The most critical moment in this chain of events – receipt, consent, taking more decisively in the hand – is clearly that of consent. By saying either 'yes' or 'no' to the image that strikes us, we use the active power of our soul, which is our essential self. The *assensio* is deliberate, and depends on an assessment and therefore on a decision.

There is, however, a problem in a situation of this kind: the duration and speed of the sequence. While we are deciding, it may be that the images demand an immediate adherence, simply because they are evident. 'Just as a set of scales has to bend under the weight placed on one of its plates, so the soul concedes to evidence' (Cicero, *Lucullus*, 12). Because of this physical harmony between the *phantasíai*, when they are clear and distinct, and the soul, with which the human animal is equipped, the perceptive and cognitive processes proceed unceasingly and feed into mental activity: the memory, notions of things, knowledge and science are formed and enriched by the soul's incessant and diligent work in filtering the appearances and regulating understanding. Two powers confront each other: that of the evidence inherent in the object (*perspicuitas*), which tends to impose itself on the soul, and the force (*vis*) of the soul itself, which carries out the role of judge. We need to distrust what appears to be crystal clear and reset the scales mechanically.

This is where we meet up again with desire, because consent is a genuine movement of desire (to understand), whereas desires (relating to love or other matters) are, conversely, forms of consent (*assensio*). Things strike us by appearing. This shock releases an appetite. The drive to grasp comes to us directly from the impulse of perceived things (*appetitio ab his pulsa sequeretur*), from the impact of the image on the soul. This is physiological; we are made to be open to the world and to attach ourselves to knowledge – to embrace it (*amplecti*, *Lucullus*, 10). Knowledge is therefore the result of an emotional drive. We know this from Plato; but, unlike Plato, the Stoics were what we might call 'sensualists'. Whereas Plato distinguishes and contrasts the parts of the soul on which desires and knowledge variously depend, the Stoics refuse to separate them. The mind and the senses are the same thing. The soul and the body are the same thing. Emotions are at the same time thoughts (approval of a judgement) and physical shifts (contractions and dilatations) of the *pneûma* (Pigeaud, 1981a: 17–18; 1981b: 265–353). For the rational animal, there is no activity that does not depend on a judgement and its ratification: every act or behaviour commences with an arousal (*inritatio*), followed by a propulsion (*impetus*) and its confirmation: *deinde adsensio confirmavit hunc impetum* (Seneca, *Letters to Lucilius*, 113, 18). All tendencies are consents (Voelke, 1973: 50–5).

This indistinctness, which is generally called 'monism', is clearly fundamental to ethics and sexuality. According to the Stoics, every inclination, volition or action derives from the good or bad use of the consenting reason. It is because of this that sexual drives are acts of an intellectual and intentional order, rather than bestial and instinctive cravings emanating from the soul's inferior intestinal and genital depths. We think and feel with the same organ, an undifferentiated soul that first judges and then leaps towards the *phantasíai* which it has chosen. We therefore desire freely, deliberately and almost too willingly. The problem of the rapidity of this mental, emotional, psychic and physical response is even more crucial in the case of sex than in situations of purely cognitive consent. Ancient philosophers considered emotions to be a natural phenomenon and extraneous to reason. Moreover, they located them in a particular part of the soul, and they put reason in another part. Zeno, the founder of the Stoic school, asserted that all the soul's emotional disturbances are voluntary. They arise from ill-founded judgements and, more precisely, from an excessive haste (Cicero, *Academica*, i, 10).

We need to examine these two ideas – the intellectual nature of feelings and the importance of time – in greater detail. All disturbances of the soul derive from errors of assessment. We overestimate a danger, and therefore have fear of it. We exaggerate a current disaster and therefore we suffer from it. We put great store by an asset and thus we are happy to enjoy it. We idealise a future asset and thus we burn with desire to possess it. All disturbances of the soul can be interpreted as the effects of opinions which we have consented to on the basis of appearance. Desire, in particular, is consent to the virtual enjoyment of an object which seems to us to be extremely beautiful, precious and worthy of esteem. It is a fever, a boundless appetite, out of all proportion to the objective value of the goal we have set ourselves. As with all the other passions, the value is not be found in the thing in itself (*in re*), but in the soul of the desirer who exaggerates.

Like Plato, the Stoics link desire and pleasure to an error of judgement. However, the judgement in question is factual for Plato – you think that you are enjoying something, but actually you are desiring and therefore suffering, whereas it is a value judgement for the Stoics – you believe that possessing a certain thing is marvellous, while the thing is not actually worth it, whether today or tomorrow. The difference leads to a substantial divide, because pleasure for Plato is made impossible by the paradoxical lack of being of concrete things and by the endless movement which takes them from our presence, while pleasure for the Stoics is excessive but real: desire is unjustified, but capable of creating enjoyment in anticipation of possession. Pleasure is the enjoyment of present things; desire is the impatience to enjoy them.

For the Stoics, desire is not, therefore, the hidden face of a pleasure which is nothing more than an illusion. It is the hope of enjoyment; it is enjoyment in anticipation, because a current sensation, which the object will provoke when it is present, is already being experienced in desire itself. It shows us where we aim to go. A representation is not a presence, this is true, but in the imagination we are already fantasising about what we will enjoy and how we will enjoy it. The presentiment is not vain and abstract, because the body prepares to enjoy the desired object as though the object were actually there. 'This was why', Poseidonius asserted, 'some people let themselves be taken over by desire while listening to a story' (Galen, *On the Opinions of Hippocrates and Plato*, v, 6). It has to be stressed again that desire is immediate consent to a future or virtual pleasure that promises to be extraordinarily wonderful. Enjoyment is consent, with excessive enthusiasm, to the overvalued object, once it is present. However, in a definition that creates a kind of superimposition of desire and pleasure, desire is 'the opinion of a future good that we will love as though it were *already* present and within our reach' (Cicero, *Tusculan Disputations,* iv, 7, 14). The anticipation, which is expressed in the 'already', is inherent to the reality of desire, because we would not start to value the object if it were not already depicted within our imagination. And, if we had not already started to await it with trembling expectancy, we would not of course desire it. The deliciousness of desire is in the impatience to have in our presence the future good we will love, and is caused by the wish to accelerate our enjoyment of it.

In other words, a desire is a 'yes' spoken too hastily; the approval has been thought out, but it has not been thought out well, and the approval is of a *phantasía* which the eyes have allowed to be presented to the mind and which, as an image, starts to create real pleasure. Through this idea, Stoicism opened the way to the Christian concept of moral responsibility: external actions are not alone in being the result of deliberate decisions, for this is also true of internal actions, that is, intentions. Using the temporal notion of 'hastiness', Stoic discourse considers the source of moral guilt to be a sort of speeding. And, using a psychosomatic concept of subjectivity, Stoic materialism explains the simultaneous nature of mental and physical responses. The acceptance of an image at the same time implies undergoing alterations in the *pneûma*.

This is why, for Christians, covetousness (*concupiscere*) means consenting immediately 'already', as Tertullian would say in his Stoic reading of St Matthew (*Exhortation to Chastity*, ix, 2): anyone who looks at a woman with desire has already (*iam*) raped her in his heart. Given that the immediate consequence is the appropriation of the *phantasía*, desire means possession. Thus the enjoyment is in the imagination, of course, but it is also current and physical, because the consent provokes a resonance within the body (*usque ad carnis fluxum*, in the words of St Augustine). This priority of desire over pleasure is, according to Michel Foucault, what characterises the Christian interpretative attitude to sexuality, which has to be unmasked in its very first movements. It reveals something more interesting; it reveals the pleasure in desire.

CONCLUSION
INDEFINITE DESIRE

The appetite which men call 'lust', and the fruition that appertaineth there-
unto, is a sensual pleasure, but not only that; there is in it also a delight of
the mind: for it consisteth of two appetites together, to please, and to be
pleased; and the delight men take in delighting, is not sensual, but a pleasure
or joy of the mind, consisting in the imagination of the power they have so
much to please.

Thomas Hobbes, *The Elements of Law Natural and Politic*, 1640, IX, 15

Having opened our exploration of ancient sensuality with a Greek doctor,
Galen, let us close it with a modern philosopher, Thomas Hobbes. Great clas-
sicist and great materialist, Hobbes offers us a perfect ending. Lust is a sensual
pleasure, he claims, but this pleasure is made up of two forms of desire. Desire
not merely to feel delight of the senses, but also a joy of the mind: it is a feeling
of power, the power to please or, in other words, the successful and cultivated
wish to be desired.

Sometimes attached to a particular person, love is naturally indiscriminate.
'The passion is one and the same indefinite desire of the different sex, as natural
as hunger' (idem.). Like Galen, Hobbes interlaces sex and sensuality, nature and
desire, pleasure and sexual difference. 'For as much as this passion cannot be
without diversity of sex, it cannot be denied but that it participateth of that
indefinite love' (16). That indefinite love is what, for Galen, gives humans the
marvellous and indescribable eagerness to make use of their sexual parts. It is
the *venus volgivaga* of Lucretius, the light-heartedly unfaithful little *Amor* of
Ovid, the natural tropism of the Platonic gendered bodies in the *Timaeus*, the
physiological attraction to pleasure that accomplishes the work of generation
for Aristotle.

I would happily part here with the most patient of my readers, if I did not
feel the need for a final apology. There are so many things that might have been
added to this book, that I owe you at least a table of virtual contents. Had I

chosen to explore the culture of sensuality following different genres, I could have included, for instance, a chapter on the novel. I could have shown how the Greek novel, in particular Longus' *Daphnis and Chloe*, plays with the didactic intent of the *ars amatoria* by staging a story of sensual education in a bucolic setting, to come to the conclusion that nature has nothing to teach, and that desire – male desire – has to be learned from a feminine and technical source. The pleasure of the senses is, again and again, a skilful expertise, which men derive from women and which has to find the right intensity between rape and incompetence.

I could have given space to comedy. Attic comedy is full of sex because of the conventions which define the comic in contrast with the tragic. The language of tragedy, as even a superficial reading will reveal, conveys the intentions, the motives, and the emotions of the characters. All these sentiments are overwhelming and painful: tragic passions are felt as profound suffering, as the aching of the soul through anger, shame, fear, mourning, jealousy, hatred, or unrequited love. There is not much joy in tragedy, while the potential for derision is just sinister. Comedy, obviously, is the locus of pleasure and laughter, as much for the audience as for the characters themselves, who are eager to trigger each other's hilarity. Now, the basic resources of laughter are what Hobbes would call the 'onerations and exonerations' of the body: the loading and unloading of luggage, the eating, drinking, defecating, urinating, passing wind, and, also, sexual arousal and the need for erotic relief. The equivalent of what is burdening, anguishing, or crushing for the tragic soul are the overpowering encumbrances and swellings which tax the comic body, demanding physical catharsis. But hydraulic sex is not sensuality. I could have found a tenuous thread of sensuality in ancient comedy for two reasons: firstly, cross-dressing is one of the recurrent sources of laughter; therefore comedy has to play with the performance of femininity and artful seduction. Secondly, the female universe is absorbed by the sensual delights of the domestic space; therefore women seem uninterested in anything but gratifying their erotic urge by reforming the laws of the city to this effect, for instance, or by bringing home, to bed, their belligerent and brutish men.

I could have dedicated much more space to erotic poetry. But there already exists an extensive and ever-growing scholarship on the intricate aspects of this literary genre in both Greece and Rome. Instead, I have moved freely within the corpus of ancient love poetry, choosing to highlight the themes that seemed important to the scenario of sex and sensuality.

Firstly, I have looked at the significance of offering and addressing a poem to a beloved, as a gesture, as an act of erotic performance. This occurs in a situation, in a time-space, because it is the absence or, worse, the distraction of the beloved that causes longing and demands the sending of a message. That written gift will voice the disappointment, hope, yearning generated by the situation itself. Love poetry, at the beginning, is rarely a simple panegyric upon the object: it is an appeal to a missing, elusive, distant subject. Think of Sappho. Think also of that inaugural scenario of courtship which is the *Odyssey*, where Penelope's suitors are famously unable to invent an *ars amatoria*. Used to the performances of sung poetry and to the traditional gifts of cattle, the boys from Ithaca fail to discover the power of the poetic love letter.

Secondly, I have looked at the Roman poets as the only heirs to the Greek philosophers, in their role of advisors on love. After Plato and Epicurus, in Rome we have Lucretius, Catullus and Ovid. And we have a completely new situation: the big city, with its haunts and dating places, its single scenes, cruising neighbourhoods, theatres, gardens, revolving doors and complicitous windows. The Roman poets design a landscape, a time–space for courtship, seduction, adultery, reconciliation, which carries us very far not only from the rustic court of Ulysses, but also from the streets of Athens. Here comes a particular form of erotic experience: urban love. This love is modern and artful, adult and sophisticated. The poet is its theorist because he has learned at his own expense, and he has learned one basic truth: that women are the masters of love because they are the masters of civilisation. Civilisation is a process which starts with hardship and hardness, only to progress to softness. It begins with sex and progresses to sensuality. The sexual encounter brings men to live with women, and ultimately it produces the feminisation of life: a cosy hut, a yielding mattress, tenderly cooked dinners. Softened by his artful endeavour but still virile enough, the poet is the perfect lover. He can take a woman because he knows how to wait, praise, weep, and make believe – just like a woman, but not too much.

I have focused on sensuality because it is a pivotal notion for the cultural elaboration of sex in antiquity. It allows us to establish the distinction of genders (what is feminine, what is masculine) and to describe the manners of erotic activity (what is fast and rough, what is lingering and refined). Sensuality is the pleasure of the senses, kept alive by a persistent craving, the need to take, embrace, hold a yielding body, but, even more, to please a willing soul. Sensuality bridges the corporeal and the intentional. To be yielding and willing I have to be soft, or to soften. The malleable, pliable, moist flesh of a woman is the paradigm of the disposition to feel that insatiable desire, which lies at the core of ancient sexuality. The categories of the basic logic of the concrete, to borrow the felicitous expression of Françoise Héritier, are dry, hot, humid and cold. Feminine and masculine are intertwined with these elementary qualities. Woman is humid, thus soft. The child, humid and warm, is just a variation of the same logic. Paederasty, therefore, is a variation of the same logic.

Sensuality is so important for the ancients that it does not remain confined to the philosophical discussions of sexual difference or to frivolous evocations of indulgent hedonism. The process of softening, I have insisted, coincides with the process of civilisation. There are two major scenarios of sensuality. One is marriage, sedentary domestic life. This is why I have insisted on those spaces where women create and keep alive the affective existence of a family, where they stay close to their conjugal bed, raise their children and wait for their wandering husbands or welcome their occasional lovers. They also kill, themselves or others, in those same rooms, on those same beds. The dialectics of love and desire occurs for women in a framework made of places, times, rules, prohibitions – the social setting where they feel all their passions. It is a polyphonic representation of norms and practices, fictional characters and historical institutions, rights, habits and bodies, that I intended to recapture. It is the anthropology of ancient sensuality – not another history of philosophical or literary ideas about the erotic experience – that I have tried to bring to life.

The other scenario of sensuality is the aristocratic universe of the gymnasium and symposium. Here women fade into the background, whereas older and younger men share dining-beds, music, conversation, wine and seduction. Is femininity out of the picture? I do not think so, for the reasons I have discussed in the previous chapters. Like Jean-Baptiste Reignault, the painter who invented the allegorical composition on the cover of this book, I see old Socrates pulling young Alcibiades from *la volupté* – the embrace of those sensual, fleshy, inviting ladies.

★ ★ ★

It would be difficult to write a history of ancient sex, particularly one that covers the ancient world and early Christianity, without relating one's own position to Michel Foucault's. His presence is, to say the least, formidable, and his *History of Sexuality*, which was suspended at the end of the second volume on the ancient world, *The Care of the Self*, before the expected publication of the volume on Christianity, *The Confessions of the Flesh*, constituted a strong disincentive, from the eighties onwards, for anyone thinking of venturing into this field. Here, I shall attempt to outline the sense of Foucault's project.

In 1976, Foucault published *The Will to Know*, a slim volume which immediately created a sensation because of its paradoxical thesis. It was then generally accepted, he argued, that Christian morality is repressive and phobic about sex, whereas psychoanalysis had revealed the importance of sexuality as a cause of neurosis and in the formation of our characters, in other words, as the decisive factor in determining out identity. We were supposed to be thankful to Freud for having freed us to speak about sexual experience, something that had been prohibited, punished and turned into a constant source of guilt by two millennia of Christian censure. Foucault saw things in a very different light. In truth, talking about sex had never been impeded by Christian morality. Quite the opposite, Christianity has always encouraged us to pour out our own sexual history, to manifest, acknowledge and name our desire and to talk about our pleasures. What is confession if not an exercise in eloquence, telling secrets and indiscretions about our sex life, and particularly telling the lead-up to any acts – in the inner space where intentions are formed? Only the naive would credit Freud with having loosened our tongues: psychoanalysis does nothing more than *reassert* the centuries-old exhortation to acknowledge sex and talk about it.

Presented as the first volume in a history of sexuality which was to follow, *The Will to Know* inaugurated a polemical, provocative and militant project. The editorial plan was a plan of battle against an unmistakable and extremely unpleasant adversary: psychoanalysis, which is an extension of Christian morality, just as the 'talking cure' is a medicalised version of the confession of sins in all their forms – of thoughts, words, works and omissions. This amounted to saying that Freud had discovered nothing, and had simply shifted a situation of extorted sincerity from the confessional to the couch. The centuries-old claim that everything regarding sex should be put through a 'masher' of words clearly brought analysis and confession together in a single inquisitive practice, on which the value judgement passed sounds contemptuous and sarcastic. Both the confessional and the couch lead to an *injunction*, and both are violent and abusive. There is no need to have a deep knowledge of Foucault's work to feel that these hard-hitting texts expose the power, which is not well concealed behind the obligation of the penitent, or patient, to report and answer for his or her inner sexual life. It is thus immediately clear that the intention of *The History of Sexuality* is to unmask the intrusive violence hidden in practices based on self-confession and to relativise such practices by examining their archaeology – that is, their appearance and establishment over time.

Foucault treats psychoanalysis in different ways. He explicitly refers to Freud as just one of the nineteenth-century psychiatrists, who became more prominent by making himself the most famous ear of our time. Freud contributed personally to the history of sexuality by introducing the sexual into the 'apparatus of alliances' and thus reinforcing the structure of the family. Freud did not discover incestuous desire; he simply eroticised kinship. Most interestingly, Foucault *alludes* to psychoanalysis without actually naming it. Passages of this kind are very important because they reveal what Foucault actually had in mind when he spoke of the nineteenth century and the *scientia sexualis*. They show how psychoanalysis was for him a dominant thinking that cast its shadow across the entire scientific culture of the nineteenth century. The establishment of the medical extortion of sexual confessions was made possible by the concurrence of the following factors: the clinical codification of the injunction to speak; the postulate of a widespread sexual determinism; the principle of an inherent latency in sexuality; an interpretative method; and the medicalisation of the effects of the confession, which are considered therapeutic. Within this framework psychoanalysis is not mentioned, but where could you possibly find all these elements together other than in the Freudian clinical technique? Foucault is certainly not referring to previous psychiatric practices, which, up to Charcot, observed hysterical women, rather than attempting to listen to them.

In the pages of *The Will to Know*, psychoanalysis is often mistreated, and often watered down with a supposed tradition of the science of sexuality, but it is always misunderstood. I will not dwell on the reduction of the Freudian discovery of infantile sexual theories to a simple cultural montage, since the 'introduction' of the sexual into the family, in the form of incest, had already occurred in classical tragedy, itself based on mythology. I would, however, like to examine more closely this amalgam of confession and psychoanalytic cure. As I have already said, Foucault's thesis in this book is that the 'talking cure' was nothing more than a revival of the long-running injunction to confess one's own evil intentions.

Medicalised confession, confession with therapeutic pretensions and confession that has to be interpreted are all synonymous with psychoanalysis. On this point, I cannot say whether Foucault is being negligent or acting in bad faith. An honest debate on Freud would, at the very least, have required an examination of the Freudian texts on the similarities and differences between confessing sins and enunciating one's own free associations. Of course, the Catholic confession has the appearance of being the same thing as psychoanalysis, Freud acknowledges, but in reality it is entirely different. In the first case, one receives an order to admit to everything one knows about one's own sexual sins and indeed other sins, while in the second case, one is encouraged to say everything that ultimately one does not know. Confession, as is well known, demands an examination of one's *conscience*; psychoanalysis makes it possible to discover one's *subconscious* thoughts, desires and conflicts. This means that the person undergoing psychoanalysis has a subconscious and the treatment presupposes and takes as its desired outcome the possibility of transforming into words that which has evaded the conscious. The reduction of the psychoanalyst's couch to a therapeutic confessional means ignoring the theoretical heart of Freud's discoveries. A historicisation or a genealogy of psychoanalysis as a nineteenth-century variant of the confessional amounts to a refusal to acknowledge the theory of the subconscious.

When reading *The Will to Know*, one has the feeling that the moment in which the 'apparatus of sexuality' makes its appearance corresponds to a break with the preceding epoch, in which sex was spoken of in a very different manner. Foucault started to work on Greek and Roman antiquity in order to find this temporal universe, this lost paradise when ethics did not demand the telling of personal secrets. This was a world before Christ and before Freud, in which no one thought that talking about sex could be good for the soul or the body: this is what ancient culture, or rather philosophy, has to offer to the archae-ologist of sexuality. Foucault therefore approached ancient societies with a very clear working hypothesis: find a background against which to cast that epoch-making break which is the birth of Christianity. In the meantime, between 1976 and 1984, the years in which *The Use of Pleasure* and *The Care of the Self* were published, Foucault came to realise the importance of a notion that was marginal in *The Will to Know* by comparison with his insistence on confession as a scenario: the idea of a 'hermeneutics of desire' and a 'hermeneutics of the self'. This theme became central to the two volumes on ancient sexuality and the unpublished volume on early Christian ethics, *The Confessions of the Flesh*.

When therapeutic extortion of the truth about sex takes over from religious extortion and becomes psychoanalytic, the confessor becomes an interpreter. Given that the truth in question appears and remains obscure for the very person who discovers it in himself and utters it, it is up to the person who hears the confession to carry out the task of deciphering it. 'The one who listens will not be simply the master of forgiveness, the judge who condemns or absolves; that person will be the master of truth. His/her function is hermeneutic' (Foucault, 1976: 89). This is an ambitious role: the hermeneutics of desire co-incides with a hermeneutics of the self, given that the essential claim of the *scientia sexualis*, of which psychoanalysis constitutes the clearest example for Michel Foucault, is to induce us to know *ourselves* through the interpretative understanding of our sexual desire. Sex therefore becomes our truth, the authentic, profound but also obscure truth about who we are. Yet already, by the seventeenth century, following the Council of Trent, the Catholic Church intensified its pastoral interests in sins of the flesh, and the variety of sexual acts and their circumstances were overshadowed by the examination of the inten-tions, the agitation and the desire, 'given that this is an evil that strikes man as a whole and in the most secret forms'. There are here two assertions: that the truth confessed *in psychoanalysis* demands an interpretation by the analyst; and that the important truth in the Catholic confession was already that of desire as an evil that affects the whole man.

In the volumes on the sexuality of the ancients, these two assertions come together. Foucault now argues that Christian morality had *always* involved an interpretative approach, not on behalf of another person but by the sinners, who are not so much asked to reveal themselves to others – as Foucault wrote in the *Will to Know* – as required to decode for themselves their own inclination in their nascent state. 'Hermeneutics and the purifying effects of deciphering desire': this was announced to be the content of the volume on the Church Fathers, *The Confessions of the Flesh*. This is what distinguishes Christian morality from Greek and Roman ethics (Foucault, 1984a: 99–107; 1984b: 269–74).

This point has to be made absolutely clear: according to Foucault, early Christians invented a form of attention to oneself that consisted in interpreting the symptoms of desire. The ancients, on the other hand, never introduced the idea of a hermeneutics of desire, even though they developed techniques of spiritual exercise and ethical self-improvement, the 'care of the self' that provided the title to the volume on Seneca, Plutarch and late antiquity. After all, a hermeneutics of desire implies that desire should be uncovered and would reveal our truest and most intimate being. However much and deeply the ancients had thought about the ways of knowing oneself through care of the self, they were still 'very far away from what would be the hermeneutics of the self' (Foucault, 1989: 159–60).

There was, therefore, a clear continuity between *The Will to Know* and the next two volumes, but we must also take note of an important and highly understandable change of viewpoint. The early Christians give interpretations like the doctors of the *scientia sexualis* and they spy on the birth of passions like the seventeenth-century confessors, but obviously outside of the setting of the confessional and the couch. In going back to the origins of Christian philosophy, Foucault loses the duet scene of the extortion of the truth, and finds himself faced with a solitary, reflective and self-analytical practice. His reading of the Church Fathers, particularly of St Augustine, was undoubtedly decisive in this discovery of a hermeneutics of desire and of the self. This occurs between the self and the self, or between the self and God, in silence and independently from an interlocutor in a position of power, who interrogates and obliges the subject to speak. This means, therefore, the disappearance of the confession, which in 1976 represented the trial of strength from which the apparatus of western sexuality emerged, and which appeared in the *Confessions*, the founding text on intimacy with oneself. The practice of the will to know, as it is embodied in the sacrament or in therapy, gives way to techniques of the self which consist of spiritual exercises, self-discipline and reflection. The whole question of power has to be re-examined in terms of subjugation to norms instead of a docile willingness to open up to the confessor–analyst.

The Use of Pleasure is a programmatic title. It is a way of announcing the content of a book on the sexuality of the ancients, and above all defining the boundaries within which one can, and should, talk of a sexuality of the ancients. The Greeks perceived the problems of sex to be its use, organisation and measured dosage. Instead of worrying about desire, they concentrated their ethical interests on acts and pleasures of all varieties and magnitudes: how, when, with whom, in what climate, how many times, and such like. In other words, an examination of the mores of sensuality, an art of love made up of restrictive but fundamentally positive norms preceded the Christian inquisition into, and anguish over, desire. Foucault called for a counterattack against the confessional apparatus of sexuality, which would take the body and the pleasures as the starting point. This counterattack was not to be found in the utopia of a future in which sex could be enjoyed without taking any responsibility for anyone else, but rather in the reconstruction of a past in which Greek philosophers and doctors became serene distributors of erotic advice. In *Care for the Self*, he illustrates the idea that the management of one's own sexual activity is nothing more than a part of the techniques for taking care of oneself that Greek and Roman philosophers developed.

The project is therefore redefined in more traditionally philosophical terms. Foucault does not describe behaviour or institutions, but rather comments on texts which theorise the task of putting pleasures to good use and of taking care of oneself. He constantly repeats that he is now interested in a history of the subjectivisation which explains how, and on the basis of what alterity, the West reached the impasse of the hermeneutics of desire construed as the hermeneutics of the self.

At this stage, it is the definition of 'sexuality' that needs to be thought out again. In 1976, 'sexuality' was an 'apparatus', a collection of knowledge, power, theories and practices, whose origin had to be identified in confession. There was also a date of birth: the 'apparatus of sexuality' came into existence in the seventeenth century, with the post-Tridentine codification of the examination of one's conscience, an examination directed more towards bad intentions than towards impure acts. In 1984, 'sexuality' is a phenomenon which seems to evade the chronological boundaries and which apparently goes back not only to the first centuries of Christianity but way back into pre-Christian antiquity, where the confession and the hermeneutics of desire were not to be found. In the introduction to *The Use of Pleasure*, we are somewhat surprised to encounter a definition of sexuality which is no longer valid solely for the historical period in which the word started to be used, namely the nineteenth century, but is valid 'for a culture', by which Foucault literally means any culture (Foucault, 1984a: 10). If we analyse the correlation between types of knowledge, types of normative systems and forms of subjectivity, we can then speak of sexuality in any place and at any time.

Foucault uses this looser definition, which can be applied far beyond the boundaries outlined in *The Will to Know*, to modify substantially his hyperhistoricist viewpoint. While it is true that sexuality is never a biological given (as desire, too, has to be historicised), it is also true that it is not a unique phenomenon, as specific as the Catholic confession of sins after the Council of Trent. Perhaps in spite of himself, Foucault abandoned a contingent notion and defined a transferable concept. This renunciation of rigid historicism and its associated nominalism demonstrates Foucault's exemplary ability to distance himself from principles that prove to be an obstacle to his research. 'The very term "sexuality" was late in appearing – not until the nineteenth century. This is a fact that should be neither underestimated nor overinterpreted (*sur-interprété*)' (Foucault, 1984a: 9). Sadly, this advice has not been followed by those who obstinately continue to attribute Foucault's historicism and nominalism of the seventies to the later Foucault. They are clearly insensitive to the simple fact that the books on antiquity are part of *The History of Sexuality* and their author did not consider them to be a prehistory, a 'before sexuality'.

Seen in this light, the critique of psychoanalysis changes tone, but continues to play a decisive role as a polemical reference point. In *The Will to Know*, Freud's discovery was relativised twice: in relation to the Christian tradition and in relation to nineteenth-century *scientia sexualis*, which therefore became a hermeneutic variant of the inquisition on sex. Here the discovery is alluded to as something that could engender a bad history of sexuality, a history which is not sufficiently 'historicised'. In this work, Foucault once again sets himself against a Freudian mode of conceiving the historicisation of the sexual. He energetically rejects the idea that, on the one hand, there is sexual desire as a real entity in itself, independent from history, and, on the other, there is censure, the only variable phenomenon whose transformations over time can be identified in historical terms. Foucault does not explicitly say that this is a psychoanalytical model of the periodisation of sexuality, but it is enough to read Freud's *Interpretation of Dreams*, *The Future of an Illusion* and *Civilization and its Discontents* to discover how he contrasts a universal and immutable desire, which is examined in his theories of infantile sexuality, and the progress of repression, which becomes increasingly powerful in Western history from one century to the next.

Freudian thought is, however, more nuanced. The elementary desires to kill, devour human flesh and have sexual intercourse with a parent are intrinsically human, whatever one's cultural identity. However, culture is established to *modify* these desires through sublimation or repression (Freud, 2002). Throughout the progressive, evolutionary process of Western civilisation, the original desires have been impeded by the increasing rationalism of morality, or inhibited in relation to their end and transformed into art and science. The renunciation of infantile drives provides an historiographical model for social and cultural phenomena. We read, for instance, in *The Interpretation of Dreams* that the progress of censure accounts for the difference between Sophocles' *Oedipus King* and Shakespeare's *Hamlet*: in the Greek tragedy, the subconscious desire for incest and homicide is manifestly represented by Oedipus' destiny, while in the Elizabethan drama the same desire is enigmatically symbolised by

Hamlet's neurosis. The onward march of civilisation and censure has by now made impossible a literary expression that acknowledges such desires.

According to psychoanalysis, prohibitions and sublimations are the engine of social history. They do not restrict themselves to formulating rules and models for and against an unchanging desire, but they alter individuals and the way they desire. It would therefore be imprecise to say that the human soul has not undergone any evolution between primitive times and the present day. The soul has a history, given that culture is internalised, assimilated and made partially subconscious in the super-ego. The working of culture, which profoundly affects the individual, superimposes itself on the original desires by moulding and redefining his or her drives. It is true that these drives are not destroyed or sublimated forever: they are reborn with each child, but on each occasion they are transformed through the restrictions that civilisation imposes and through the prospects it offers. The individual reproduces both the history of humanity and the history of the cultures in which he or she grows up. For psychoanalysis, the desirous individual is constructed by history to the point of acquiring a culturally-specific super-ego, even though desire in itself can never be definitively defeated or abolished. Every baby starts from zero, although a Victorian adolescent would not desire in the same way as a Californian teenager of the 1970s. The influence of different cultural models produces two different souls, with disparate super-egos.

Foucault asserts that everything, including, and in particular, desire, has to be understood as an historical fact, a construct. It is not enough to reconstruct events concerning prohibitions when it comes to reflecting on sexuality in history. In his opinion, the *history* of sexuality continues therefore to constitute an alternative to the analytical theory of the sexual. Like many historians, Foucault undervalues the historical dimension that psychoanalysis already admits to, and he principally sees the fixity of desire, against which he directs his arguments. The Freudian idea that the soul, which is subjectivity, is moulded by time and by culture is not enough for him. Or rather, Foucault provides us with a schematic and impoverished representation of psychoanalysis: desire can only encounter a prohibition and not a sublimation, and he appears to attribute no significance to the fact that the super-ego is subconscious and therefore anything but external to the self. The manner in which individuals subject themselves to the norms is for him an essential element, but he seeks out arguments and criteria (the ethical substance), while contemptuously ignoring the subconscious. In the new context, where he is no longer interested in reducing analytical practice to confessional practice, the polemic restricts itself to the conception of the relationship between time and desire. In a way, the critique of psychoanalysis is the only thing *The Will to Know* and the books on the ancients have in common.

Given the importance of Foucault's antipathy for psychoanalysis, it was to be expected that at least one psychoanalyst would point this out to him. Jacques-Alain Miller (1989) emphasises not only the sarcasm, but also the obstinacy with which Foucault equates the specific nature of Freudian thought with the nebulousness of nineteenth-century *scientia sexualis* and with the Christian discipline of the confession, which are, Miller insists, forms of knowledge that psychoanalysis was established *to counter*. Foucault found in the ancient world the realisation of his desire for an eroticism of the body and pleasures, beyond castration and independent from any deficiency.

It is now time to declare what we consider to be positive about Foucault's work, which so manifestly precedes this book. The most important contribution, in my opinion, is the concept of 'care'. Foucault uses the category of *Sorge*, namely 'care', as developed by Heidegger in *Being and Time* (I believe he hasn't been given sufficient credit for doing this), and uses it remorselessly against Heidegger's recommendations, that is, as a precious concept in describing the content of ancient ethics. In *Being and Time*, we should briefly recall, Heidegger analyses at length all the possible semantic nuances of the concept of 'care': to concern oneself with, to worry about, to be interested in, to desire, to understand, to be with others, to be uneasy about, to anguish over. In other words, he examined all the possible modifications of that which he considers to be the genuinely human way of being in the world. 'Care', for Heidegger, belongs to a literary and philosophical tradition which, through Goethe and Herder, goes back all the way to the ancients. It represents that from which human beings cannot escape, because they are mythologically its children. We are the children of Care, which is demonstrated by the fact that *everything* we do, feel or think can be traced back, without exception, to the many different forms of 'to take care of'. The most elementary of these forms, which is always presupposed by the others, is the care of the self (Heidegger, 1927). It is as care of the self that human beings attempt to understand themselves in a reflective mode, which is unavoidably one of interpretation. As intellectual activity is not a glance at an object through a transparent *medium*, but rather an effect of being concerned with something, we attempt to know ourselves by turning ourselves into the exegetes of our own selves.

Foucault does not acknowledge Heidegger's influence on his decision to analyse ancient ethics in terms of 'care'. He allows this need to emerge from the very language of the authors he examines. However, if we take into account his own statements on the decisive and ongoing importance of reading Heidegger on his philosophical journey, it becomes more than plausible to claim the existence of an intertextual significance involving *The Care of the Self* and the chapters on *Sorge* in *Being and Time*. It is not difficult, on the other hand, to understand why Foucault has not acknowledged the Heideggerian background to his theory. Precisely because *The History of Sexuality* wishes to provide us with an *archaeology* of hermeneutics of the self (that is, a reconstruction of its history as though it had only started to exist in a given moment rather than constituting a timeless form of the human condition), Foucault uses Heidegger not only without Heidegger, but also against Heidegger. He uses the 'care of the self' as a category suited to a period and to a particular culture – the ethics of late antiquity as it prepares the ground for Christianity. He uses the 'hermeneutics of the self' as a specific characterisation of Christian morality, in contrast with historical periods in which such hermeneutics did not take place. He therefore separates two ideas which in Heidegger go together and are valid for all time, and he applies them to an historical model, which is explicitly directed against a general and universal theory of being in the world and the relationship of human beings with themselves.

Moreover, the hermeneutics of the self, for Foucault, culminates in psychoanalysis, a technique of enquiry and interpretation he does not approve of, to say the very least. Psychoanalysis therefore becomes the baleful and contingent implementation of what Heidegger defined as human in its most absolute form, namely the opaqueness of the relationship with oneself and the inevitability of interpretation. The reduction of Freud to a predictable incident in Christian and scientific culture in the nineteenth century means relativising Heidegger as well. It is as though Foucault were saying: 'the hermeneutics of the self is a notion which is relevant not in general, as Heidegger would have it, but in particular, in order to portray psychoanalysis, whose derivation from the confession of sins I have already demonstrated. The hermeneutics of the self therefore remains a valid notion only for describing an historical phenomenon, which has had a beginning and perhaps will have an end. Freud proved to be contingent, and then Heidegger provided me with a good idea, but he was wrong to universalise it.' Such is Foucault's ambition to provide us with a definitive philosophy of being in the world that his historicist attack on Freud is accompanied by a silent dismemberment of Heidegger's ontology. Whereas Foucault shows no interest in Freud's categorisation, he quite freely recycles Heidegger's.

The notion of 'care' constitutes an excellent recurring theme which reveals the central concern of ancient ethics. It is a pity, however, that in periodising the transformation of the use of pleasures into the hermeneutics of desire through the intermediary moment of the care of the self, Foucault identifies a rift between philosophy in the classical era and Hellenistic philosophy that does not correspond to the facts. The concept of 'care' was as important for Seneca as it was for Plato; indeed, the entire question of the way of life (that is, of the duration for which moral choices can be valid), has to be seen as a series of variations on this theme. The concept of the 'use of pleasure', on the other hand, is important, particularly for the Epicureans, but not to the extent that Foucault would have us believe. The pragmatic, instrumental and organisational relationship with the matters of love (*aphrŏdísia*) which were supposed to typify the ancient approach to sex constitutes the otherness of the Greeks when compared to us, that is, in relation to our will to know our desires. Pleasure instead of desire, use instead of inquisitive interpretation: finally he had discovered a world in which the substance of ethics (that which is treated as problematic) is made up of sexual acts. There is a deep misunderstanding on this point: for, quite the contrary, the reasons why sexuality appeared disturbing and therefore worthy of philosophical analysis were related systematically not to pleasures and their management, but to desire and its makeup. Desires for food, drink, sex and money have a common 'nature' and a single mechanism: they are insatiable. If we give in to them, we allow ourselves to be taken over by a way of life in which we risk losing all our time. The persistent and repetitive nature of desires linked to the body can be rationalised through a certain use of pleasure. But the essential point for this theory is indeed desire. Sexuality poses a problem for philosophers as a form of sensuality: no one who follows their own boundless inclinations can avoid making it their full-time occupation, in which a self-sustaining emptiness is created.

Heidegger helps us to understand the connection Greek philosophers established between desire and temporality, and therefore between desire and 'care'. Desire generates a certain kind of activity on, preoccupation with and attention to certain objects. Given that desire is insatiable, what is already owned is never enough, and therefore one *still* continues to desire. One incessantly pursues an unobtainable satisfaction, within an endless movement. In practice, there is no reason to stop. We could apply Heidegger's analysis of habituation to the manner in which desire operates, just as Plato describes it in the *Gorgias*, the *Republic* and the *Philebus*: a 'running after', as though up a slope, while being attracted by something that never ceases to precede us and to avoid our grasp. The virtually infinite duration of this activity depends on the particular type of 'care' that constitutes the insatiable desire.

Unfortunately, Foucault does not use Heidegger to demonstrate this. Quite the opposite, he restricts the relevance of the care of the self to Hellenistic philosophy, reads classical philosophers as though they were doctors, sexologists or marriage councillors, and completely ignores the arguments on the nature of desire that constitute the theoretical nucleus of the ethics of sexuality. It is simply not true that the Greeks restricted the substance of ethics to sexual acts and the sexual delights they can savour, and equally it is not true that ancient philosophy ignored the problem of interpreting the manifestations of desire. One of the more curious aspects of Platonic ethics is precisely the affirmation that the impression of enjoyment can be mistaken, in other words, that

the experience of sensation can be interpreted incorrectly. The error of interpretation results from the fact that pleasure is always mixed with pain, the pain
of loss and of desire. One must become aware of the component of desire
which accompanies enjoyment (we are always desiring more, because desire is
insatiable) in order to understand that what we experience and understand as
pleasure is not ultimately true and pure pleasure. There is a hermeneutics of the
self founded on the hermeneutics of desire, also, and most especially, in Plato.

Michel Foucault has underestimated the Stoics' disjunction between ancient
philosophy and Christian philosophy, with its extremely important consequences for the phenomenology of perception and for the valorisation of the
imaginary. In Plato, *eros* was conceived as the inexhaustible source of emptiness,
the fountainhead of loss, and the absence of pleasure; it was an illusion which
had to be exposed for what it was. For the Church Fathers, it became a reality
which was increasingly enjoyable: a presence which had to be revealed. The
profound transformation brought about by Christianity did not coincide with
the abandonment of a supposed pragmatism – the use of pleasure – and the
discovery of the opaqueness of desire, but rather with a shift of attention in
theoretical matters, from the pernicious boundlessness of insatiability to the
efficacy of pleasurable expectancy. Whereas desire made pleasure impossible for
the ancients, for the Christians it made pleasure all too real, because of its hallu-
cinatory powers. With the Stoic theory of *phantasía*, Christianity invented
tedium, pornography, courtship and courtesy.

BIBLIOGRAPHY

Adams, J. (1982), *The Latin Sexual Vocabulary*, Baltimore.

Bahut, D. D. (1963), 'Les Stoïciens et l'amour', *Revue des Etudes Grecques*, 76, 55–63.

Bailey, D. S. (1975), *Homosexuality and the Western Christian Tradition*, London.

Baladier, C. (1999), *Eros au Moyen Age*, Paris.

Baldwin, J. (1994), *The Language of Sex. Five Voices from Northern France around 1200*, Chicago.

Balibar, E. (1989), 'Foucault et Marx. L'enjeu du nominalisme', in *Michel Foucault philosophe. Rencontre internationale, Paris, 9, 10, 11 janvier 1988*, Paris, 54–76.

Bardon, H. (1965), 'Rome et l'impudeur', *Latomus*, 24, 495–518.

Bettini, M. (1995), *Il ritratto dell'amante*, Turin.

Bléry, H. (1909), *Rusticité et urbanité romaines*, Paris.

Bloch, R. H. (1991), *Medieval Misogyny and the Invention of Western Romantic Love*, Chicago.

Bodei, R. (1986), 'Pouvoir politique et maîtrise de soi', *Critique*, 471–2, August–September, 898–917.

Bollack, J. (1975), *La Pensée du plaisir*, Paris.

Bollack, M. (1978), *La Raison de Lucrèce*, Paris.

Boswell, J. (1980), *Christianity, Social Tolerance, and Homosexuality: Gay People in Western Europe from the Beginning of the Christian Era to the Fourteenth Century*, Chicago.

Boyarin, D. (1993), *Carnal Israel. Reading Sex in Talmudic Culture*, Berkeley.

Brown, P. (1988), *The Body and Society. Men, Women and Sexual Renunciation in Early Christianity*, New York.

Burguière, A. et al. (eds) (1992), *Histoire de la famille*, 2 vols, Paris.

Calame, C. (1992), *I Greci e l'eros. Simboli, pratiche e luoghi*, Rome and Bari.

Cameron, A. (1994), 'Early Christianity and the discourse of female desire', in L. Archer, S. Fischier and M. Wyke (eds), *Women in Ancient Societies. An Illusion of the Night*, New York, 152–68.

Cantarella, E. (1981), *L'ambiguo malanno: condizione e immagine della donna nell'antichità greca e romana*, Rome.

Cantarella, E. (1988), *Secondo natura: la bisessualità nel mondo antico*, Rome.

Cantarella, E. (1998), *Pompei: i volti dell'amore*, Milan.

Cantarella, E. (2002), *Itaca. Eroi, donne, potere tra vendetta e diritto*, Turin.

Cartledge, P. (1981), 'The politics of Spartan pederasty', *Proceedings of the Cambridge Philological Society*, 27, 17–36.

Clarke, J. (1998), *Looking at Lovemaking: Constructions of Sexuality in Roman Art, 100 BC–AD 250*, Berkeley.

Cohen, D. (1987), 'Law, society and homosexuality in classical Athens', *Past and Present*, 3–21.

Cohen, D. (1992), *Law, Sexuality and Society. The Enforcement of Morals in Classical Athens*, New York.

Cohen, D. and Saller, R. (1994), 'Foucault on sexuality in Greco-Roman antiquity', in J. Goldstein (ed.), *Foucault and the Writing of History*, Oxford, UK and Cambridge, MA, 35–59.

Cole, S. (1984), 'Greek sanctions against sexual assault', *Classical Philology*, 79, 97–113.

Dalla, D. (1978), *L'incapacità sessuale in diritto romano*, Milan.

Dalla, D. (1987), *'Ubi venus mutatur'. Omosessualità e diritto nel mondo romano*, Milan.

Davidson, A. (1987), 'Sex and the emergence of sexuality', *Critical Inquiry*, 14 (1), 16–48.

Davidson, J. (1997), *Courtesans and Fishcakes. The Consuming Passions of Classical Athens*, London.

Dean-Jones, L. (1994), *Women's Bodies in Classical Greek Science*, Oxford.

Dover, K. J. (1978), *Greek Homosexuality*, Cambridge, MA.

Dreyfus, H. (1989), 'De la mise en ordre des choses', in *Michel Foucault philosophe. Rencontre internationale, Paris, 9, 10, 11 janvier 1988*, Paris, 101–24.

Dreyfus, H. and Rabinow, P. (1983), *Michel Foucault: Beyond Structuralism and Hermeneutics*, Chicago.

Dupont, E. (1981), 'Rome: Des enfants pour le plaisir', *Raison présente*, 59, 63–76.

Dupont, E. (1989), *La Vie quotidienne du citoyen romain sous la République*, Paris.

Dupont, E. and Eloi, T. (1994), *Les Jeux de Priape. Anthologie d'épigrammes érotiques*, Paris.

Dupont, E. and Eloi, T. (2001), *L'Erotisme masculin dans la Rome antique*, Paris.

Durry, M. (1956), 'Le Mariage des filles impubères dans la Rome antique', *Revue Internationale des Droits de l'Antiquité*, 3 (3), 227–43.

Edwards, C. (1993), *The Politics of Immorality in Ancient Rome*, Cambridge.

Eribon, D. (1992), *Michel Foucault*, Paris.

Eyben, E. (1972), 'Antiquity's view of puberty', *Latomus*, 31, 678–97.

Fantham, E. (1991), '"Stuprum": Public attitudes and penalties for sexual offences in Republican Rome', *Echos du Monde Classique*, 10, 267–91.

Fischer, N. (ed., transl. comm.) (2001), Aeschines, *Against Timarchus*, New York.

Fitzgerald, W. (1988), 'Power and impotence in Horace's "Epodes"', *Ramus*, 17, 176–91.

Fitzgerald, W. (1992), 'Catullus and the reader: The erotics of poetry', *Arethusa*, 25, 419–43.

Fitzgerald, W. (1995), *Catullan Provocations. Lyric, Poetry and the Drama of Position*, Berkeley, Los Angeles and London.

Flacelière, R. (1969), 'Les Epicuriens et l'amour', *Revue des Etudes Grecques*, 70, 3–43.

Flandrin, J.-L. (1983), *Un Temps pour embrasser. Aux origines de la morale occidentale*, Paris.

Foucault, M. (1976–), *Histoire de la Sexualité*, Paris, 6 vols (English translation: The History of Sexuality, New York *c*. 1978–*c*. 1986).

Foucault, M. (1976), *La Volonté de savoir*, Paris (English translation: *The Will to Know*, London 1998)

Foucault, M. (1984a), *L'Usage des plaisirs*, Paris (English translation: *The Use of Pleasure*, London 1998).

Foucault, M. (1984b), *Le Souci de soi*, Paris (English translation: *The Care of the Self*, London 1990).

Foucault, M. (1989), *Résumé des cours 1970–1982*, Paris.

Freud, S. (1989), *The Future of an Illusion*, New York (original publication: 1927).

Freud, S. (2002), *Civilization and its Discontents*, London (original publication: 1929).

Freud, S. (2005), *The Interpretation of Dreams*, New York (original publication: 1900).

Frontisi-Ducroux, E. and J.-P. Vernant (1997), *Dans l'oeil du miroir*, Paris.

Galimberti, U. (1987), *Il corpo*, Milan.

Gardner, J. (1986), *Women in Roman Law and Society*, Bloomington.

Giardina, A. (ed.) (2006), *L'uomo romano*, Rome and Bari.

Golden, M. (1984), 'Slavery and homosexuality at Athens', *Phoenix*, 38 (4), 308–24.

Goldhill, S. (1995), *Foucault's Virginity*, New York.

Gourevitch, D. (1982), 'Quelques fantasmes érotiques et perversions d'objets dans la literature gréco-romaine', in *Mélanges de l'Ecole Française de Rome, Antiquité*, 94, 823–42.

Gourevitch, D. (1984), *Le Mal d'être femme*, Paris.

Griffin, J. (1976), 'Augustan poetry and the life of luxury', *Journal of Roman Studies*, 66, 87–105.

Grimal, P. (1979), *L'Amour à Rome*, Paris.

Hadot, P. (1989), 'Réflexions sur la notion de "culture de soi"', in *Michel Foucault philosophe. Rencontre international, Paris 9, 10, 11 janvier 1988*, Paris, 261–8.

Hadot, P. (1992), *La Citadelle intérieure: introduction aux pensées de Marc-Aurèle*, Paris.

Hallet, J. (1989), 'Female homoeroticism and the denial of Roman reality in Latin literature', *Yale Journal of Criticism*, 3, 209–27.

Hallet, J. and M. Skinner (eds) (1997), *Roman Sexualities*, Princeton.

Halperin, D. (1989), 'Plato and the metaphysics of desire', in J. Cleary and D. Shartin (eds), *Proceedings of the Boston Area Colloquium in Ancient Philosophy*, Vol. 5, Lanham, 27–52.

Halperin, D. (1990), *A Hundred Years of Homosexuality and Other Essays on Greek Love*, London and New York.

Halperin, D. (1994), 'Historicizing the subject of desire: Sexual preferences and erotic identities in the Pseudo-Lucianic "Erotes"', in J. Goldstein (ed.), *Foucault and the Writing of History*, Oxford, UK and Cambridge, MA.

Halperin, D., J. Winkler and E. Zeitlin (eds) (1990), *Before Sexuality. The Construction of Erotic Experience in the Ancient Greek World*, Princeton.

Heath, J. (1986), 'The supine hero in Catullus 32', *Classical Journal*, 82, 28–36.

Heidegger, M. (1927), *Sein und Zeit*, Halle.

Henderson, J. (1991), *The Maculate Muse*, New York.

Héritier, F. (1997), *Les deux filles et leur mère*, Paris.

Hopkins, K. (1965), 'The age of Roman girls at marriage', in *Population Studies*, 18, 309–27.

Hubbard, T. (ed.) (2000), *Greek Love Reconsidered*, Wallace Hamilton Press.

Hubbard, T. (2003), *Homosexuality in Greece and Rome*, Berkeley.

Janan, M. (1994), *When the Lamp Is Shattered. Desire in the Poetry of Catullus*, Carbondale.

Johns, C. (1982), *Sex or Symbol? Erotic Images of Greece and Rome*, Austin.

King, H. (1998), *Hippocrates' Woman: Reading the Female Body in Ancient Greece*, London and New York.

Laqueur, T. (1990), *Making Sex: Body and Gender from the Greeks to Freud*, Cambridge, MA.

Lilja, S. (1983), *Homosexuality in Republican and Augustan Rome*, Helsinki (*Societas Scientiarum Fennica Commentationes Humanarum Litterarum*, 74).

Lissarrague, F. (1987), 'De la sexualité des Satyres', *Métis*, 11(1), 63–79.

Lloyd, G. E. R. (1966), *Polarity and Analogy: Two Types of Argumentation in Early Greek Thought*, Cambridge.

Loraux, N. (1989), *Les Expériences de Tirésias: Le féminin et l'homme grec*, Paris.

McGinn, T. (1998), *Prostitution, Sexuality and the Law in Ancient Rome*, New York and Oxford.

McMullen, R. (1982), 'Roman attitudes toward Greek love', *Historia*, 31, 484–502.

McMullen, R. (1984), *Christianizing the Roman Empire (AD 100–400)*, New Haven.

Meeks, W. (1993), *The Origins of Christian Morality. The First Two Centuries*, New Haven.

Miller, J.-A. (1989), 'Michel Foucault et la psychanalyse', in *Michel Foucault philosophe. Rencontre internationale, Paris, 9, 10, 11 janvier 1988*, Paris, 77–84.

Narducci, E. (1989), *Modelli etici e società: un'idea di Cicerone*, Pisa.

Narducci, E. (1995), *Processi ai politici nella Roma antica*, Rome.

Nelli, R. (1963), *L'Erotique des troubadours*, Paris.

Nussbaum, M. (1978), *Aristotle's "De motu animalium"*, Princeton.

Nussbaum, M. (1994), *The Therapy of Desire. Theory and Practice in Hellenistic Ethics*, Princeton.

Nussbaum, M. and J. Sihrola (eds) (2002), *The Sleep of Reason. Exotic Experience and Sexual Ethics in Ancient Greece and Rome*, Chicago.

Nygren, A. (1944), *Eros et Agapè. La notion chrétienne de l'amour et ses transformations*, Paris.

Olender, M. (1986), 'Priape le mal taillé', *Le Temps de la Réflexion*, 7, 373–88.

Paduano, G. (ed. and transl.) (1997), Gaius Valerius Catullus, *Le poesie* (with commentary by A. Grilli), Turin.

Pagels, E. (1988), *Adam, Eve and the Serpent*, New York.

Patterson, C. (1998), *The Family in Greek History*, Cambridge.

Petrocelli, C. (1989), *La stola e il silenzio. Sulla condizione femminile nel mondo romano*, Palermo.

Pigeaud, J. (1981a), 'Le Rêve érotique dans l'antiquité romaine', *Littérature, Médecine, Société*, 3, 10–23.

Pigeaud, J. (1981b), *La Maladie de l'âme*, Paris.

Pollack, M. (1982), 'L'homosexualité masculine ou: Le bonheur dans le ghetto?', *Communications*, 35, 37–55.

Pomeroy, S. (1997), *Families in Classical and Hellenistic Greece. Representations and Realities*, New York.

Rahe, P. (1992), *Republics Ancient and Modern. Classical Republicanism and the American Revolution*, Chapel Hill.

Ramage, E. (1973), *Urbanitas: Ancient Sophistication and Refinement*, Oklahoma.

Richlin, A. (1992a), *The Garden of Priapus. Sexuality and Aggression in Roman Humor* (new edition), New York.

Richlin, A. (1992b), *Pornography and Representation in Greece and Rome*, Oxford.

Richlin, A. (1993), 'Not before homosexuality: The materiality of the cinaedus and the Roman law against love between men', *Journal of the History of Sexuality*, 3–4, 523–73.

Robert, J.-N. (1997), *Eros romain*, Paris.

Rougement, D. de (1938), *L'amour et l'Occident*, Paris.

Rousselle, A. (1983), *Porneia. De la maîtrise du corps à la privation sensorielle, IIe-IVe siècles de l'ère chrétienne*, Paris.

Ryan, E. (1994), 'The "Lex Scantinia" and the prosecution of censors and aediles', *Classical Philology*, 89 (2), 159–62.

Schroeder, J. (1988), *The Vestal and the Fasces: Hegel, Lacan, Property and the Feminine*, Berkeley.

Shaw, B. (1987), 'The age of Roman girls at marriage: Some reconsiderations', *Journal of Roman Studies*, 77, 30–46.

Sissa, G. (1983), 'Il corpo della donna. Lineamenti di una ginecologia filosofica', in S. Campese, P. Manuli and G. Sissa, *Madre materia. Sociologia e biologia della donna greca*, Turin, 83–145.

Sissa, G. (1987), *Le Corps virginal. La virginité féminine en Grèce ancienne*, Paris. English transl.: *Greek Virginity*, Harvard.

Sissa, G. (1990a), 'Philosophies du genre. Platon, Aristote et la différence sexuelle', in G. Duby and M. Perrot (eds), *Histoire des femmes en occident*, Vol. 1, *L'antiquité* (ed. P. Schmitt Pantel), Paris (English translation: *A History of Women in the West* (1992–94), Vol. 1, *From Ancient Godesses to Christian Saints* (ed. P. Schmitt Pantel) Harvard).

Sissa, G. (1990b), 'Epigamia. Se marier entre proches à Athenes', in *Stratégies familiales dans l'antiquité romaine*, Rome, 199–223.

Sissa, G. (1997), *Le Plaisir et le mal. Philosophie de la drogue*, Paris.

Sissa, G. (2000), *L'Ame est un corps de femme*, Paris.

Sissa, G. (2000), 'Sexual Body-Building', in J. Porter (ed.) *Constructions of the Classical Body*, 147–68, Michigan.

Sissa, G. (2003), 'L'amour urbain ou l'art d'aimer chez les Romains, *Les Lettres de la Société de Psychanalyse Freudienne*, 9, 17–36.

Skinner, M. (1989), ' "Ut decuit cinaediorem": Power, gender, and urbanity in Catullus 10', *Helios*, 16, 7–23.

Skinner, M. (1993), '"Ego mulier". The construction of male sexuality in Catullus', *Helios*, 20, 107–29.

Thomas, Y. (1990), 'La division des sexes en droit romain', in G. Duby and M. Perrot (eds), *Histoire des femmes en occident*, Vol. 1, *L'antiquité* (ed. P. Schmitt Pantel), Paris.

Thornton, B. (1997), *The Myth of Ancient Sexuality*, Boulder.

Vegetti, M. (1986), 'Foucault et les Anciens', *Critique*, 471–2, August–September, 925–32.

Veyne, P. (1978), 'La Famille et l'amour sous le Haut-Empire romain', Annales ESC, 33, 35–63.

Veyne, P. (1982), 'L'homosexualité à Rome', *Communications*, 35, 26–33.

Veyne, P. (1983), *L'Elégie érotique romaine*, Paris.

Voelke, A.-J. (1973), *L'Idée de volonté dans le stoïcisme*, Paris.

Wallace, R. (1996), 'Law, freedom, and the concept of citizens' right in democratic Athens', in J. Ober and C. Hedrick (eds), *Demokratia. A Conversation on Democracies, Ancient and Modern*, Princeton, 105–20.

Williams, B. (1992), *Shame and Necessity*, Berkeley.

Williams, C. (1999), *Roman Homosexuality. Ideologies of Masculinity in Classical Antiquity*, New York and Oxford.

Winkler, J. J. (1990), *The Constraints of Desire. The Anthropology of Sex and Gender in Ancient Greece*, New York.

Wyke, M. (2002), *The Roman Mistress: Ancient and Modern Representations*, Oxford.

Zeitlin, F. (1996), *Playing the Other*, Princeton.

INDEX

abstinence from pleasure 52–3
  and reason 67–9, 70, 82
  see also asceticism; chastity
Achilles 64–5, 140–1
Adam 174, 180, 182–3
adolescents and sexual activity 159–60
  see also paederasty and puberty
adoption 93, 99
Aegisthus 33, 34, 103–4, 105–6, 112, 114, 115
Aegyptus 98
Aeschines
  Against Timarchus 2, 53, 54–6, 58–65, 69, 70, 162
Aeschylus
  Clytemnestra in the *Oresteia* 99, 104, 105–9, 110
  Electra in *Choephoroe* 110–12, 113, 114, 115
Agamemnon
  and Clytemnestra 103–4, 105–6, 108, 109, 110, 143
  and Elektra 110–16
Agathon 67, 69, 70
Alcibiades 57, 63, 67–9, 70–1
anal eroticism 60–2
  as learned behaviour 62, 153–4, 159, 161, 163
  puberty and paederasty 153–4, 158–63
āndáneīn 33
anthropology
  ban on incest 123–4
  see also kinship relations
anticipation and desire 190–1
Antigone 2, 98
anxiety
  and desire 48–9

of marriage and family life 175–7
Aphrodite 8, 17, 18, 33, 72
Aphrodite Pandemia 66
Aphrodite Urania 66, 68
aplēstía 41, 61, 101
Apollo 99, 107, 108, 111
Areopagus 108
aristocracy
  and homosexuality 101
  see also symposiums
Aristogiton 64–5
Aristophanes 63, 65, 69, 140
  Wasps 51
Aristotle 8, 12, 54, 192
  and anal eroticism 60–2
  on desire 134
  on division of sexes 4
  on erection 81–4, 85–6, 134
  on female body 90, 152
  and female sensuality 86–7, 160
  on male body 3
  and *Medea* 120
  and *mollitia* 152–3
  Poetics 99–100, 101–2, 122
  Politics 97
  Problems see Pseudo-Aristotle
  on reproductive biology 98–9
  Rhetoric 58, 122
  on voluntary and involuntary actions 17–18
art of love 10–11, 136–49, 194
  see also seduction
Artemidorus Daldianus 80
artificial femininity 143, 163
asceticism
  marriage and sexual continence 183–5
  marriage as sinful alternative 182–3

asceticism (*cont.*)
    and viability of Christianity 170, 171,
        172, 173, 179
    see also abstinence from pleasure; chastity
Athena 20, 39
    in *The Odyssey* 26, 27, 28, 30, 34, 104
    in the *Oresteia* 107–8, 113
Athens
    atīmía punishment 53–4, 55, 58
    inheritance and *ēpíklērŏs* 95–6, 114, 115
    legal status of children 92–4
    public and private spheres and
        democracy 54–8
    and sexual difference 2
    sexual morality and love between men
        62–9, 70, 161–2
atīmía 53–4, 55
    and Timarchus 58–62
attachment and female desire 21
Attic comedy 193
Augustine, St 12, 80, 81, 171, 174, 185–8,
    191
    City of God 185–6, 187–8
    and Foucault 199

betrayal and erotic pride 142–3, 146
bisexuality and specificity of gender 158–9
blood crimes 108
body 2–3
    and desires 41–2
    essential to ancient thought 4–5
    male body as model for female body
        3–4
    and sexual difference 72–88
    and soul 189
    see also female body; male body
boys and sexual activity 159
    see also puberty

Caesar, Gaius Julius 10, 157–8
Cage aux folles, La (film and play) 159
Callicles 43, 44, 53
Calypso 21, 25–6, 34, 35, 38, 105
'care' in Foucault's work 48, 49, 203–6
'carnal Israel' 171
Cassandra 109, 143
Catullus 9, 162, 194
    Caesar as *cinaedus* 10
    Poems 151–2, 153, 159
cause and object of desire 44–5, 133–4, 135
celibacy *see* chastity
Celsus 155
censure and sexuality 201–2

chărízeīn 8
Charmides 68
chastity
    as Christian alternative to marriage 12,
        170, 171, 174–5, 179–81, 183, 185
    of Penelope 22
    see also virginity
children
    Love as child 136–8
    and marital 'community' 97, 116–18, 122
    relationships and legal status 91–4
    and woes of family life 175–6
    see also puberty
Christianity
    and erotic drive 80–1, 183
    eroticised imagery 12, 172–3, 177–8
    Foucault and Christian morality 79–80,
        196, 199, 206
    sensuality and the flesh 6, 171–7, 183–4
    and sexual morality 11–12, 167–91, 195,
        198–9
Chrysostom, St John
    On Virginity 182–3, 184, 185
Church Fathers and sexual morality 11–12,
    167–91
    and Foucault's 'hermeneutics of desire'
        199, 206
Cicero 133, 158, 188–9, 190, 191
cinaedus (male dancer) 7, 8, 150
    and insatiable desire 53, 61
    Julius Caesar as 10, 157–8
    and *mollitia* 151, 153, 157, 163
Circe 34
citizenship and legal status of children 93
civilisation and sex 154–6, 157, 194, 195
class distinctions and democracy 57
Clytemnestra 27, 33, 34, 102, 103–9, 176
    and Electra 110, 111, 112, 113–14, 116
    jealousy and erotic pride 142, 143
comedy and sex 130, 193
community creation and marriage 97,
    116–18, 124, 168
confession and psychoanalysis 195–200,
    203
conflict resolution through marriage 97–8
consent
    soul and desire 84–5, 186–90
    and women's libido 138, 139, 140
Corpus Hippocraticum 98
couches 51, 62–3
courtly love 11, 138, 149
Cronus 75, 76–7
cruelty, eroticism of 9, 135–6

culture and softness 155, 156, 157
Cupid 156, 157
Cura 73, 74

Danaids 21, 53, 98
Danaus 98
daughters
    ĕpíklērŏs and inheritance 94–6, 97–8,
        114, 115
deceit and art of love 141–7
Deianeira 102, 103, 109–10, 140, 176
Deidamia 141
democracy and private actions 53–62
Demosthenes 69, 91–2, 97
    Against Boeotus 117
desire 15–49
    as anxiety 48–9
    body as physical manifestation 5, 11–12
    cause and object of 44–5, 133–4, 135
    Christian morality and marriage 167–91
    definitions 32–3
    and fabrication of sexual difference 78
    Foucault and interpretation of 199–206
    incompatibility with spiritual life 170
    and knowledge 189
    and lyrical poetry 35–7, 38
    marriage as antidote 183–4
    and pleasure 37–9, 48–9, 84, 133, 187–8,
        190–1, 205–6
    as primal instinct 1, 5, 11
    as punishment for the 'fall' 174, 181, 187
    and reason 67–9, 70, 82–3, 85–6
    subjectivity and locus of desire 161
    see also female sensuality and desire;
        insatiable desire; philosophy of
        desire; psychoanalysis and desire;
        sensuality
detachment and female desire 16
deviant will 187–8
Diotima of Mantinea 69, 70, 71, 178
dira libido see 'insane love'
division of the sexes see sexual difference
domestic life as tragedy 175–7, 179
Dover, Kenneth 158
dowries and inheritance 96
dreams and consent to desire 186–7,
    188–90
durable love 44–5

ĕĕldŏmaĭ 34
effeminacy and desire
    effeminacy as learned behaviour 62,
        153–4, 159, 161, 163
effeminacy and manliness 156–8
    and locus of desire 161; passivity of
        effeminate men 60–1, 62, 65, 163
    puberty and paederasty 153–4, 158–63
    see also cinaedus
Electra 102, 109, 110–16
emotions
    and involuntary acts 17–18, 84–5
    of mothers 176
    and reason 190
    and soul and desire 189
Epicureanism 133, 205
Epicurus 8–9, 133, 136
ĕpíklērŏs 94–6, 97–8, 114, 115
ĕpithūmētikŏn 42
ĕpithumía páscheĭn 88
ĕpithumía 41
ĕrastḗs 66–9, 70, 162, 163
erection 79–86
    female erection 87–8, 90
    as involuntary action 11–12, 20, 33,
        78–9, 80–6, 134, 187, 188
    philosophy of 79–86, 134
Erichthonius 20
Erinyes (Furies) 106–7, 108–9, 111, 112,
    113, 114
ĕrṓmĕnŏs 66–7, 70, 163
Eros 89
eros
    in Christian metaphor 12, 172–3,
        177–9
    definition 1, 5, 34
    and feminine striving 8
    Hobbes on 195–6
    and tragic heroines 121–2, 130
    as tyrant 18, 79, 81
    vocabulary of 6–7
    see also desire; libido
ĕrōs kalŏs 62–3, 65–9
ĕrōs ŏrthŏs 70–1
erotic drive 80–1, 83, 183
    see also libido
erotic poetry 193–4
erotic pride of women 142–3, 146
eroticism of cruelty 9, 135–6
Eschylus 21
ĕthḗleĭn 33, 34
ethics
    of desire 40–3, 44–9, 189–90, 206
    erection and Stoic ethics 84–5
    and Foucault 204–6
    Greek tradition and Christian sexual
        morality 11–12, 167–91, 205–6

Eumenides 108, 109
eunuchs 153, 159–60
Euripides 20, 91
　　Electra 110, 114–16
　　Hippolytus 19, 21
　　Ion 92
　　Medea 15–17, 18–19, 32, 97, 116–23
exchange of goods and marriage 124,
　　170–1

'fall' of Adam 174, 180, 182–3, 187
family life
　　woes of 175–7, 179
　　see also children; marriage
fathers
　　daughters and *ĕpíklērŏs* 94–6, 114, 115
　　see also paternity
fear as wife's condition 176
female body
　　Christianity and maternal metaphor
　　　178–9
　　heart and mother's empathy with
　　　children 176
　　as inversion of male body 3, 20, 86
　　as receptive container 3–4, 5
　　see also womb
female erection 87–8, 90
female sensuality and desire 15–19, 33,
　　86–8
　　and art of love 138–49
　　and comedy 193
　　and 'insane love' 138, 140, 157
　　and Medea's tragedy 121–2
　　and theatrical performance 20–1, 101,
　　　109–10, 130
flux and philosophy of desire 46–7, 48
Foucault, Michel 6, 79–80, 101, 191,
　　195–206
　　The Care of the Self 48, 49, 195, 198, 199,
　　　200, 203
　　The Confessions of the Flesh 195,
　　　198–9
　　The Use of Pleasure 48–9, 198–200
　　The Will to Know 195–202
freedom in personal life 54–5
Freud, Sigmund 123, 125, 127, 163
　　and Foucault 196–9, 202–5
friendship *see phĭlía/phĭloí*
Furies *see* Erinyes

Galen 1, 3, 5, 11, 12, 86
　　on female erection 87–8
　　ignorance of hymen 90, 91

on indefinite love 192
gender roles *see* sexual difference
genealogy in mythical tradition 102
genetic bilateralism 98
gods
　　humans and divine intervention 106
　　separation from men and appearance of
　　　women 72–3, 76
Greek lyrical poetry 35–7, 38, 39
Greek philosophical tradition and
　　Christianity 11–12, 167–91, 206
Gregory of Nyssa, St
　　On Virginity 175–7, 178, 179, 183
gymnasiums *see palaestrae*

Halperin, David 158
Harmodius 64–5
heart
　　and involuntary action 82, 83, 85–6
　　and mother's empathy 176
hēdŏnē 50–71
　　and history of Rome 157–8
Hegesander 65
Heidegger, Martin
　　Being and Time 74, 203–5
Helen 21–2, 50, 143, 145
Hellenised Judaism 171–2
Hephaestus 20, 39
Hera 33, 34, 35
Heracles 103, 109–10
Heraclitus 46–7, 48
Héritier, Françoise 124–5, 127–8, 194
'hermeneutics of desire' 198–206
'hermeneutics of the self' 198–9,
　　204–6
Hermes 26
Herodotus 40
Hesiod 39–40
　　Theogony 72–3, 74, 76, 79
　　Works and Days 40, 73, 74–5, 76
hetairai 51, 52, 59
hĭmĕrŏs 33, 34, 35, 37
Hippocrates 3, 86, 98
Hippolytus 19
historicisation of desire 201–2
Hobbes, Thomas 192, 193
Homer 40
　　desire and pleasure in 37, 38
　　The Iliad 17, 24, 34, 103, 104
　　The Odyssey 17, 22–32, 33–5, 38–9, 50,
　　　103–5, 156–7, 194
　　see also Penelope
homosexuality

and Athenian sexual morality 65–9, 70, 161–2
and desire 60–1, 153–4
érōs kalós 65–9
Greek attitudes towards 62–9
as modern concept 158, 161
and mollitia in Roman world 149–54, 156–8, 160, 162
and Oedipus myth 127–8
and philosophy 101
puberty and paederasty 153–4, 158–63, 194
sensuality as feminine trait 8–9
and specificity of gender 158–9, 161, 162
subjectivity and locus of desire 161
Timarchus' behaviour 58–62
see also anal eroticism; effeminacy and desire
humĕnaĩŏs 91
Hyginus 74
hymen 90–1, 151
Hymenaeus 91
hysteria 78–9

immortality and love 1, 12
incest
ban on incest 123–4
Oedipus 123–30, 201
Phaedra and Hippolytus 19
proximity of relations 124–5
and psychoanalysis 201–2
indefinite love 192
infantile desire and incest 123–4
infidelity
Christianity and Greek tradition 169, 185
deceit and art of love 141–7
inheritance and kinship relations 93–6, 102
bilateral nature and biological difference 98–9
ĕpíklērŏs 94–6, 97–8, 114, 115
'insane love' (dira libido) 133–6
of women 138, 140, 157
insatiable desire 39–43, 133
and eroticism of cruelty 135–6
female insatiability 39–40, 72, 162, 194
and homosexuality 60–1, 153–4, 162, 163
and philosophy 40–3, 44–5, 47, 49, 52–3, 79
and time 205
in tragedy 101

intention and passion 17–18
see also volition
intertextuality of tragedy 103, 109
intestines and reason 79
involuntary actions
erection as 11–12, 20, 33, 78–9, 80–6, 134, 187, 188
love as external force 17–18
Iole 109
Iphigenia 105, 106, 108, 109, 110
Isaeus 97
Isocrates 54–5

Jason 15–17, 19, 21, 116–17, 118–23
jealousy
and art of love 142–4, 145, 146
and sexual proximity 125
Jesus of Nazareth 168–9, 180
Jocasta 8, 92, 123, 125, 127–30, 140
Judaism in Greece 171–2
Juvenal 151, 162
Satires 149–50, 153, 159–60

Kallipolis (Plato's 'City of Beauty') 3
kinship relations
exogamous marriage and exchange of goods 124
and inheritance 93–6, 102
and legal status of children 91–4
sex and tragedy 99–130
see also incest
klĩnaĩ 51
knowledge 46–7, 48
and desire 189
koīnōnía 97, 98, 116–17, 124
kúriŏs 95, 96

Lacan, Jacques 136
Laius 125, 126–8
lasciviousness and homosexuality 60, 61, 62
law
inheritance and kinship relations 93–6
'legal principles' in tragedy 106–9, 113–14
legal status of children 91–4
sexual difference and inequality 98–9
Lévi-Strauss, Claude 97, 124, 125, 127
lex Scantinia 162
libido
dira libido of women 138, 140, 157
and love 135
and sexual difference 138–40
see also eros; erotic drive; female sensuality and desire

Longus
    Daphnis and Chloe 193
love
    art of 10–11, 136–49, 194
    as external force 17–19
    indefinite love 192
    as means to immortality 1, 12
    as transformation of physiological
        response 135
Lucretius (Titus Lucretius Carus) 10,
        194
    On the Nature of Things 7, 9, 133, 134,
        135–6, 137, 145, 146, 147, 154,
        155–6, 192
lust 192
luxury and softness 154–5
Lycurgus 155
lying *see* deceit and art of love
lying down and symposiums 51–2, 62–3
lyrical poetry 35–7, 38, 39
Lysias
    Funeral Oration 2
    On the Murder of Eratosthenes 186

malakía 51, 154, 155
male body
    as model for female body 3–4, 86, 87
    parts for men and women 160, 161
    see also erection; penis; puberty
male desire 20–1, 25–6, 33, 193
    as paradoxical vulnerability 134
    Penelope's suitors 30, 31, 34, 35, 194
    in Plato 43
    as pornographic 130
male vir 159, 163
marriage 89–99
    and Christian sexual morality 11,
        167–85
    and community and kinship relations
        96–9, 107–8, 116–18, 124, 168
    and conflict resolution 97–8
    exogamous marriage and exchange of
        goods 124
    and inheritance laws 94–6
    legal status of children 91–4
    and Penelope's virtue 22–35
    of prepubescent girls in Rome 162
    ritual of 90–1, 92
    and sensuality 195
    and sexual continence 181–2, 183–5
    as tragedy 175–7, 179, 195
    weddings 89–91
Martial 151, 160

masculinity
    development of 159–60
    see also male body; male desire; virility
maternity
    Christianity and maternal metaphor
        178–9
    and 'legal principles' in tragedy 106–9,
        118–19, 120
    and legal status of children 91–3, 118–19
Matthew's gospel 185, 186, 191
Medea 8, 15–17, 18–19, 21, 22, 32, 102,
        116–23, 140, 176
menstrual blood 83, 84, 99
metallic 'races' 75
metaphor
    eros and Christian imagery 12, 172–3,
        177–9
    female body as inversion of male 3
    fire and sex 181, 185
Methodius of Olympus, St 178, 183
Miller, Jacques-Alain 15, 203
Misgolas 65
modesty and art of love 139
mollescere 154, 156, 157
mollitia (softness) 9, 10, 51
    and art of love 139, 156, 194
    as feminine property 156, 194
    and process of civilisation 154–6, 157,
        194, 195
    in Roman world 149–58, 160
    and 'unmanly love' 149–54, 157–8, 162
monism 189–90
mora (delay) and art of love 139, 145
morality *see* ethics, of desire; sexual
        morality
Moravia, Alberto 134
mothers
    and adoption 93, 99
    and *ĕpíklērŏs* inheritance 94–6
    legal status in tragedy 106–8
    maternity and legal status of children
        91–2, 118–19
    and woes of family life 175–6
    see also Clytemnestra; Jocasta; Medea
Muses 50
mûthos in tragedy 102
mythical tradition and genealogy 102–3

'natural' children 91–2
naturalness of desire 82–4
negative freedom in Athens 54
Nevolus 149–50, 152
novel 193

Numa, king of Rome 9–10, 155, 156, 162

oaristús 8
Oedipus 92, 123, 125–30, 201
ontology of desire 49
Orestes 103, 106–9, 111–12, 114
Origen 178
original sin 174, 180, 181, 182–3, 187
Ovid 194
    Art of Love 7, 8, 10–11, 136–49, 155,
      156, 159, 192
    Metamorphoses 77

paederasty and puberty 153–4, 158–63, 194
    and Greek sexual morality 62–3, 65–9,
      161–2
palaestrae 62, 69–70, 101, 195
Pandora 73
passions see emotions
passivity
    of effeminate men 60–1, 62, 65, 163
    of female body 86–7
paternity
    dominance of 99, 108, 119
    and legitimacy of children 91–3
Patrocles 64–5
Paul, St (Paul of Tarsus)
    letters to the Corinthians 11, 167–8,
      170–5, 179–81, 181–2, 183, 184
    letters to the Ephesians 178, 180, 181
Pausanias 66, 67, 68, 69, 135, 162
Penelope 22–32, 33–5, 38–9, 92, 143
    and Clytemnestra 103, 104–5, 112
    female attachment and desire 21
    portrayals of 25–9
    as sensual figure 7, 29–32
    and time 22, 25–9
Penia 39
penis 78–9
    phallus and Roman symbolism 150–2
    see also erection
perfection
    sexual difference and loss of perfection
      75, 76
Pericles 54, 56, 57, 93
personal life and private and public spheres
    54–8
    shameful behaviour 58–62
perversa voluntas 187–8
Phaedra 19, 21, 22, 140
phallus and Roman symbolism 150–2
phantasía 188, 189–90, 191, 207
phīlía/phĭloí 99–100, 101–2, 105, 118, 120

Philo of Alexandria 178–9
philosophy of desire 17–19, 32–5, 38–9,
    40–9, 133–4
    Christian philosophy 185–91, 206
    Epicureanism 133, 205
    and erection 79–86
    and homosexuality 101
    insatiable desire 40–3, 44–5, 47, 49,
     52–3, 79
    see also ethics
phratry and legitimacy of children 92, 93
Plato
    Charmides 68
    and Christian philosophy 12
    and eros as tyrant 18, 79, 81
    and ethics of desire 40–3, 44–9, 52, 82,
     189, 190, 205
    Gorgias 43, 53
    the Laws 70
    on love between men 62–3
    Phaedrus 43, 70, 79
    Philebus 136
    physical training for girls 3
    the Republic 42–3, 51, 54, 97
    sexual difference and the Statesman
     76–7
    soul and desire 189
    Symposium 66, 69–71, 135, 136, 162,
     178
    Theaetetus 178
    theory of Forms 47
    Timaeus 41–2, 47, 77–8, 79, 81, 192
    tripartite soul 84–5
Platonic love 8, 11, 64, 68
pleasure
    abstinence from 52–3, 67–9, 70
    and Christian sexual morality 11–12,
     183–5, 186–7, 206–7
    and desire 37–9, 48–9, 85, 133, 187–8,
     190–1, 205–6
    hedone 50–71, 157–8
    politics and public and private behaviour
     53–62
plot in tragedy 102
plovers and insatiable desire 42, 43, 47, 53
Plutarch 10, 68, 155, 162
    Conjugal Precepts 97, 117
    Life of Caesar 158
    On Moral Virtue 85, 86
pneûma
    and involuntary movement 82, 84
    soul and desire 189, 191
poet as model of manliness 156–7, 194

poetry *see* erotic poetry
  Greek lyrical poetry
  Roman poetry
poïkílŏs 66, 67
politics and public and private behaviour 53–62
pornography and comedy 130
Poseidonius 191
power relations and sex 150, 152, 158
Praxiteles
  Aphrodite statue 3
Priapus 150
private sphere *see* public and private spheres
procreation
  and Christian purpose of marriage 181–2
  legal status of children 91–4
  and marital 'community' 97, 116–18, 122
Procris 144
Prometheus 72
prostitution and public life 54
  Timarchus shameful behaviour 58–62
Protagoras 46–7
Proteus 141
Proust, Marcel 137
proximity and incestuous relations 124–5
Pseudo-Aristotle
  Problems 60–2, 153, 159
Pseudo-Demosthenes
  Against Neaira 52, 93
Psyche 178
psychoanalysis and desire 16
  Foucault on 195–204
  incest and Oedipus myth 123–4, 125, 127, 201
puberty
  medical theories 5
  and *mollitia* 153, 160, 163
  and pederasty 153–4, 158–63, 194
  and sexual desire 133–4
public and private spheres: and democracy 54–8; symbolism of marriage 89, 90

Rahe, Paul 55
rape
  and art of love 140–1
  of the Sabine women 10, 140
  and virginity 185–6
reason and desire
  and consent 189–90
  and pleasure 67–9, 70, 82–3, 85–6
Reignault, Jean-Baptiste 195

relationships 89–130
  and sex in tragedy 97–8, 99–130
reputation and public and private spheres 55–8
resistance
  and art of love 130, 139
  virginity as 115–16
rhetoric
  and feminine sensuality 8–9
  and gender roles 2
  and shame 58–9
Roman love and sexuality 131–58
Roman poetry 9, 194
romantic poetry 39
Rome
  foundation myths 9–10, 140, 150–1, 155
Rumor 56

Sabines
  rape of the Sabine women 10, 140
Sallust 10
Sappho 21–2, 36–7, 38, 194
scientia sexualis 196, 198, 199, 201
secretions of female body 87, 88
seduction: and marriage ritual 90
  and pederasty 162
  and sensuality 8, 10–11
  and sexual violence 140–1, 186
  see also art of love
semen
  male and female semen 98–9
Seneca (the Younger)
  Epistles 160
  Medea 116
sense perceptions and sex 46, 47, 48, 189
sensuality 194–5
  and bitterness and betrayal 9
  civilising influence 154–6, 157, 194, 195
  and comedy 193
  definitions 7, 8
  as feminine property 8, 20, 87
  as fluid 45–7
  of Penelope 7, 29–32
  and tragedy of Medea 121–2
  vocabulary of 6–7
  see also female sensuality and desire
sex
  definitions 7
  and metaphor of fire 181, 185
  and process of civilisation 154–6, 157, 194, 195
  and relationships in tragedy 97–8, 99–130

and tragedy of Medea 121–2
sexual activity 5–6
  advice on sexual positions 147
  Christian antipathy to 183–5
  deflowering in marriage ritual 90–1
  involuntary act in male 20–1
  and Plato's ethics 48–9
  and puberty 133–4
  puberty and paederasty 153–4, 158–63,
    194
  sensuality as constant craving 52–3,
    194
  and social bonds 96–9, 117, 155
sexual difference 1–2, 72–88
  and concept of homosexuality 158–9,
    163
  demanding females 39–40, 73, 74–5
  erection 79–86
  fabrication of 77–9
  female sensuality 86–8, 138
  and inequality in law 98–9, 106–8
  and libido 138–40
  myths of female creation 72–9
  and nature of sex and sensuality 7–8
  and representations of body 2–4
sexual morality
  Christian sexual morality 11–12,
    167–91, 195–6, 198–9, 206
  Greeks and love between men 62–9, 70,
    161–2
sexual organs
  creation of 1, 77–9, 81
  female body as inversion of male 3, 20,
    86
  see also penis; womb
sexuality
  use of term 6, 201
Shakespeare, William
  Hamlet 202
shame 57–8
  Timarchus and shameful behaviour
    58–62
social bonds of sex 96–9, 117, 124, 155
social construction of gender 1
Socrates 43, 45, 53, 69–70
  and Alcibiades 67–9, 70–1
softness see malakia; mollitia
Solon 40
sophists 46–7
Sophocles
  Electra 109, 110, 112–14, 115
  Oedipus King 92, 123, 125–30, 201
  Trachinian Women 109–10

Soranus 90–1
soul
  desire and consent 84–5, 186–90
  as female body 178
  and involuntary action of erection 84–5,
    187, 188
  and rape of virgins 185–6
Sparta 3, 155
speech
  and desire 34–5
  see also rhetoric
Stoics 9, 11, 18, 176, 188–91, 206
structural anthropology 97, 127
subconscious desires 198, 203
subjective sexuality
  homosexuality and locus of desire 161
  and tragedy 101
submission and female body 5, 10–11
Suetonius
  Julius Caesar 157–8
suffering and pleasure 38
super-ego 202–3
symposiums 50–2, 62–3, 65–71, 162,
    195

tà dēmósia 55
tà ídia 55, 56
Tarchetius 150–1
Telemachus 26, 27–8, 29, 30–1, 104, 112
Tertullian 6, 183–4, 185, 191
  On Monogamy 180–1, 183
theatre
  and female sensuality and desire 20–1,
    101, 109–10, 130
  performance of desire 20–1, 32–3
  performance of gender roles 2
  see also comedy; tragedy
Thucydides
  on Alcibiades 57
  Pericles Funeral Oration 54, 56
Timarchus 54–6, 58–65, 161
time
  fluidity of sensuality 45–7
  and insatiable desire 205
  and Penelope 22, 25–9
  and sexual difference 75–6
tragedy 5, 22, 194
  and desire as feminine characteristic 8
  domestic life as 175–7, 179
  ingredients of 99–100
  and philosophical questions 18–19
  sex and relationships in 97–8, 99–130
triclinium 51

Ulysses 20–1, 22–32, 33–5, 38–9, 103, 104, 105
'uranic' love 66–7, 68
urban love 10–11, 138, 145, 149, 194
uterus *see* womb

vendettas in tragedy
    Electra 112–16
    Oresteia 106–7, 107, 108, 110–12
Venus 154, 155, 156, 157
Venus *volgivaga* 135
Vesta 151
violence: and art of love 139, 140–1
    and kinship in tragedy 99–100, 101–2, 105–9, 110–12, 113–14, 120–1, 122–3, 125
    see also rape
virginity
    and Christian sexual morality 11, 167–8, 171, 172, 174–5, 177–81, 183, 185
    deflowering and existence of hymen 90–1
    and devotion to God 177–9
    of Electra 114–15
    eros in Christian metaphor 12, 177–8
    and question of rape 185–6
    and Roman myth 151
    see also chastity
virility
    and art of love 10, 140, 141
    and history of Rome 157
    and model of manliness 156–7
    and 'unmanly love' 151–2, 153–4, 159–60, 161
Virro 150, 152, 160
volition
    deviant will 187–8

erection as involuntary action 11–12, 20, 33, 78–9, 80–6, 134, 187, 188
    love as external force 17–19
    reason and consent 189–90
    see also consent
voluptas 9, 133, 156

weddings 89–91
wife awaiting husband's return motif 22–35, 103, 104–5, 109–10
    fear as wife's condition 176
womb
    animal-like nature of 78–9
    Christianity and maternal metaphor 178–9
    and female erection 87–8
women
    and inheritance laws 94–6
    'insane love' (*dira libido*) 138, 140, 157
    myths of invention of woman 72–9
    see also female body; female sensuality and desire
work
    and demands of woman 74–5
    sex as chore 76, 77

Xenophon
    Memorabilia 65
    Oeconomicus 97, 117

young men and sexual activity 159–60
    see also paederasty and puberty

Zeno of Citium 188, 190
Zeus 33, 39, 72, 73, 74, 75, 76
    in *The Odyssey* 26, 35, 103–4